SCYTHIANS

CASPIAN SEA

CHORASMIA

SCYTHIANS

GANDARA

SOGDIANA

MARGIANA

ECBATANA

BACTRIA

ARACHOSIA

MEDIA

PARTHIA

SUSA

ARIA

ON

PASARGADAE
PERSEPOLIS

CARMANIA

INDIA

PERSIAN GULF

RABIA

ARABIAN SEA

MAP BY

SUSAN DAVIS

Best wishes to our
good friends, Wallace
and Irene —

Doris A. Paul
March, 1979

با بهترین آرزوها تقدیم به دوستان عزیزم گردید.

نصرت ایثارگری
مارس - ۱۹۷۹

A Picture of Persia

A
PICTURE
OF
PERSIA

Mohammad Ali Issari
and Doris A. Paul

An Exposition-University Book

EXPOSITION PRESS

HICKSVILLE, NEW YORK

Acknowledgment is hereby given for permission to reprint:

Quotations from *Springs of Persian Wisdom,* Herder and Herder, New York. Copyright by Leobuchandlung 1970. Used by permission of McGraw-Hill Book Company.

[Lines] Reprinted by permission of G. P. Putnams' Sons from *The Gulistan of Sa'di,* translated by Edward Rehatsek. Copyright © 1964 by George Allen & Unwin Ltd.

FIRST EDITION

© 1977 by Mohammad Ali Issari and Doris A. Paul

All rights reserved, including the right of reproduction in whole or in part, in any form or by any means, electronic or mechanical, including photocopying, recording, or by any information storage and retrieval system, without permission in writing from the Publisher. Inquiries should be addressed to Exposition Press, Inc., 900 South Oyster Bay Road, Hicksville, N.Y. 11801.

ISBN 0-682-48410-5

LIBRARY OF CONGRESS CATALOG CARD NUMBER: 76-678

Printed in the United States of America

To Joan and Wilson,
without whose understanding, patience
and cooperation this book could not
have been written

Contents

Preface

For many years, Iran (or Persia) was generally thought of as a small country "somewhere in the Middle East" known for its carpets and poetry. Suddenly during World War II, it became known as the "Bridge of Victory," for it served as a vital pathway for the shipment of supplies to Russia. It was catapulted into the news when it became the host country for the Tehran Conference where Roosevelt, Churchill and Stalin met to design their war strategy. At this time the world at large gained a little more information about the geographical location of Iran, and some insight into its identity.

Sporadic news about the country following the war centered around the young Shah who ascended the Peacock Throne in 1941, when his father was forced by the Allies to abdicate. In recent years, Iran (which has its roots in the 2,500-year-old Persian Empire), under the rule of Mohammad Reza Shah Pahlavi, has found its place in the news of the world with headlines such as these: "Iran, One of the Fastest Growing Countries," "Iran Commandeers the Persian Gulf," "The Rising Power of Iran," and "Iran's Shah: Key to U.S. Aims in Mideast."

To understand fully how this Mideastern country has worked its way to the forefront of international recognition, one should delve deeply into the history of what has happened within its boundaries—particularly since the present Shah came to power.

The major motive in writing this book is to present the country
—its history and social, economic and political life—through the
eyes of a man who was born there, received his basic education
there and who (through his involvement with numerous pioneering social projects, and particularly his involvement with a comprehensive mobile cinema operation that took him the length and
breadth of the land) rubbed elbows with the villagers, nomads
and peasants. In addition he spent ten years as the official cinematographer of the Shah, and was thereby privileged to see government in action at firsthand.

Collaborating with an American authoress, he has told his story
in a leisurely, informal fashion, taking time to reminisce about
matters appealing to human interest, hoping to provide a panoramic
picture of Persia for the Western reader, and to show Iran as it
was and as it *is* today, following decades of struggle—under the
virile and progressive leadership of its dedicated, determined Shah.

A Picture of Persia

1
The Other Side
of the Page

It was about nine-thirty on a Thursday morning in February of 1956, in Tehran, when I received a telephone call from a friend of mine who was adjutant to H.I.M. Mohammad Reza Pahlavi, Shahanshah of Iran.* "Do you have a passport?" he asked.

"No, I don't. I don't need a passport."

"Yes, you do; you're leaving for India on Saturday morning."

"I am?"

"Yes. So go to the passport section of the police department and get your passport at once."

In Iran the "weekend" holiday starts Thursday noon and I was sure that the passport office would be closed within a couple of hours. And anyway, why should I be going to India?

"You have been chosen as the Shah's official cameraman on his state visit to India. You are to leave for New Delhi the day after tomorrow and your assignment is to make a documentary of Their Majesties' visit to that country," he told me.

"It is a great honor for me to be asked to make a film of Their Majesties' visit to India," I said. "But I am not sufficiently qualified as a cameraman to have full responsibility on such an important mission. May I take a cinematographer with me?" He told me there was only one seat on the plane reserved for a cameraman,

---

*Shahanshah means King of Kings; Shah is the short form of Shahanshah.

3

assured me he thought I could do the job, and put down the receiver.

Frankly I was terrified! To be given such an opportunity was the dream of any young man of my status, but I felt that undertaking such an assignment required considerably more experience and expertise than was mine at the time. My knowledge of cinematography was really quite limited.

Torn between cognizance of my lack of adequate technical competency and the elation of having been honored by the court (with His Majesty's approval), I went to the proper authorities to get my passport before the office closed for the weekend.

The chief of the passport division welcomed me by saying, "You're Mr. Issari, aren't you? Sign here, and sign here." I knew that photographs would be necessary in getting a passport and I had brought them with me. At that time in Iran, it took several weeks to get this document, but that day mine was in my hand within a very short time.*

With this business settled, I decided I'd better learn as *much* as possible about taking motion pictures as *quickly* as possible. I had actually photographed with a movie camera several times in my life, but always as one of several cameramen photographing the same event. I went to a friend who worked for me as a cameraman/director and told him my problem.

"Starting Saturday morning I am scheduled to accompany His Majesty to India as his official cinematographer, and frankly it scares me. As you know, my experience in cinematography is very limited and I want to do a good job—worthy of my assignment." Being an experienced cameraman, he realized my situation and agreed to help me. We worked together the remainder of the day, throughout the night and into Friday, as he taught me the rudiments of the operation—loading the camera, lens characteristics, camera angles, depth of field, film emulsions, composition, exposure meters, indoor and outdoor filming, shutter speed, filters, etc., etc.

Then we discussed photographic problems that might come up in the particular kind of situation to which I had been assigned. He knew (as did I) that in making a newsreel documentary such as this the photographer can't suddenly cry out in the middle of a ceremony involving two heads of state, "Hold it! Sorry, but I

---

*Today a passport may be obtained within as short a time as twenty-four hours.

missed that! Would you mind doing it again?" or "Wait a moment while I wind my camera." Such comments may be tolerated from American photographers, but certainly from no one else. He very patiently gave me pointers, based on his many years of experience as a cameraman, that were to be quite helpful as I photographed that historic first state visit of the Shah and Queen of Iran to India.

Before going into the reason I was chosen to be the Shah's official cinematographer for this trip, it is necessary to outline briefly what I was doing at the time. I was with the United States Information Agency (USIA) in Iran as assistant motion picture officer.

Preceding my acceptance of the position there in 1950, I had worked for almost eight years as head of the Joint British Council/ British Embassy Film Division. We sent mobile cinema units throughout the country, showing films to about four million people each year. My job was to procure these films, screen them, deciding whether or not they were suitable for Iranian audiences, have those chosen for showing translated into the Persian language, and then supervise their distribution.

I built the division almost from scratch but when it was fully developed I became more and more dissatisfied with the job because of two things: I seemed to be doing the same thing over and over with little personal creativity involved, and I felt the pay was not commensurate with the work being done. However, during these eight years I learned a great deal about documentary films by just seeing hundreds of them and analyzing their value for Iranian audiences.

It was during this period that I met the Shah in person for the first time. In August of 1948 we were asked to show a 35-minute film on new British aircraft to His Majesty at his summer palace, Sa'ad Abad, about twelve miles north of Tehran in the skirt of the beautiful Alborz mountains. The film was sent to us by the British Ministry of Information and knowing the Shah's interest in aviation and piloting we thought he might like to see it. The British Ambassador, Sir John LeRougetel, approached the Imperial Court and made the arrangement. I was instructed to handle the showing. My boss felt that I should go along with the projectionist to be available in case of any questions or technical problems.

When the projectionist and I arrived at the palace and went through the normal security inspection, we were shown the building where the viewing was to take place. It was one of several palaces in Sa'ad Abad, the residence of the Shah's oldest sister, Princess Shams, and her husband, His Excellency Mehrdad Pahlbod. As we were moving our projection equipment into the palace, suddenly a very little girl appeared from nowhere and engaged us in pleasant if childish conversation. "Who are you?" "What are you going to do in the palace?" "What is this piece of equipment?" "Do you know how to play volleyball?" and so on and on. Recognizing Princess Shahnaz, the only daughter of the Shah from his first marriage with Princess Fawzieh of Egypt, I had no alternative but to respond attentively in spite of the fact that we were behind schedule. She struck me as being an extremely intelligent girl, very kind-hearted and compassionate, and I never changed my mind in later years.

As pleasant as our conversation was I had to get into the building and get ready for the show. But you cannot excuse yourself in the presence of royalty no matter how young they may be. A God-sent governess appeared after about ten minutes and told Her Highness that it was time for dinner and going to bed. Her Highness very politely excused herself—or rather excused us—and ran off.

My projectionist and I dashed into the palace and started setting up equipment. The film had to be shown in a long hallway which was most unsuitable for any such purpose. During the hustle and bustle of setting up our projection equipment and tying our screen to the walls (we did not have the modern, easily raised screen on tripod) a few men who seemed to be employees of the court passed through the hallway, each one offering help or suggestions. I politely thanked them and said that we were doing all right and did not need help. Just as we had tied our screen securely to the wall in front of a large window with no shades, another man came toward us and started telling me why I should not put the screen there and how much better it would be to move it a couple of feet to the right! This broke the last thread of my patience and I had to tell him very firmly, but politely, that I knew my business and did not need any advice at this time. The man shrugged his shoulders and left.

We managed to test our equipment and complete all preparations only a few minutes before the party arrived: the Shah, accompanied by his sister, Princess Shams; Sir John LeRougetel, the British Ambassador; Lady LeRougetel; their son, who was a lieutenant in the British Navy; their daughter, whom I knew (we had acted together in the dramatic plays presented at the Anglo-Persian Institute); and the man who had been telling me where to put the screen for the show. To my embarrassed surprise, I discovered he was Princess Shams' husband and the Shah's brother-in-law, His Excellency Mr. Mehrdad Pahlbod. Although I had seen his picture in the daily papers, during the rushed preparation of getting ready for the show I had not recognized him.

The Ambassador introduced me to the Shah and the rest of the party and we started the film. For about five minutes everything went as smoothly as clockwork; but then I felt that something was wrong. I looked back and saw the projector's take-up reel was not working; the projectionist was trying desperately to fix it, but without success. I quietly slipped back to the projector and discovered that the spring turning the take-up reel had broken and there was no way to repair it without stopping the showing. The projectionist and I took turns winding the take-up reel with our fingers (we had no pen or pencil with us) but after perhaps ten minutes neither of us could keep it up. In desperation, not wanting the Shah and his party to realize that we were having technical difficulties, I cut the film and let it drop to the floor. (It goes without saying that we had brought with us a brand-new projector which I had tested myself in the morning, when it worked perfectly.) I went to my seat and the rest of the showing went without a hitch.

When the end title came on the screen I sighed with relief. The Shah expressed his pleasure and said that he had enjoyed the film. He talked about the planes with the Ambassador and his son, and just before getting up to go he turned to me and said, "You had some technical difficulty, didn't you?" I could have sworn that no one in the audience could possibly have realized we were having trouble. Other members of the party were as surprised as I at his comment, but I explained our problem.

It was then and there that I discovered how intelligent and observant the Shah is and how he can sense things happening around him of which other people are not even aware. When they left their seats of course everybody could see the pile of film on the floor at the back of the projector.

The Shah thanked me and left. A few minutes later the Grand Master of Ceremonies appeared, inviting me to go to have dinner with His Majesty and the other guests. We ate on the veranda of Princess Shams' palace and it was one of the most memorable evenings of my life. I made my peace with the Shah's brother-in-law, and came to know the Shah of Iran as a warm, kind and intelligent person. I realized how dedicated he is to his role as leader of his people, not because he inherited the throne but because he has a deep desire to prove himself their devoted leader and friend.

It was in April of 1950 that my counterpart in the American Embassy, John Hamilton, told me he needed an assistant and asked me to recommend someone for the position. I introduced several capable young men to him, but he wasn't satisfied with their credentials. One evening at dinner with him and his wife, June, I asked, "How much can you pay this assistant you're trying to find?" He quoted a wage that was almost half again as much as I was getting at the British Embassy as Films Officer.

"You're paying 'way above the market, John!" I said, thinking that this is often true of Americans. I told him how much I was being paid and June immediately said, "My goodness! Why don't you come to work for John?"

I hesitated to change jobs, but after the offer of a position with the American Embassy came to me in writing, and frustration at work piled up more and more, I tendered my resignation. I was ready to accept the new offer when I received a call from John's boss:

"I've heard a lot about your ability and your qualifications as a film expert, but I can't offer the job to you at this time."

When I said, "You wrote to me about the position," he answered, "Yes; but we don't want to threaten our relationship with the British." It became apparent that the news of the American's offer to me traveled faster to my boss than to me, for he immediately complained to the British Ambassador that the Americans were stealing well-qualified employees because they were able to offer higher salaries. The two ambassadors discussed the situation, and word was passed to the Public Affairs Officer of the American Embassy to withdraw their job offer.

I decided to work for neither. I was teaching Persian to members of the foreign community, and found I could fill classes four or five hours a day, making more money than either embassy could offer. When I handed in my resignation, my boss at the British Council gave me an even better offer than the American Embassy, but I declined. I was not a pawn to be moved around in a game between the British and American chess players!

I had been doing some translation work for John Hamilton and, needing some money for a vacation before going into teaching, I delivered the completed work. When I was leaving his office he casually said, "Where are you going?"

"To a resort on the Caspian Sea for a week's vacation."

"Why?" he asked. "I thought you didn't have any vacation this year. That's what you told me a couple of months ago."

"Right! I did say that," I answered. "But today the British Council accepted my resignation officially and I am a free man again!"

He immediately got up from his chair, called his secretary, and said, "Close all the doors. Don't let Ali go out. He has just started working as my Assistant—as of *now*." Turning to me he said, "There's your office, next to mine. I hope you like it."

I lost my week's vacation, but started a new phase of my career. The Americans were interested in developing and promoting new ideas, and their motives were to help Iranians help themselves. Here I found a challenge!

The first project to which I was assigned was a festival of American films, which proved to be a gratifying success. The second project we launched upon was the development of a cinema mobile unit operation. The plan continued to expand as the days passed, until we had thirty-six mobile units touring the remotest villages in the country, on a regular basis, showing educational, agricultural, health and hygiene films to the farmers.

Perhaps the most popular of all the films distributed was one showing the Shah's visit to the United States in 1948, his first visit, with President Truman as his host. This was the first time that most of the villagers had seen their Shah that close and their excitement was boundless.

We soon discovered that some of the films of an educational nature were not understood by our target audiences—not so much because of the language barrier, but because they were related to the life of the rural American rather than to that of the Persian villager.

One humorous incident occurred when we showed an American cartoon film on malaria, depicting what caused the disease, how to prevent it, and how to treat it. Having seen almost no films in their lifetime, some people thought the huge close-ups of the mosquitoes represented their actual size. Their reaction was, "No wonder your people worry about them. You have such big mosquitoes in your town! Ours are very small!"

John **Hamilton**, my American boss, who was deeply devoted to helping Iranians, although strongly against wasting the American taxpayer's money, opposed the use of such films. He wrote memo after memo to the State Department in Washington recommending production of locally made films on local problems in local situations. If, through the medium of films, we were to help the villagers have a better life, such films should deal with the actual problems facing these people in their own environment. There was no point in showing better farming methods through use of American farm machinery to Iranian villagers for whom the most sophisticated equipment at the time was a new wooden plow and a pair of oxen. And how could a film on prenatal care made in the United States for an American audience help Iranian village women whose cultural, religious and socioeconomic backgrounds were totally different from those of the women of the United States?

The newly established USIA separated from the State Department at this time, and a very understanding man, Herbert Edwards, became the head of the motion picture division in Washington. As a result of John Hamilton's intercession with Mr. Edwards, we were finally authorized to produce our own films on subjects such as prenatal care, how to take care of infants, how to plant trees, how to plow, and how to fight malaria—the simplest things that touched the daily lives of the rural Iranians. This program proved to be highly successful and one that was emulated in other developing countries. (More about this aspect of our work later.)

After a time it occurred to us that we were exerting all our efforts toward the benefit of people living in the countryside, forgetting the needs of the city population. It was decided that we should make films depicting the latest news events, showing new developments in the nation, and the activities of the government. We thought that the more people knew about the events taking place in their country, the more willing they would be to support new programs for social change; the more they knew about their country the more they would be devoted to it. I was given the responsibility of initiating such a project.

Limited production facilities hampered our efforts, but we were able to cover three or four subjects in a ten-minute newsreel each month. We had a crew on contract and when news broke some place, I would call the contractor and go out with his crew to cover the events. Our newsreels giving national coverage were in great demand and soon film distributors across the country were asking for them.

One of the most popular features of these newsreels had to do with the activities of the Shah. I knew a number of people in the court, a situation that served to expedite matters when I accompanied the newsreel crew. (At that time, there were no authorized court photographers.)

In the winter of 1955, a newsreel crew and I went out to Masjid-e-Suleiman, a town situated in the south of Iran in the very center of the oil fields, to cover a visit of the Shah in this area. Out in the field, His Majesty began talking to a simple laborer. Here was a meeting of the man holding the highest rank in the land, and a laborer representing the humblest class of people in Iran, engaged in animated conversation, meeting on common ground. The laborer was so awed by the presence of his ruler that one could almost visualize an aura of light about his head; his facial expression defied description. I thought to myself, "We have *got* to record this on film!"

I looked around to see that my cameraman was about three feet from me, behind one of the guards. I whispered, "Hey! Cover!" He was slightly deaf and did not hear me. Not willing to let the magic moment pass, I grabbed the camera, advanced within four feet of the Shah, pointed the camera and pressed the trigger. The Shah shook hands with the laborer, who stood there in a golden daze, and moved on. I returned the camera, apologizing to the cameraman for my impulsive action, and said, "That was such a great shot, why didn't you get it?"

He answered, "They [meaning the guards] won't let me as close to the Shah as they allow you, Mr. Issari." I exploded, "Of course they will! Find the right position for a good shot and go ahead and take it! You have to take these things when they happen!"

As usual, I viewed the rushes of the Shah's trip, and suddenly there on the screen appeared this beautiful two-shot of the Shah and the laborer, well composed and correctly exposed. The picture told the story exactly as I wanted it told. Beginner's luck was with me, I suppose!

We included the footage in the newsreel, and as usual sent it to the court for the Shah's viewing. Subsequently, I heard that he was very much pleased with the coverage, and this encouraged me to try my luck with a movie camera.

A number of my colleagues in the press and some government officials who were present that day later saw the newsreel and complimented me on that lucky two-shot. And so it was that I started experimenting with the medium of motion pictures.

A few months later, authorities of the royal court, making plans for Their Majesties' state visit to India, selected me as the official cinematographer in the entourage, a decision which met with the approval of the Shah.

Accordingly, two days following my telephone call from the adjutant to the Shah, I launched on a career that I pursued for ten years.

In that time I got to know His Majesty from a close-up angle, to use a filmmaker's term, and share his dream for his beloved country, as I photographed him on visits in the provinces of Iran and in countries across the world.

I am reminded of something Nezami, a Persian poet, wrote many years ago:

> Everything that happens and everything that befalls us has a meaning, but it is often difficult to recognize it.
>
> Also in the book of life every page has two sides: we human beings fill the upper side with our plans, hopes and wishes, but Providence writes on the other side, and what it ordains is seldom our goal.[1]

I had not dreamed of such an association with the Shah, but it would appear that Providence wrote it "on the other side" of the page.

Because of my work with the mobile cinema operation and my extensive travels with the Shah, I have been able to see Iran through a prism, viewing a wide spectrum. Unfortunately, few

---

[1]*Springs of Persian Wisdom*, Herder and Herder, New York, copyright by Leo-buchandlung, 1970 (pages not numbered). Used by permission of McGraw-Hill Book Company.

people in the Western world are as well informed about my country as I should like them to be. I attribute this to the fact that what most people learn is limited to material found in sketchy newspaper stories, short magazine articles or brief glimpses on their television screens.

My motive in writing this book is to give the reader a comprehensive picture of Persia as I saw it, a panorama of the history of the country from its earliest years to the present day, showing on a wide screen the economic, political, cultural and social life of the people from the lowliest peasant or nomad to the members of the ruling class. I propose to show Persia in broad perspective, with emphasis on what I saw and learned about the Shah during my association with him in the ten years I served as his official cameraman.

I shall begin with a quick look at ancient Persia, "pan" to Persia as Reza Shah rose to power, then to the country as his son Mohammad Reza Shah Pahlavi found it when he succeeded to the throne, and finally to Persia as it stands today—one of the most stable and progressive countries in the Middle East.

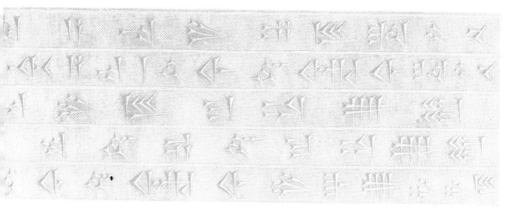

2
An Overview
of Persian History

Part I: The Pre-Islamic Period

Reading the "begats" in the Book of Genesis is far from inspiring or entertaining unless one is truly interested in the genealogy of Biblical characters, or is spurred by some other definite motive. Some readers may place capsules of history, with their lists of who conquered whom and when and who reigned for how long and why he was dethroned, in the same category. However, history is fraught with drama, filled with stories of treachery and steadfastness, deceit and courage, cowardice and bravery, despair and triumph. And one cannot understand the problems that beset a head of state of an ancient empire, if he has little or no knowledge of what transpired before the monarch's ascendancy: the death struggles of religion against religion, church versus state, the power-hungry against the peasant, and the terror of ravaging invaders.

For this reason I shall relate briefly the story of the Persian Empire from its inception up to the time the present Shah assumed leadership in my country. (A chronological list of major events appears at the end of this chapter.)

The destiny of Iran has been influenced greatly by her geographical position on the land bridge connecting Europe and the Far East. Persia is an ancient country, known throughout the ages as the romantic land of poetry and song, the "rose and the nightingale," and the "wise men of the East." Although recorded history of the country goes back only about 2,500 years with the rise of the Achaemenian Empire, archeological evidence points to the existence of man on the Iranian Plateau for perhaps 7,000 years. The Elamites were among the first peoples of the area, creating their capital at Susa.

One of the strongest tribes to invade the plateau was the Aryans from whom the country derived its name, for Iran stems from the word meaning "land of the Aryans."

The authentic history of the country begins with the Medes (a branch of the Aryans) and the Parsees (Persians), spoken of in the Bible. At some remote period—some say 1500 B.C.—these two Aryan tribes are believed to have come from the steppes of central Asia (although there is a growing claim that they originated on the Iranian Plateau), the Medes settling in the northwest and the Parsis in the province of Pars (known today as Fars) farther south. They did not come in one massive invasion, but rather in different migrations over a period of time, spreading out over the Iranian Plateau. The Medes were more civilized than the Persians at the time, owning cattle, sheep, goats, horses and even wheeled vehicles. By the sixth century before Christ, they had established rule over many tribes, including the Persians.

The Persians, however, had their own king, Achaemenes, who united the various Persian tribes and established the Achaemenid dynasty. His grandson Cambyses married the daughter of the Medean king, Astyages, and from the marriage was born a son whom they named Cyrus. This child was to become known through history as Cyrus the Great.

About 553 B.C., the Persians, inspired by their great leader, Cyrus, revolted against their Medean overlord, Astyages, and captured the capital, Ekbatana (presently the city of Hamadan). All ancient Iran was united under the rule of Cyrus the Great.

Nations forming the Persian Empire retained most of their autonomy and enjoyed an era of relative peace and prosperity. The great king allowed them freedom of worship according to their beliefs, and encouraged them to continue their way of life as dictated by their individual cultures.

One writer has said,

> The seed and origin of modern systems of government and civil government and civil administration, road transport, army organization, revenue and taxation, judicial administration, postal communication, police and

coinage are all to be found in the Achaemenian policy and mode of government.[2]

A major contribution of the early Persians was their empire form of government, supported by many technological achievements. In his book *Mission for My Country*, the Shah says,

> As the American anthropologist, Dr. Coon, has pointed out in his book, *Caravan*, "it was the earliest true empire in the world, in that it constituted a government of many different peoples under a single ruler. While kingdoms had existed during the Bronze age, in Egypt, Sumeria, Babylonia, China and elsewhere the technological facilities (such as the Persians developed) for rapid transport and communication needed by an imperial government had not been invented. In China this came about three hundred years later."[3]

Iran was also the first nation to affirm staunchly the importance of the individual. The Shah goes on to say,

> The rights of all the subject nations were upheld, and their laws and customs respected. Indeed, I see in our first empire something of the spirit of the United Nations of nearly 2,500 years later.[4]

Preceding the time of Cyrus the Great, ruling power was determined by the size of armies and brute strength. An ancient inscription, said to be authored by Assurbanipal, famous Assyrian king, reveals the unbelievably sadistic violence of the age:

> On the order of Ashur and Ishtar, the great gods who protect me, I conquered in a single attack the city of Ginabou, thanks to my soldiers and war chariots. I decapitated 600 enemy soldiers on the spot and burned alive 3,000 prisoners: I did not spare even one official to keep as hostage. I carved up the governor with my own hands and, after impaling his body, hung it opposite the city wall. From where I left for the city of Ur. The inhabitants did not beg for mercy nor did they want to submit. Therefore, I attacked the city and conquered it; I let 3000 people feel my sword; I grilled others on a fire; I cut off the hands, fingers, ears and noses of a large number of prisoners; ripped thousands of eyes from their sockets and tongues from their mouths; I made huge mounds of the bodies of the victims, and I exposed the cut-off heads of the city's losses. Then I conquered the city of Susa; I opened the treasures of the kings of Elam who had long been storing them away; I sent to Assur the gold,

---

[2]P. N. Vachla, *Iran, Ancient and Modern*, by the Consulate General of Iran in Bombay, 1956, p. 9.

[3]Mohammed Reza Shah Pahlavi, *Mission for My Country*, Hutchinson of London, 1961, p. 21.

[4]*Ibid.*

silver, rich costumes and palace furnishings that I found as well as the golden, silver, bronze and stone statues. Then I razed the temples to the ground and suppressed their gods. I transformed into a vast desert all of a region over a distance of a march of a month and 25 days; I sowed salt and thorns. I took to Assur the sons and sisters of the king and some princes, as well as all the members of the royal family, governors, officers, armourers, artisans, men and women, troops more numerous than the waves of locusts.

In sharp contrast, Cyrus the Great uttered a declaration of human rights, miraculously preserved for posterity on a baked-earth cylinder, found by archaeologists in Mesopotamia in 1879. (It now rests in the British Museum in London.) A part of the declaration, translated from the Babylonian text (inscribed in cuneiform characters) reads:

> I, Cyrus, King of Kings, son of Cambyses, grandson of Cyrus, whose dynasty has been blessed by the gods and whose reign is based upon the heart, when I entered the city of Babylon all the people welcomed me with joy. I assumed the throne of the king. Marduk, the god of Babel, whom I have taken in and whom I have loved, won the noble hearts of the people of Babel for me. My great army entered this city without incident. The holy places of the city moved my heart. I accorded to all men the freedom to worship their own gods and ordered that no one had the right to bother them. I ordered that no house be destroyed, that no inhabitant be dispossessed. The great god accorded to me and to all my army his benefits. From Babel to Assur, from Susa to Addak. . . . and in all the regions long inhabited on the other side of the Tigris, I wished that the temples that had been closed be reopened, that all the statues of the gods be returned to their place, and that they remain there forever. I reassembled the inhabitants of these regions and had their houses, which had been destroyed, rebuilt. I saw that the gods of Sumer and Akkad were returned to their places which are called "the joy of the hearts." I accorded peace and quiet to all men.

On conquering Babylon, Cyrus the Great not only restored the images of gods to those cities from which they had been removed, but he also freed the Jews from slavery, returning to them gold and silver vessels and other treasures, and bidding them to return to Jerusalem to rebuild their Temple which had been destroyed.

Cyrus is mentioned repeatedly in the Old Testament of the Bible in the books of Ezra, Isaiah, Jeremiah and Daniel, and is prophesied *by name* as the one who would deliver oppressed people from bondage.

Cambyses, Cyrus the Great's successor, who added Egypt to the Empire, was followed by two other great leaders: Darius and Xerxes. The manner in which Darius was chosen to rule, from among leaders of the seven great Persian families, is of interest. According to the historian Roger Stevens, Darius' father was Hystapes, and in all probability a third cousin once removed of Cyrus and "well qualified to uphold the imperial tradition of the family."[5] In fact, he was next of kin to Cambyses and was therefore naturally his successor. However, according to Herodotus, a very strange test was arranged to determine which of the representatives of the seven great families should rule.

He related that the king was chosen by hippomancy—divination by the horse. It was agreed that the man whose horse neighed first at sunrise should be declared king. The groom who took care of Darius' horse—either through his own ingenuity or his master's—formulated a plan. He took the horse beforehand to the appointed spot where he let him see a mare. The next morning when the horse recognized the place, he started neighing in joyful anticipation of another meeting with the mare. It is said that by this ruse, Darius was declared to be the one to wear the crown. No matter the route by which Darius ascended the throne, he proved himself worthy.

One of his most remarkable achievements was the construction of a road over fifteen hundred miles in length extending along the west coast of Asia Minor from Susa to Sardis, complete with posting stations along the way. It was Darius who built Persepolis and Xerxes (who followed him) who expanded it to be a special court where the king could receive the homage and gifts of the people of captive lands within the empire. Friezes on the ruins of Persepolis show processions of men bearing gifts of all description. The empire at its height (about 500 B.C.) extended from the Indus up into southern Russia, included part of Greece as we know it today, all of Turkey and Cyprus, a great portion of present-day Egypt and some of Libya. It was Darius who made the first attempt to connect the Persian Gulf and the Mediterranean Sea (through the Suez Canal area) to promote trade between nations. Cambyses is said to have been the first non-Egyptian to be accepted by the Egyptians as their Pharaoh. And so we see that during the Achaemenian era the Persian Empire brought a period of prosperity and peace to most of the known world of the time.

---

[5] Roger Stevens, *The Land of the Great Sophy,* Methuen and Co., Ltd., London, 1965, p. 11.

By 330 B.C. (after a period of about 220 years) the great empire was beset by internal jealousies and treachery, and consequently fell victim to the forces of the youthful, ambitious Macedonian, Alexander the Great. It was during this period that the Greek historians gave Iran the name Persia, which has remained in the language of the Western world. Alexander became fond of his subjects, married Roxana, the daughter of Darius III, and encouraged his officers and soldiers to marry Persians. But for some strange, undetermined reason, he set fire to Persepolis, the capital of the Persian Empire, and a few years afterwards died in Iran.

About 248 B.C. a less civilized Aryan tribe from the northeast, the Parthians, overcame the successors of Alexander and held supremacy over the land for more than four centuries. The Parthian feudal state lasted until 224 B.C. when Ardeshir, a vassal king of the province of Fars, revolted, won his cause, and established the Sassanian dynasty, which endured until A.D. 641. (The name "Sassanian" probably came from an old Persian title *Sasan,* which meant "commanders." It later became a family name.)

During the time of the Parthians and the Sassanian dynasty, the persistent Romans tried to expand eastward, but they were met with strong resistance, and were never able to defeat the proud Iranians.°

Later in the period, Shapur the Great, a Sassanian king, defeated the Roman army and captured Emperor Valerian in a battle. This is recorded in a rock carving on the arch of Bostan near Kermanshah in western Iran.

Religion began to play a major role in the collision of the Roman and Sassanian Empires, the Romans having embraced Christianity in the fourth century. The Iranians were, in the main, followers of Zoroaster, a prophet of great stature. Zoroastrianism (originally monotheistic) preached harmony between God and man which was said to be necessary to the functioning of the universe. Zoroaster's message sharply distinguished between that which was good and that which was evil. The core of the belief was that man, through Zoroaster, the prophet, could be brought into what amounted to a direct partnership with "the wise Lord," Ahura

---

°The Parthians and Romans fought often, and finally at the battle of Carrhae a Persian general *Surena* defeated *Crassus* (who had suppressed the famous Spartacus revolt in Rome), and thus the plains of Mesopotamia became an established boundary between the great empires.

Mazda, or to Ahriman, the evil spirit. These thoughts influenced later religions and philosophy. The ideal of the Zoroastrian was "good thoughts, good words, good deeds."

In the seventh century, this idealistic creed of the Iranians fell into decadence, partially due to corruption among the priests, despite the efforts of some monarchs to reform it. For example Anooshirvan Sassani, who was given the title "Just," is reported to have had a bell hung from his palace gates with a long chain so that anyone who thought himself to be unjustly treated could ring the bell and receive personal attention from the king. One day a strayed donkey scratched his neck against the chain and caused the bell to ring. When the Shah came to his balcony to see who was asking justice he found his guards beating the donkey, trying to drive off the stubborn animal. Anooshirvan stopped them saying, "Even a donkey may have justice," and instructed them to find the owner and return the beast with no more blows. It was also during the reign of Anooshirvan the Just that the Prophet Mohammad was born. It is said that Mohammad took great pride in having been born during a period when such a just king ruled Iran.

The Sassanian dynasty gave the empire a period of remarkable stability and development. Towns were built, roads were constructed, taxation on land was graduated, art flourished, and the first university—Jondi Shapur—was founded in the province of Khuzestan. Polo and chess became two popular games in Iran at this time.

The weakening and collapse of the Sassanian Empire marked the end of what some historians have called the Pre-Islamic Era. The Islamic Era, ushered in by conquering Arabs in A.D. 651, has continued to the present day.

Part II: The Islamic Era

Fired by their young Islamic faith, the Arabs swept over the land, overcoming the Persian armies, establishing a rule that endured into the thirteenth century.

Mohammad, founder of the Islamic religion, was not only a prophet, but also a great leader, legislator and judge. (The caliphs or "successors" to Mohammad inherited and assumed all his roles.)

Mohammad did not found the nucleus of the great Moslem Empire by religious persuasion alone, but by political maneuvers and power of the sword.

He had arisen from the position of caravan leader, then Meccan tradesman; but he had nurtured an insatiable desire to restore the religion of Abraham and the belief in *one* God. He realized fulfillment of this burning desire at the age of forty.

All of Mohammad's teaching is embodied in the Koran (the Holy Book of Islam). In less than a century, the Moslem belief (based essentially on the premise, "I submit to the will of Allah") encompassed half of the known civilized world. Today it is the second largest religion of the world, with more than five hundred million followers.

The Persians have shown uncanny ability throughout the years to survive under foreign or tyrannical home rule, outwardly supporting their monarch, but maintaining their own beliefs and true identity. Under Arab domination in the tenth century, they adopted a branch of the Moslem faith known as Shi'ism, rather than Sunnism practiced by the Arabs. Generally speaking, the Sunnites place their faith in the holy word of God or in the Law; the Shi'ites' faith is exemplified in the *Imam*, or divine representative of Allah to his people on earth. The Shi'ites believe that the first true caliph (or unquestioned successor to Mohammad) was Ali, Mohammad's cousin and son-in-law, rather than the direct successor of the Prophet, Abu-Bakre. Shi'ites recognize the first caliph to be Ali (although he was the fourth in succession), then his sons Hassan and Hossein and their descendants.

The Shi'ites, though spinning off from the Sunnites, are divided into sects, one of the most prominent being the Ismaili community, whose leader is Agha Khan. The present leader is Agha Khan IV, who is the forty-ninth Imam of the sect and the leader of Ismailis in East Africa, Pakistan, India and (in small numbers) Iran.

During the Arab domination, a number of local dynasties rose to limited power, the greatest being the Ghaznavids (A.D. 1005), who eventually ruled over most of Iran. After a time, a Turkish tribe of nomads called Seljuqs overran Iran and Iraq, setting up their capital in Rey (south of present-day Tehran) in A.D. 1058. Once again the small dynasties were united under a single power.

During this period there was a strong revival of intellectual activity, spurred by a deep interest in science, architecture and literature. This was the period that produced Omar Khayyám, a famous poet and scientist who deserves greater recognition than the mere mention of his name in this brief history of Persia.

It is said that Hakim Omar Khayyám, along with two close friends, studied under a great and wise man named the Imam Movaffak of Naishápúr. It was the belief at the time that every boy who sat at the Imam's feet to study would attain honor and happiness. The three students made a pact that should one of them "attain honor" he would share it with the other two. One *did*, becoming administrator of affairs during the rule of Sultan Alab Arsalan. Omar Khayyám approached his friend, reminding him of the schoolday vow, saying, "The greatest boon you can confer on me is to let me live in a corner under the shadow of your fortune, to spread wide the advantage of Science, and pray for your long life and prosperity."[6] The wish was granted and the poet-scientist was given a yearly pension of twelve hundred *mithkals* of gold.

Omar Khayyám is remembered by the Western world particularly for his *Rubáiyat,* although during his lifetime he was more noted for his contribution to science. Along with eight other men, he built an observatory for the study of astronomy, and compiled the astronomical tablets known as Zeije Malek Shahi.

One of the most frequently quoted stanzas in the *Rubáiyat* is:

Here with a Loaf of Bread beneath the Bough,
A Flask of Wine, a Book of Verse—and Thou
    Beside me singing in the Wilderness—
And Wilderness is Paradise enow.[6]

Edward J. Fitzgerald, one translator of this poet's verse, says

---

[6]*Rubaiyat of Omar Khayyám,* Hartsdale House, New York, 1932: XI.

Khayyám fell back upon *Today* as the only ground he had to stand on—as may be seen in these two stanzas taken from the same work:

The Worldly Hope men set their Hearts upon
Turns Ashes—or it prospers; and anon
Like Snow upon the Desert's dusty Face
Lighting a little Hour or two—is gone.[7]

Ah, fill the Cup:—what boots it to repeat
How Time is slipping underneath the Feet:
Unborn Tomorrow and dead Yesterday,
Why fret about them if Today is sweet![8]

Ferdowsi, the great epic poet of Iran, was also a product of this period. According to one historian he "outshone them all."[9] Ferdowsi had reached middle age when he came to the court and began his great epic the *Shahnameh* ("Book of Kings"), which when completed comprised some sixty thousand rhyming couplets. One of his best-known stanzas follows:

It was a night like no other. . . .
You came, oh my beloved!
You made the night into blessed day,
You sang music and graciously poured wine,
And you said the words, primeval and holy,
that I have never forgotten,
and the evil night disappeared like smoke.[10]

Although the Arabs conquered Iran and brought the religion of Islam to it, the Persian culture and administrative system became the pillars upon which Islamic civilization was built. During this period art, science and literature flourished, and Iran produced great philosophers and physicians (as well as poets) such as Avicenna, the father of modern medicine; Razi, one of the greatest physicians of the Moslem world and Rudaki and Daghighi, eminent poets, along with Khayyám and Ferdowsi.

---

[7]*Ibid.*, XIV.
[8]*Ibid.*, XXXVIII.
[9]Donald N. Wilber, *Iran Past and Present*, Princeton University Press, Princeton, New Jersey, 1967, p. 41.
[10]*Springs of Persian Wisdom*, op. cit. (pages not numbered).

About A.D. 1220, the Mongols under the ruthless Genghis Khan swept into the country, crushing the Arab rule and initiating a century of destruction and terror. The conquerors, however, found it necessary to rely on the Persian people as administrators, architects and writers. After several decades, ironically the conquerors began to adopt the Persian culture; and the Khan's great grandson, Ghazan Khan, became a Moslem, announcing his independence from the great Khan.

The Safavids (a Persian dynasty) ruled Iran once again when Shah Ismail asserted his power in the northwest and was crowned in Tabriz in A.D. 1502. Of the three strong kings of the Safavid dynasty, the outstanding monarch was Shah Abbas the Great (1587-1629), who promptly installed the Shi'ah faith as the state religion.

The Safavid period in general, and the forty-year reign of Shah Abbas in particular, are regarded as golden eras in Iran's history. Shah Abbas is known especially for his administrative ability, his reconstruction of the country, and his great support of the arts. In 1598 he moved his capital from Ghazvin to Esfahan and rebuilt it as a beautiful city with some of the finest mosques in the world. Esfahan became the center of eastern Moslem art and culture for almost two hundred years. Most of the great buildings in Esfahan constructed under Shah Abbas stand largely unchanged today, and the city is one of the major tourist attractions of Iran. Shah Abbas was also responsible for the construction of roads and caravanserais (inns) all over the country, encouraging travel and communication among all parts of the nation. It was during his reign that diplomatic contact was made with European countries and ambassadors were exchanged for the first time.

Historians point out that he failed to train administrators to follow him; consequently succeeding kings were somewhat inept as rulers. An Iranian proverb states that "when the great Prince ceased to exist, Iran ceased to prosper." The last of the Safavid dynasty, Shah Sultan Hossein (1694-1722) was in many ways the opposite of Shah Abbas. He was a very religious man; he built the Madresseh Chahar Baq, a religious school and one of Esfahan's finest mosques; but he spent most of his time there discussing religious matters rather than ruling his country. As a result, he lost not only his mosque, but his throne and his head as well to the Afghani invaders.

Chahar Bagh Mosque and Theological School, built during the reign of Shah
Sultan Hossein (the last of the Safavid kings) at Esfahan

Minarets of Masjid-e-Shah, the largest mosque of the Safavid era in Esfahan

Full view of Masjid-e-Shah, built by the master architect, Aliakbar Esfahani during the reign of Shah Abbas the Great, in Esfahan

View of Ali Qapu, the Residential Palace of Shah Abbas the Great, in Esfahan

A view of Chahar Bagh Mosque and Theological School

Mehrab (prayer niche) of Sheikh Lotfollah Mosque, Esfahan

Details of faience decorations on Sheikh Lotfollah Mosque, Esfahan

A few hundred years before the Safavids, Omar Khayyám wrote a quatrain which nicely summarizes both extremes of the dynasty:

> Alike for those who for today prepare
> and those that after a tomorrow stare,
>   A muezzin from the tower of darkness cries,
> "Fools, your reward is neither here nor there."[11]

In 1736, the Safavid dynasty was followed by the Afshar dynasty, established by a great general of simple origin, Nader Shah. One of the things for which he is remembered is his invasion of India, from where he returned bearing fabulous treasures.

Nader Shah is remembered also for reconquering territory (including Bokhara, Kiva, presently in Russia, and Iraq), that had been lost from the empire to invading enemies. He was assassinated in 1747.

In the north, the Turkish tribe of Qajar became so powerful that in 1794 their chief, Agha Mohammad Khan, was crowned Shah. Following his assassination a year later, the dynasty continued under Fath-Ali Shah. Unfortunately, the Qajar dynasty nearly bankrupted the country. Iran lost some of its northern provinces to Russia, and finally assumed the geographical boundaries that exist today.

Foreign infiltration became a sinister problem; religious leaders wielded far too much power in civil affairs; and tribal matters got out of hand. Toward the end of the nineteenth century, the people rose up in apprehension and frustration to demand the formation of a constitution. In 1905 the ruler of the country, Mozaffar-ed-din Shah, gave his promise to satisfy the urgent request, but he did not honor his word. In 1906, the Constitutionalists renewed their demands. Two years later, they won their case when the Parliament (Majlis) took form. Iran was the first country in Asia to fight for and win a constitution. (An American missionary named Baskerville lost his life in Tabriz, helping Iranians to gain their Constitution.)

However, the step toward a more democratic form of government did not succeed. Results were disastrous. The illiterate Persians, particularly, like their ancestors, could not understand or

---

[11]*Rubaiyat of Omar Khayyám*, XXIV.

accept authority from anyone but the Shah—the supreme power. World War I added to the chaos, and in 1921 a powerful soldier who had risen from the ranks of the Persian Cossack Brigade wrested the reins of government from the Qajar dynasty, after marching on Tehran with a few thousand men. In 1925, he set up the Pahlavi dynasty (named for an ancient form of the Persian language). This soldier was Reza Shah, father of the present Shah.

When he was later crowned, this common soldier who had been illiterate into his teens was proclaimed Shahanshah (King of Kings), Shadow of the Almighty, Vice-Regent of God, and the Center of the Universe. (Under Islam, rulers were considered to be "the shadow of God upon the earth.") However, Reza Shah differed in many ways from his predecessors on the throne. Richard N. Frye in his book *Persia*, describes him in this way:

> Reza Shah decided that Iran was not ready for the paraphernalia of Western parliamentary government so he ruled benevolently by fiat. Yet he passionately believed in a modern, powerful Iran which could prosper, in his opinion, only if the underbrush of the Safavid and Qajar past could be cleared away. This meant the divorce of church and state, the creation of a new secular society.[12]

Reza Shah abolished the judicial rights of the Mullahs (Moslem priests), established courts and revised laws concerning many facets of living. Previous to this time an alien criminal could not be tried in a Persian court. Reza Shah took away this privilege of immunity from the foreign lawbreaker.

Mr. Frye sums it all up when he says that "the brave new world of Iran began with the Reza Shah." He was tireless in his work, giving the smallest detail his meticulous attention; he revised the tax structure, established a national bank, founded factories, started the building of modern harbors, founded a new modern army, built thousands of kilometers of new roads, created a uniform system of coinage, fought illiteracy, and built the Trans-Iranian Railroad from the Caspian Sea to the Persian Gulf—perhaps his greatest achievement.

The Shah wanted his country to be independent of other powers, but when he introduced industrialization and a sort of

---

[12]Richard N. Frye, *Persia*, Schocken Books, New York, 1969, p. 34. For a detailed study of this Shah, see Donald N. Wilber, *Riza Shah Pahlavi: The Resurrection and Reconstruction of Iran*, Exposition Press, Inc., Hicksville, New York, 1975.

"crash" program of education he found it necessary to import technicians with ready skills, engineers, and teachers, in large numbers. Most of these specialists came from Germany to assist in furthering the progress of the "new Iran." German architects and engineers built government buildings, designed machinery for the new factories and built the Trans-Iranian Railway. The close association, although very helpful at the time, was to give the government serious problems later.

Reza Shah established a university in 1935, uniting various existing colleges in Tehran. Thousands of Persian students were sent abroad to study—in Europe and in the United States. But from this elevation of education grew a strange problem: the average educated man would not deign to use his hands in manual labor. The faculty of law was the most popular in the university because the graduates were promised government posts which would not require manual labor. Unfortunately, this attitude toward working with one's hands still persists to some degree in Iran today.

Reza Shah, although sometimes less than sagacious, with his forceful character, led the country out of conditions reminiscent of the Middle Ages. One of his greatest achievements was the emancipation of women. Before the Pahlavi era Iranian women were kept ignorant, and those in upper-class Persian families never set foot outside their homes without being veiled.

By 1930, many of the women of the higher classes had adopted European dress for wear in their homes, and sometimes at mixed parties; a few of the more daring appeared occasionally on the street unveiled. By 1935 women teachers and schoolgirls were forbidden by law to wear the veil in schools. And then on January 8, 1936, the Queen and two of her daughters appeared unveiled with Reza Shah at a public official ceremony, thereby placing the stamp on the right of women to appear at all times in all places unveiled. Unfortunately the reign of Reza Shah did not last long enough to establish Iran firmly on her course of development.

The tragedy of World War II descended with dire effects for the regime of Reza Shah. Persia proclaimed her neutrality at once, but after Germany's merciless onslaught against Russia, it was obvious that the Soviet Union could survive only if Britain and the United States came to her aid. But how could arms and supplies be routed to reach the Soviet Union without traversing enemy territory? Once again, Iran's geographical position affected her destiny. The only plan that seemed feasible was to proceed through the Persian Gulf and across Iran by way of the newly constructed Trans-Iranian Railway.

It was common knowledge that thousands of Germans in technical and educational work resided in Iran. These highly disciplined Germans were able to convince people in high places that Germany would win the war. Secret agents organized groups of sympathizers among tribesmen in southwestern Iran as well as in Tehran and Esfahan.

Great Britain and Soviet Russia, apprised of these activities, used them as an excuse, and put pressure on Reza Shah to correct the situation. However, perhaps because of his strong nationalistic feelings against interference in Iran's internal affairs by other countries, Reza Shah refused to act. The Allies demanded the expulsion of the German nationals, but Reza Shah and his government, again declaring their neutrality, refused.

Consequently, on August 25, 1941, British troops entered Iran across the Iraq frontier and landed at the head of the Persian Gulf, while the Russians invaded the country from the northwest in a simultaneously-timed operation. British ships attacked Iran naval forces at Khorramshahr, sinking every vessel—a bitter blow. Iranian troops saw defeat as inevitable, and after three days, the Prime Minister resigned and his successor sent out the order for all forces to cease resistance.

On September 9, the newly appointed Prime Minister, acting with the consent of Parliament, agreed to the demands of the Allies, whose authorities had halted their forces some distance from the capital city. However, when the Persian government procrastinated in keeping their part of the bargain, the impatient Allies gave notice that their troops would enter Tehran on the afternoon of September 17.

Seeing the handwriting on the wall, Reza Shah announced his abdication on the morning of the sixteenth, and on that day his son, Mohammad Reza Pahlavi, succeeded to the throne. (Reza Shah died in exile in Johannesburg, July 26, 1944.)

Assadollah Alam, the present Court Minister of Iran, reminisces about that day with reporter Amir Taheri, in an article published by *Kayhan International* on December 14, 1972. Alam remembers that on that rather hot gray September day, a crowd of several thousand watched as the new King Mohammad Reza Shah Pahlavi drove to Parliament to take the oath as the second of the Pahlavis before "demoralized, browbeaten and disheartened Majlis deputies."

According to the article,

> At first there was no "sparkle" and the people watched in gloomy silence. Then someone in the crowd shouted, "Long Live the Shah!" The response from the rest of the people was slow in coming. But when it did come it produced something like a "thunderclap." In the young, pensive, but faintly smiling prince, who was to be sworn in as the Shahanshah of Iran, the people of Iran saw what appeared to them as the only figure between them and perdition.

Alam remembers that what had begun as a somber, silent procession developed into one of "veritable passion" as everyone tried to get closer to the Shah. The people were undoubtedly fervently hoping that with the new sovereign sworn in, Iran would be allowed to resume its life as an independent nation. But this was merely a prologue to a great drama.

Chronology of Events in Iranian History
from 1500 B.C. to A.D. 1941

Elamites lived on the Iranian Plateau in pre-historic times.

Part I: The Pre-Islamic Era

1500 B.C.:	Medes and Persians settled in the plateau of Iran
553 B.C.:	Persians of Achaemenid dynasty overthrew the rule of the Medes. Great kings of this dynasty: Cambyses, his son Cyrus the Great, Darius and Xerxes
330 B.C.:	Alexander the Great conquered Persia
248 B.C.:	Parthians came to power
A.D. 224:	Ardeshir established the Sassanian dynasty
A.D. 651:	Arabs conquered Iran

Part II: The Beginning of the Islamic Era

A.D. 1005:	The Ghaznavid dynasty was established
A.D. 1058:	The Seljuq dynasty was established
A.D. 1220:	Mongols under Genghis Khan crushed Iran
A.D. 1499:	Shah Ismail established the Safavid dynasty
A.D. 1736:	Nader Shah established the Afshar dynasty
A.D. 1794:	Agha Mohammad Khan established the Qajar dynasty
A.D. 1925:	Reza Shah the Great established the Pahlavi dynasty; later forced to abdicate in favor of his son.
A.D. 1941:	Mohammad Reza Shah Pahlavi succeeded to the throne

3
Turbulent Years

Assuming the role of monarch at the age of twenty-one was a gargantuan undertaking for Mohammad Reza Shah Pahlavi. In his own words, he was at once "plunged into a sea of trouble." A state of conflict and tension plagued the country, for Iran was torn by factions made up of people with diverse loyalties. Some intellectuals went underground, aiding the Germans, whose ultimate aim appeared to be crossing Iran to conquer India.

Some of the unrest among the tribes was the direct result of the unyielding rule of Reza Shah, who had not hesitated to incarcerate tribal leaders whom he thought to be wielding unwarranted power in the provinces. Sons of these imprisoned tribesmen foresaw liberation of their fathers and return of their family lands, if Hitler were successful in invading the country and toppling the government. As might well be expected, these young tribal chiefs exerted prime influence in quietly furthering German espionage.

The people, accustomed to obeying orders from their unquestioned leader, were confused after Reza Shah was forced to abdicate and his young, untried son ascended the throne. Members of Parliament, used to voting only according to the wishes of the Shah, were at a loss. Some openly sided with the Allies; others were uncertain and wavering in their loyalties, or they covertly worked for the German cause.

After occupation and the total disintegration of the Iranian armed forces, the Allies dictated policies through their embassies, emasculating the power of the already weakened Majlis and the central government. For example, if the request for permission to cut down a forest to facilitate movement of war supplies were presented to the Ministry of Agriculture, through one of the embassies of the Allies, there was nothing the government could do but comply.

The domestic economy was directly affected by the dire situation: inflation set in, prices skyrocketed out of control, and bribery for favors from those holding certain reins flourished.

In the face of all this, the young monarch held the awesome responsibility for maintaining courage among his divided people and instilling some sort of confidence that the nation would survive the ordeal of occupation and would once again—on a brighter day—enjoy autonomy.

Meanwhile the Western Allies sent more than five million tons of supplies to the Soviet Union through Persia in less than three years. The Trans-Iranian Railway carried a little more than half of the total tonnage, the remainder being sent by road. Most of these roads first had to be built, and then safeguarded against German sabotage.

Facilities of the railway and the Persian fleets of trucks were severely taxed, and were found to be totally inadequate. The British and Americans sent rolling stock, locomotives and thousands of trucks to add to the facilities.

To offset the dire consequences of the disastrously disrupted economy, the Americans and British also sent tons of food and supplies. The American Lend-Lease program was responsible for sending technical help in agriculture, health, finance and police.

In November 1943, British Prime Minister Winston Churchill and Franklin D. Roosevelt, President of the United States, met in conference at a villa near the pyramids in Egypt. It had become increasingly apparent in this delicate phase of prosecution of the war that a high level meeting of the three big powers was necessary. Tehran was agreed upon as the meeting place with Stalin; and on November 27, at dawn, the Prime Minister and the President flew out of Cairo in different planes, proceeded by different routes, arriving at different times.

Mr. Churchill discusses the British Legation's failure to follow utmost safety precautions for his arrival in his book, *Closing the Ring*. He comments that he "could not admire the arrangement" made for his arrival in Tehran, where he was met at Mehrabad Airport by the British Minister in his car. Churchill writes about the drive to the Legation:

> As we approached the city, the road was lined with Persian cavalrymen every fifty yards, for at least three miles. It was clearly shown to any evil people that somebody of consequence was coming, and which way. The men on horseback advertised the route, but could provide no protection at all. A police car driving a hundred yards in advance gave warning of our approach. The pace was slow. Presently large crowds stood in the spaces between the Persian cavalry, and as far as I could see there were few, if any, foot police.[13]

The crowds grew denser and got closer to the car as the procession reached the city; and if someone had wanted to attack Mr. Churchill and the British Minister, there would have been no defense. A block from the Legation a traffic jam, caused by a large truck at an intersection behind the Russian Embassy, held the car stationary in the crowd for about four minutes. I was working in the British Legation at the time, and I watched the situation with deep personal concern until police arrived to untangle the traffic, allowing the official cars to proceed.

In his book *Closing the Ring*, Churchill writes sarcastically:

> If it had been planned out beforehand to run the greatest risks, and have neither the security of quiet surprise arrival nor an effective escort, the problem could not have been solved more perfectly.[14]

In spite of Churchill's opinion regarding the lack of security measures taken by the British Legation, great care had been shown at the Legation to protect visiting dignitaries. We had devised a foolproof system whereby no member of the British Legation staff or anyone else could enter without a validated pass signed and sealed by one person, and with a special code known only to the security guards. I was responsible for informing the Guards (Indians) in charge of Embassy security of regulations set especially for the Tehran Conference. They were told that nobody under any circumstances could walk in without his pass, whether or not he was well known.

---

[13]Winston Churchill, *Closing the Ring*, Houghton-Mifflin, Boston (also Riverside Press, Cambridge), 1951, p. 342.
[14]*Ibid.*, p. 343.

A few days before Mr. Churchill's arrival, I appeared at the Embassy with my driver, and the guard (a good friend) saluted and said, "Good morning, Mr. Issari! May I see your pass, please?" Unfortunately, I had forgotten to bring mine with me that morning and I said, "I'm sorry. I left it at home. I'll make sure to have it with me when I come back after lunch."

He walked back, opened the door and said with great authority, "Sir, please get out of the car." And to the driver who had shown his pass, he said, "You can go in, but I don't know this gentleman." He called one of the Indian soldiers and told him to escort me out of the Legation. I knew then that Mr. Churchill or anyone else coming to the Legation would be absolutely safe. Similar security measures were taken at other legations.

The American security system was better prepared for Roosevelt's arrival. According to information in the President's log[15] of his trip to Tehran, his plane arrived at 3:00 P.M., having covered 1,310 miles from Cairo in about six and a half hours' flying time. His plane and others bearing members of the American and British delegations landed at a military field, unknown at that time to many Iranians (Gale Morghe Airport), about five miles south of the capital city.

Only one official greeted the President (as per request): Major General D. H. Connally, Commanding General of the Persian Gulf Service Command.

Mr. Roosevelt entered a waiting U.S. Army motorcar and, unescorted by the usual number of armed vehicles (appropriate for wartime security measures), proceeded to the American Legation through back streets of the city.

Before leaving Cairo the President had been urged to set up his headquarters at the British or Russian legations, but, wishing to be independent during the Tehran Conference, he expressed preference for living at the American Legation. (Another reason for his decision rested in the fact that he had been approached first by the British, and should he have accepted their offer of hospitality, the Russians might have been offended.)

The problem then arose as to where the Big Three should meet —the British and Russian compounds were across the street from

---

[15]*Foreign Relations of the United States Diplomatic Papers: The Conferences at Cairo and Tehran 1943;* United States Government Printing Office, Washington, 1961.

each other, but the American Legation was about a mile away. The German intelligence network was very strong in Iran at this time, and opportunities for assassination had to be kept to a minimum. Churchill states,

> Molotov, who had been in Tehran twenty four hours before our arrival, produced a story that the Soviet Secret Intelligence had unearthed a plot to kill one or more of the "Big Three", as we were regarded, and the idea of one or the other of us continually going to and fro through the streets filled him with deep alarm. "If anything like that were to happen," he said, "it could produce a most unfortunate impression." This could not be denied.[16]

On being apprised of this personal danger to heads of state, Roosevelt moved into the Russian compound for the duration of his stay. Two streets on each side were blocked off, thereby making the two compounds into one security complex, giving easy access and freedom of movement to the Big Three and their staffs.

One happy personal incident, related to the Conference, comes to mind—a party for Winston Churchill on his sixty-ninth birthday, November 30. It was a beautiful autumn day when all members of the Legation staff (both British and Iranian)—sixty or seventy of us—gathered in front of the Chancery to wish him "many happy returns." Churchill came out of the building with Anthony Eden at his side and smilingly acknowledged our gesture of good will and affection by raising his right hand in a V for victory sign with two fingers. He had his famous cigar clenched in his teeth and looked happy and content. The traditional birthday cake and tea were served, of course.

Mr. Churchill does not refer to this tea party honoring him in his report of the Tehran Conference in *Closing the Ring*, but he does give an account of his birthday dinner:

> Hitherto we had assembled for our conference or meals in the Soviet Embassy. I had claimed however that I should be the host at the third dinner, which should be held in the British Legation. This could not well be disputed. Great Britain and I myself both came first alphabetically, and in seniority I was four or five years older than Roosevelt or Stalin. We were by centuries the longest established of the three Governments; I might have added, but did not, that we had been the longest in the war; and finally, November 30 was my birthday.[17]

---

[16]Churchill, *op. cit.*, p. 343.
[17]*Ibid.*, p. 384.

The other two powers agreed but the Russians insisted on searching every inch of the British Legation beforehand, and the armed Russian police guarding the place were almost matched in number by American security men. Stalin and Roosevelt arrived in a good mood and Churchill writes the following about the event:

> This was a memorable occasion in my life. On my right sat the President of the United States, and on my left the master of Russia. Together we controlled practically all the naval and three-quarters of all the air forces in the world, and could direct armies of nearly twenty millions of men, engaged in the most terrible of wars that had yet occurred in human history.[18]

But what did the Conference purport for Iran? The people of the country were wondering, now that the "Big Three" were guests in their capital city, whether Iran's sovereignty would be respected. Would the Allies pull their forces out of the country after the war if they won? Would the Germans invade Iran as they had many European countries? An air of tension prevailed not only in Tehran, but in the whole country.

The one person most concerned was of course the young Shah, captain of a ship on a stormy sea. The Shah met with the three great Allied leaders to obtain some answers to these questions. The result was the Declaration of the Three Powers Regarding Iran,[19] issued December 1, 1943:

> The President of the United States, the Premier of the U.S.S.R., and the Prime Minister of the United Kingdom having consulted with each other and with the Prime Minister of Iran, desire to declare the mutual agreement of their three Governments regarding their relations with Iran.
> The Governments of the United States, the U.S.S.R., and the United Kingdom recognize the assistance which Iran has given in the prosecution of the war against the common enemy, particularly by facilitating the transportation of supplies from overseas to the Soviet Union.
> The Three Governments realize that the war has caused special economic difficulties for Iran, and they are agreed that they will continue to make available to the Government of Iran such economic assistance as may be possible, having regard to the heavy demands made upon them by their world-wide military operations and to the world-wide shortage of transport, raw materials and supplies for civilian consumption.
> With respect to the post-war period, the Governments of the United States, the U.S.S.R., and the United Kingdom are in accord with the

[18]*Ibid.*, p. 385.
[19]Included in *Foreign Relations of the United States Diplomatic Papers, The Conferences at Cairo and Tehran 1943*, pp. 646, 647.

Government of Iran that any economic problems confronting Iran at the close of hostilities should receive full consideration, along with those of other members of the United Nations, by conferences or international agencies held or created to deal with international economic matters.

The Governments of the United States, the U.S.S.R., and the United Kingdom are at one with the Government of Iran in their desire for the maintenance of the independence, sovereignty and territorial integrity of Iran. They count upon the participation of Iran, together with all other peace-loving nations, in the establishment of international peace, security and prosperity after the war, in accordance with the principles of the Atlantic Charter, to which all four Governments have subscribed.

> Winston S. Churchill
> J. Stalin
> Franklin D. Roosevelt

After the war, true to the spirit of the pact agreed upon at the Tehran Conference, the British and American troops withdrew; however, the Russians had something else in mind. They had established a rebel puppet government in Azarbaijan—one of the provinces they occupied, fully intending to retain rule there.

On March 3, 1946, Russian troops in Tabriz, capital of Azarbaijan, divided into three columns. One headed in the direction of Iraq, one toward Turkey, and the third toward Tehran. Subsequently, hundreds of tanks and numerous army units started pouring into Iran from Russia, moving in three directions—toward Iraq, Turkey and Tehran. The Soviet Union deployed troops along Turkey's European frontier, and at the same time initiated diplomatic and propaganda action against Iran—an intimidating offensive.

In effect, Russian troops had separated a province of Iran from the rest of the country. Ahmad Qavam, the shrewd Prime Minister of Iran, in a unique move offered certain concessions in establishing a joint Russian-Iranian Oil Company, recognizing the Azarbaijan government and—most important of all—withdrawing Iran's complaint against the Soviet Union before the United Nations, in exchange for withdrawal of all Russian forces from Iran.

The Prime Minister was aware that a well-known tactic of the great Communist power is to "nibble away" at border territory during times of vulnerability. It was conceivable, should Russian troops be allowed to remain in the area, that—following the pattern of the takeover of Azarbaijan—other neighboring provinces on the 1,100-mile border between the two countries, such as Gilan, Mazanderan and Khorassan, might eventually fall into their hands. He was willing to risk the one province (Azarbaijan), at least for the time being, to save others.

Nevertheless, Ambassador Hossein Ala (later Minister of the Imperial Court), who was serving as the head of the Iranian delegation to the United Nations at the time, refused to retract the Iranian complaint from the Security Council.

The Shah writes in *Mission for My Country:* "He [Ala] knew that I wanted the complaint to stand, and he realized that it was because of Soviet pressure that Qavam had requested its removal."[20] At the next session, held on the twenty-first of March, Mr. Ala discussed in an extremely forceful manner the problem of the continued occupation of a portion of Iran by Russian troops, demanding the withdrawal of Russian forces immediately in accordance with the terms of the Tehran Declaration of 1943. Five days later Mr. Gromyko, the head of the Soviet delegation, announced that all Soviet forces would proceed at once to evacuate the country.

By the ninth of May all were gone. This was the first true test of the effectiveness of the great peacemaking organization, the United Nations. Had the Russians not been stopped in Iran, Turkey and perhaps Iraq might have subsequently felt the iron heel also.

The rebel Azarbaijan government collapsed under the pressure of Imperial Iranian forces led by the Shah, and all remnants surrendered in Tabriz on December 15 of the same year (1946), their leaders fleeing to Russia. This date is celebrated as a national holiday called Azarbaijan Day. It commemorates the recovery of that important province—in many ways the cradle of Persian culture and civilization, and the home of many national heroes.

Sometime after the Azarbaijan Affair, we put a film together using footage showing much of what actually happened—the manner in which the army commanded by the Shah maneuvered to quell the rebellious forces, and their eventual triumph. The film was shown all over Iran, especially in the army barracks, and it has been shown in subsequent years across the country on Azarbaijan Day.

Bitter about losing the province, the Russians set up radio stations over which they beamed propaganda almost endlessly. In

---

[20]Mohammed Reza Shah Pahlavi, *op. cit.,* p. 116.

addition they installed public address systems on their side of the border in the Azarbaijan area. Towers were erected from which Russian soldiers monitored the movements of the Iranians on our side of the border.

In 1951 when we were setting up our cinema mobile unit operation in the country, I arrived at a small town called Astara with a unit to present movies for the people of the region. The gendarmerie authorities welcomed us with open arms, saying, "We had heard you were coming. We're glad because the Russians put up one of their public address systems right across the river and they broadcast propaganda every few hours—even while we're having lunch! We have no way to counterattack this. What can you do to help?"

I answered that we'd do the same. We were expecting a crowd of two to three thousand people from the nearby towns and villages to view the movies in the open air. We set up our screen in such a way that it would face Russia; and on our first evening there, we presented the popular motion picture showing the Shah's visit to the United States. We turned up the volume so that those on the other side of the border could not only see the picture, but could also hear the narrative. When the close-up of the Shah appeared on the screen, the cheers from the villagers filled the night!

When we used the public address system for explanation or announcements, we were very careful not to say anything derogatory about the neighbors listening in across the river. We wished our project (a joint American-Iranian project) to act as a positive deterrent. Our method worked. The next day the Russian loudspeakers were completely silent. Our counterattack had been successful.

In a country fraught with internal problems and still insecure as to its place in the family of nations, after being victimized as a side effect of the devastating war, a struggle for power was almost certain to ensue. Two main elements were striving for ascendancy at the time.

The first was the Tudeh Party, highly influenced by international communism, which attracted a great number of educated and semieducated segments of the population. The second was the Nationalist Front, composed of those who did not sanction the communist doctrine, but who on the other hand did not believe in absolute monarchy, fearful of another period such as Reza

Shah's reign, during which democratic procedures had been suppressed in favor of national development.

And of course the Shah, feeling a deep concern for the country and its future, thought only to unite the people and lead them toward the most urgently needed social and economic progress.

In the late forties, Dr. Mohammad Mossadegh, whose blood line was connected with that of the Qajar dynasty, rose to lead the Nationalists, comprised of people from all walks of life, from shopkeepers to engineers and laborers to university professors. He had at various times held a number of responsible positions in the government: Minister of Finance, Minister of Justice, Minister of Foreign Affairs; and he was long a member of Parliament.

To understand the rise and fall of these various factions in the 1950s, which eventually led to what is now referred to as the "Revolution of the Shah and People" in 1963 (during which oil was a major factor in Iranian politics), one ought to know a little about the history of oil in Iran.

Persia was the first Middle Eastern country in which oil was discovered—in the shadow of an ancient Zoroastrian temple. Oil had been used for the "eternal fire" of the Zoroastrian temples for hundreds of years. It was utilized as a means of offense and defense in war, on flaming arrow tips shot over battlements, or in boiling cauldrons emptied on attackers scaling walls. It was also used in curing camels of mange and in caulking boats.

The discovery of the first oil well in Masjid-e-Suleiman in 1908 led to the creation of the Anglo-Persian Oil Company (APOC), and later Anglo-Iranian Oil Company (AIOC), a British-owned company which paid Iran only a small percentage of its huge income for exploring and selling Iranian oil. The agreement with the British Petroleum Company (BP, known in Iran as Benzine Pars), the mother company of APOC and AIOC, was revised a couple of times during Reza Shah's reign, but each time Iran was given only a few percent more than it had received under the previous agreement, while the oil company was realizing fabulous wealth from its activities in Iran.

After the Azarbaijan settlement, in an attempt to find new sources of revenue to pursue her development of economic and social reforms in this period of postwar reconstruction, Iran looked to her oil resources for more income. Negotiations started with the British Petroleum company but after a couple of years all efforts proved fruitless.

The difference between Iran's demand and the company's offer was only about two percent; Iran was asking for an increase in her revenue from about 16 percent to approximately 35 percent, but the company was willing to go only as far as 33 percent. At the time (1949) I was Public Relations Advisor to the AIOC in Tehran. My boss, the head of Public Relations for the company in Iran, thought that the Iranians were bargaining and that if the company would stand firm an agreement could be reached.

I had the opposite view and thought the company should meet Iran's demand and sign the agreement because this was not a sudden impulse on the part of the Iranians, but rather the culmination of many decades of frustration. I believed that refusal of the company to agree would result in their having to accept the consequences which might create a much more serious crisis. But of course no one could see into the future and the oil negotiations dragged on.

In 1950 an able man, General Razmara, became Prime Minister of Iran, and tried to bring these negotiations to a fruitful conclusion. But when he was assassinated in 1951 the negotiations broke down completely. Shortly thereafter Dr. Mossadegh, who was leading the minority in the oil dispute in Parliament, became Premier of Iran. Under his leadership and with the full support of the Shah and other factions in the country, the oil nationalization bill was unanimously approved by the Iranian Parliament. Iran took over the exploration, refining and marketing of her oil resources from AIOC, a task that raised the self-confidence of Iranians high while lowering their economic status. Mossadegh, leading the Nationalists, suddenly became a hero to the masses; unfortunately, he did not know where logic should rule over sentiment. He calculated that if he did not sell oil to the British, Europe would come to her knees within three months, particularly because he assumed the Russians in their power struggle with the West would support Iran's cause and refuse to sell their oil in the European market. The company tried to come to new terms with Iran, sending several negotiating teams, both British and American, but Mossadegh was given poor counsel by his young, inexperienced advisors and held out for better terms.

At some point I heard that one of these missions offered up to 75 percent of the oil revenue but Premier Mossadegh refused. Europe did not come to her knees in three months and the Russians *did* sell their oil in the European market. Iran was left alone with no revenue from the oil and a mountain of bills to pay. The situation deteriorated all over the country and Mossadegh, not being able to deliver on his many promises to the people, faced grave difficulties and opposition of the Parliament which had brought him to power.

Mossadegh, a unique politician, once went to Parliament to submit a bill but could not find a quorum. He came out of the house and into the street where he stood on a platform and talked to a crowd of many hundreds who gathered within a short time to hear their Premier. He said, in effect, "If your representatives conspire against me behind those walls I come to you, my *real* constituents, and ask for your support and permission to carry out my reform program." This action, in a country where the man on the street had never been given such democratic importance, created an explosion of public favor for Mossadegh.

In July 1952 in order to solve some of his problems he demanded that if he were to continue in the office of Prime Minister he must be given extraordinary powers to govern for six months without having to observe Parliamentary procedure. The Shah refused to grant him this power and appointed Ahmad Qavam to replace Dr. Mossadegh. Qavam had more than once served in this position and in fact was the premier who negotiated with the Russians for evacuation of Iran after the war. Suddenly mob rule took over, spurred by the Communist Tudeh party and Mossadegh's followers. Noting at once that the new appointee was too old and weak to restore order, the Shah suggested that he resign—after only four days. Then there was no alternative but to give Mossadegh all the powers he had demanded as he seemed to be the only one with nationwide popular support and therefore able to unite the various factions.

During these turbulent times disputes with Great Britain over oil rights and ways of conducting the industry rose to fever pitch; as a result Mossadegh broke off foreign relations with the British. Impetuously, in order to bring about his reforms, he suspended elections for the National Assembly, dissolved the Supreme Court, abolished the Senate, stifled the press, and the economy of the country was damaged to the point of bankruptcy.

In hindsight, one might conclude that Mossadegh attempted to make too many changes much too fast. I am reminded of a quatrain written by the great poet Sa'di:

O thou who desirest to reach the station
Take my advice and learn patience.
An Arab horse gallops twice in a race.
A camel ambles gently night and day.[21]

Quoting William O. Douglas in his book *West of the Indus,* "The one [reform] that triggered the explosion leading to Mossadegh's downfall was a constitutional argument with the Shah. The Shah both reigns and rules, appointing Prime Ministers · as he chooses. Mossadegh wanted the Shah to follow the example of the British monarch and reign but not rule. Mossadegh's bid was for Parliamentary control and the transformation of the Shah into a constitutional monarch."[22]

In February 1953, Mossadegh suggested that the Shah leave the country for a time, giving him more freedom to carry out his proposed plans. In early spring, after news had leaked to the people in the capital city that the Prime Minister was attempting to force the Shah into exile, hundreds of them demonstrated outside the palace in a great show of loyalty to their ruler. The Shah, heartened by this show of loyalty, remained in Tehran. To offset this display, the Communist Tudeh party, allied with great numbers of Mossadegh's followers, called for a united front against the monarchy.

The Shah shortly thereafter slipped away to a hunting lodge on the shore of the Caspian Sea, not far from Ramsar. It was here on the thirteenth of August that His Majesty, exercising his constitutional rights, spurred by the necessity of settling the line of authority once and for all, signed a decree dismissing Dr. Mossadegh as Prime Minister, appointing in his place General Fazlollah Zahedi. The Shah entrusted the delivery of his two messages for Mossadegh and Zahedi to a military aide, Colonel Nematollah Nassiry, and left the country in his small private plane, landing first in Baghdad.

Although the Iranian ambassador to Iraq probably knew of

---

[21]Reprinted by permission of G. P. Putnam's Sons, from *The Gulistan of Sa'di,* Copyright © 1964 by George-Allen & Unwin Ltd.; translated by Edward Rehatsek, edited with a preface by W. G. Archer; Story 4, p. 209.

[22]William O. Douglas, *West of the Indus,* Doubleday and Co. Inc., Garden City, N.Y., 1958, p. 286.

the Shah's actions, he disregarded them and was not at the airport
to meet him. After the plane had been refueled, the party flew on to
Rome, where the Shah was greeted only as a private individual by
royalists from the Iranian embassy.

The next few days were, in my opinion, the most crucial in
those turbulent years. Zahedi, who had once supported Mossadegh
but who was later fearlessly outspoken against him, had found it
necessary to live in hiding to protect his life. Only a few people
were aware as to his whereabouts, for he moved from place to
place—sometimes daily—in the interest of self-preservation.

Colonel Nassiry delivered the Shah's note to General Zahedi,
who agreed to serve if Dr. Mossadegh was displaced. Getting the
message to the Prime Minister was not so easy. But flanked by two
other officers, Colonel Nassiry approached Mossadegh's house un-
molested—passing the muzzles of tank guns on the way. An aide
accepted the message, delivered it to Mossadegh, and finally returned with a signed receipt. The Colonel knew the Prime Minister's handwriting and felt sure the note had been delivered. As
might be expected, Nassiry was arrested shortly thereafter by
Mossadegh's forces and jailed.

When the Iranian people found out by radio and through the
newspapers that the Shah had left the country, many assumed he
had departed in frustration or anger and they were highly verbal
in expressing their sympathy with his untenable position. But
when the news leaked out that he had issued the order that Mossadegh was to be replaced by Zahedi as Prime Minister, citizens,
unarmed or carrying sticks, stormed the prison and demanded the
release of all political prisoners. Although they were met with
shots by the guards—some were killed—they kept coming in a re-
lentless, determined mass. The guards, fearing for their lives, fled
and the prison was evacuated; along with many others, Colonel
Nassiry walked out a free man. Tehran became a battleground on
which Mossadegh's followers challenged the thousands of ordinary
people who demanded the return of the Shah.

The revolution was now in full swing. An army man drove a
tank close to Mossadegh's residence and half wrecked it with
cannon fire. The Prime Minister climbed over the garden wall and
escaped, to be captured a couple of days later.

On August 19, when victory was assured, General Zahedi
declared (by radio) the people's revolution to be a success, and

announced himself as the Shah's newly-appointed Prime Minister. Three days later on August 22, 1953, His Imperial Majesty returned to Tehran in triumph.

Dr. Mossadegh was brought to trial on November 9, charged with failure to obey imperial edicts, and with plotting the overthrow of the monarchy. On December 21 he received a sentence of three years in prison.

It was subsequently discovered that the Communists had masterminded the great plot to topple the Pahlavi dynasty. Their plan was to do away with Mossadegh, clearing the way for a complete takeover and the establishment of a new government patterned after those of other Communist countries. Stocks of arms and ammunition were discovered, awaiting the day of the final uprising by the Tudeh party—a day that was never to come. In the years that followed we made film coverage of the unearthing of some of these caches of weapons, underground printing presses, and so forth, and the footage became hot news in the biweekly newsreel we put together for release in Iranian cinemas.

Under General Zahedi's regime, mob rule ceased, martial law was brought to an end, oil flowed again for shipment to foreign countries, and Parliament was restored. It was the Shah and the ordinary people of Iran who were victorious after the years of turbulence during which conflicting factions strove for supremacy, marking the opening of a new chapter in the history of Iran.

It was the beginning of an era which gave stabilization to the country, moving it progressively forward from the position it had attained through the courageous efforts of Reza Shah.

Each year on August 19, Iran celebrates Nation Day, commemorating the return of the Shah and of law, order and stability to the country.

4
In Search of a Queen

The following years in Iran were highly significant, for with renewed vigor the Shah led the people in reconstruction of their country and restoration of their confidence in the monarchy and the future of Iran. With the line of authority clearly defined, the government was now able to proceed in solving its problems and initiating long-term development projects.

During the turbulent years, however, the people of Iran had been plagued by the question as to what might happen should the Shah's political enemies resort to personal violence to achieve their ends: there was no male heir for continuation of the Pahlavi dynasty. One must turn back a few years to examine the Shah's personal life to understand this disturbing situation.

After completing his education in Switzerland, he entered military college in Tehran, joining the army with the rank of Lieutenant in 1938. At that time in Iran, when arranged marriages were smiled upon, Reza Shah laid plans for the Crown Prince. After looking about for a young woman well qualified to become a queen, he decided upon Princess Fawzieh, sister of King Farouk of Egypt. Negotiations were carried on in Tehran and Cairo, ending with complete agreement for the proposed union. The engagement of Princess Fawzieh and Crown Prince Mohammad Reza Pahlavi was officially announced in the year 1938.

Arranged marriages have, until very recently, been an accepted procedure for royalty all over the world, but this tradition reached every social level in Iran and the custom goes back many hundreds of years.

Long ago, especially among the wealthy and influential, arrangements for marriages were often negotiated when the prospective bride and groom were still children. In more recent years, when a young man approached the marriageable age (usually in his late teens and early twenties) his parents began to look about for the right girl to become their son's bride. They visited friends who had daughters, whom they carefully appraised to see whether one of them might be a suitable wife for their son. For some girls who felt—as one said—"like a piece of merchandise to be bought," this was a rather embarrassing situation; but the custom was a timeworn practice and they had to accept it. The groom might never have seen his betrothed until the actual ceremony, and might have had no say in choice of bride. But, in still more recent years after the parents had selected a prospect, a party was arranged to which the girl and the boy were invited. The mother or the sister pointed out the eligible girl to the boy, giving him the opportunity to study and evaluate her—and perchance to talk to her during the evening.

If the boy was interested in the girl, his parents then made a semiofficial visit to her parents, asking for her hand in marriage to their son. The mother of the girl would then break the news to her daughter and ask her if she was attracted to the young man who— through his parents—had asked for her hand. If the girl's parents were particularly eager for the marriage to take place, the mother would be careful to point out all the advantages of such a match: the young man's social status (which was very important), his education, his position economically. If the mother could truthfully do so, she would praise his handsome appearance and personal charm.

This system was not quite as callous as it may seem to Westerners who moved away from arranged marriages several decades ago. In most cases the parents sincerely looked for a mate with whom they thought their son or daughter could be content, weighing all factors with judgment matured by experience. And on the other side of the scale, the boys and girls did not mix socially so the prospective spouse was usually the only member of the opposite sex the bride or groom knew, except for very close relatives. Furthermore, the girls were trained to please their husbands. Many believe there was a much higher percentage of happy marriages under this old system than under the new method of free choice.

When the girl had been informed of the proposal, unless she violently objected, parents of the two young people gathered with close friends present to discuss dowry—a meeting called "Shirini Khorun," which translated literally means the consumption of candies. The groom's parents would promise security for the girl by naming a sum of money known as the *mehrieh* (for the very wealthy, sometimes as much as $100,000) that she would receive in case of a divorce. The agreed-upon amount was often given to her at the time of the marriage in the form of jewelry, silver, land and so forth. The parents of the bride would then even the exchange by promising household goods and other assets to be brought to the marriage.

After these arrangements had been completed to the satisfaction of all concerned, the engagement was announced at a big party to which all the friends of both were invited. Rings were exchanged in the presence of the guests. (The exchange of wedding rings is a custom borrowed from the West; in olden times, gifts of a different nature were exchanged between members of the families of the betrothed.)

The next step (and the most important one) was the ceremony called *aghd konun*. Usually the guest list for this affair was confined to members of the family and the couple's closest friends. This was both a religious and a civil ceremony, performed by a Mullah with a representative from the registrar's office present.

The bride sat on a little prayer rug or cloth spread by a happily married woman, facing a mirror in a silver frame in the direction of Mecca, flanked by candlesticks on either side, the gift of the groom. (Besides the mirror, candlesticks and the ring, the bride also received a copy of the Koran from her prospective husband.)

At one side was a large tray, on which a specially made sheet of bread had been placed, the whole surface decorated with colored seeds, rice and sugar in an attractive design, symbolizing happiness, prosperity and fertility. All women guests with the exception of spinsters, widows and divorcees, congregated in the bride's room, the immediate circle being composed of happily married women to launch the young woman on a blissful marriage. A piece of fine linen was held over the bride's head, while one of the women ground two sugar cones above it, suggesting sweetness and happiness in her new life. At the same time another woman (usually from the groom's family) sewed stitches into the linen symbolizing the hope that the bride's lips would be stitched shut against saying unkind things to her husband. Some say the symbolism extended to the mothers-in-law and sisters-in-law who would attempt to refrain from criticism.

The ground sugar was made into a pudding following the ceremony to be shared by the couple the next day.

The Mullah, sitting by the groom in an adjoining room, read portions from the Koran to begin the ceremony. Then he called to the bride and asked if she would take the young man to be her husband. It was customary for the bride—not wishing to appear immodest—to remain silent after the question. The Mullah then asked a second time, but not until he asked her the third time did she answer "Yes." The groom then entered the bride's room, where he lifted the veil and gazed on the reflection of the face of his beloved in the mirror—sometimes seeing her closely for the first time! At the same time legal documents were drawn up, witnessed and signed.

The couple was now legally married and had the blessing of the Mullah. If the bride and groom were old enough and the husband in a position to begin supporting his own household, the wedding feast celebrating consummation of the marriage might be held right away—immediately following the *aghd konun* or within a few days. Often, however, the bride and groom were too young and the marriage was not consummated for some time—as long as one or even several years. However, the couple enjoyed greater freedom after this ceremony and were able to see each other whenever they wished.

At the end of the waiting period a festive reception was held at the home of the groom. The bride, in her white wedding gown, was brought from her home to the grand soiree. After celebrating with their guests the couple went to their room, while the party continued—usually into the early morning hours. (In olden times the wedding feast might last three to seven days.)

Customs varied in the past (and still vary) in different regions of the country. In Bandar Abbas in southern Iran, ceremonies have been quite simple. One unique feature in Bandar Abbas is that during the *aghd konun* all the buttons on the outfits worn by both bride and groom are left open, symbolizing that during their lives they will keep no secrets from each other. In Sushtar (another southern city) green is the dominant color for the day. The couple both dress in that color and their bridal chamber is decorated in green. Green—the color of springtime—symbolizes a blissful life.

With the westernization of Iran many such customs, some of them unique in Persian Islamic culture, have vanished.

Reza Shah followed the custom of the time, arranging the marriage of his son, but of course in a royal fashion. The union was thought to be a highly satisfactory one, for the princess was a very beautiful young woman. In addition, the marriage promised a closer tie between Iran and Egypt, two of the strongest countries in the Middle East.

And so it was that the Crown Prince went to Cairo, staying two weeks to get acquainted with his prospective bride. The religious ceremony was then performed, although none of the prince's family was present. However, a number of Persian dignitaries (selected especially for the occasion) came to Egypt from Iran to witness the rites. The young couple then traveled to Tehran, where the civil ceremony was performed, followed by lavish wedding festivities which lasted several days.

The Iranian constitution ruled that the heir to the throne must be born of Iranian parents; Reza Shah took care of this technicality by passing a law making Princess Fawzieh an Iranian.

In 1940 Fawzieh gave birth to a daughter, Princess Shahnaz (destined to become a very beautiful woman). As has been noted, Mohammad Reza Pahlavi ascended the throne just over a year after the birth of his daughter.

For reasons unknown, Queen Fawzieh was unable to bear any more children. The royal couple eventually agreed that for the good of the country they should separate, so that the Shah would be free to enter into another marriage contract, with the hope of producing a male heir to the throne. In 1948 the news media reported that the Queen had returned to Egypt for an extended stay and subsequently an announcement was made of their divorce.

Two years later, hearing about a beautiful girl named Soraya Esfandiari, at the moment living in England, the Shah sent his sister, Princess Shams, to visit her. Shortly afterwards (following Princess Shams' glowing report), the engagement made headlines.

Soraya Esfandiari was born in Esfahan. Her father came from a line of Bakhtiari tribesmen, and was one of the notable chieftains of this old, important Persian tribe. He had studied in Germany, where he met Soraya's mother, bringing her to Esfahan to live. The Esfandiaris visited Europe often, where Soraya learned to speak French, along with German, and of course her native Persian. Because of her wish to improve her English, she decided to spend the year 1950 in England. However, after Princess Shams' historic visit, Soraya returned immediately to Tehran.

Soraya's grave bout with typhoid fever prevented an immediate marriage. Unlike the Shah's previous marriage, it was decided that—because of the forced postponement—the civil and religious ceremonies with a brief wedding celebration should occur all in one day. And so, in January of 1951, in a lavish ceremony, Soraya Esfandiari became the second Queen of Iran.

However, after seven years of happy union, no child had been born to provide a male heir to perpetuate the Pahlavi dynasty. Putting the stable future of the country above his own personal desires, the Shah announced the dissolution of the marriage. The divorce became final in March, 1958.

During the following year, when the Shah was unmarried, he had only to be seen walking with an attractive young woman for rumors to spread like wildfire of a budding romance. Some thought that there was more than a casual attraction between His Majesty and Princess Margaret of England. In Holland, the Shah was observed with interest whenever he was in the company of the eligible princesses there. The French newspapers were the most active in their speculative reports.

One day in November, 1959, the press and cameramen were requested to be at Mehrabad Airport in Tehran at a certain time to photograph and report an important event—we did not know what or who was involved.

The chartered plane taxied up to the royal pavilion, and so we knew that this was a momentous occasion of some kind.

The very special passenger to disembark was the beautiful Farah Diba, with her mother and a few other companions. No announcement was made but all of us knew she must indeed be Iran's next queen. And how beautiful she was walking down the ramp—tall, slender and poised! She is the daughter of an army colonel who died a few years previous to the day we met her plane as she and her party flew in from Paris.

Her Imperial Majesty, Queen Farah Pahlavi *(Photo courtesy Iran Press Photographers Association)*

His Imperial Majesty, Mohammad Reza Shah Pahlavi Aryamehre and Queen Farah *(Photo courtesy Iran Press Photographers Association)*

The Royal Family of Iran: behind the Haft-Sean table, part of the Iranian New Year's festivities *(Photo courtesy Iran Press Photographers Association)*

The Royal Family of Iran: left to right, Princess Farahnaz, the Shahanshah, Queen Farah, Crown Prince Reza, Princess Leila and Prince Ali-Reza *Photo courtesy Iran Press Photographers Association)*

Her Imperial Majesty, Farah Pahlavi, Queen of Iran *(Photo courtesy Ira~
Press Photographer Association)*

Farah, who was a student of architecture at the Ecole Speciale d'Architecture, had returned one fateful day to Tehran to visit her family, and this is the way the fairy story began.

Princess Shahnaz, the Shah's daughter, and her husband, Mr. Ardeshir Zahedi (at the time in charge of Iranians studying abroad), who were very socially inclined, were fond of giving large parties, democratically including among their guests people from outside the magic circle of royalty and high government administration. It is said that Miss Diba, during her stay in Tehran, went to see Mr. Zahedi to discuss her education with him. There Princess Shahnaz met her and they quickly struck up a friendship.

Thinking her father might be attracted to her regal-appearing friend Farah Diba, the princess and her husband gave a series of parties during Farah's vacation in Tehran, inviting His Majesty to the festivities and hoping the two could meet.

The Shah appeared at only one of the series of social events, but this was enough. In an article appearing in the magazine *The Women,* Farah is quoted as saying,

> I was very excited. My heart beat faster when the Shah arrived. At first, he paid scarcely any attention to me. But after dinner, he hardly took his eyes off me, and asked me many questions. I was embarrassed and felt myself blushing. I saw Princess Shahnaz smiling at me.[23]

The author of the article asked the Queen how she felt at that time, knowing she was selected primarily for her heir-bearing potential. Did it disturb her to know that everyone was waiting for her to bear a son? Her answer was, "No, for it is not in my hands, but in Allah's. Besides, every woman wants a son. I am not unique in that."[24]

On November 23 the Shah proclaimed his engagement to Farah Diba at a ceremony in his private palace. (He was forty and Farah twenty-one.) Farah had returned only a few days previously from Paris, where she had arranged for her trousseau. She chose to wear for the ceremony one of the Paris creations, a blue-green silk dress with gold sequins. The Shah was dressed in a green uniform as Commander-in-Chief of the Imperial Army.

---

[23]Teresa Barbieri, "Secrets of Royal Wives," *The Women,* April, 1967, p. 24.
[24]*Ibid.*

His Majesty sat on a gold silk-covered sofa, with Farah at his right and the Queen Mother and his daughter, Princess Shahnaz, on his left. In the presence of about a hundred guests, he took from his pocket a ring with a diamond more than half an inch square, and placed it on Farah's finger; she in return gave the Shah a ring. Both appeared extremely happy. Sweets were then served, a traditional part of the ceremony.

After the ceremony, Farah moved into the palace of the Queen Mother where she would live until her marriage to the Shah.

Approximately a month later (December 21, 1959), the storybook wedding took place. The radiant bride wore a gorgeously embroidered white satin gown designed by the fashion house of Dior in Paris, after a Persian miniature of the eighteenth century; the hem of the gown was richly decorated with mink. The train, two and a half meters in length, was carried by eight girls. Farah ascended the staircase to the throne room of the Marble Palace, between lines of meticulously groomed soldiers who formed a guard of honor.

She was received by the smiling Shah, surrounded by his highest court officials and ministers. From the throne room Mohammad Reza Pahlavi, Shahanshah of Iran, and Farah proceeded to the wedding room where vows were made before the highest Shi'ah priest of the capital, Imami.

A poignant feature of the event was a tray bearing an inscription formed by colored spices reminding Farah of her duty as a wife of the Shah, and Queen of Persia: "Wishes for an heir!"

Fate smiled on the Shah when he chose Farah to share his life, for—as history has shown—she was destined to become a queen beloved by her people, a highly respected diplomat, and a shining credit to the Persian throne, as well as the mother of the Crown Prince and three other beautiful children.

5
The Persian People as I Saw Them

In 1943 (the year of the Tehran Conference) my work as personal secretary and interpreter for the Assistant Military Attaché in the British Embassy was far less confining and demanding than it became a few years later when I took charge of the joint film department of the British Embassy and British Council in Iran.

During this time I became conscious of some of the needs of the· people of my country—particularly in the area of recreation and entertainment, and set about the task of trying to help fill these needs.

Being drawn to the smell of greasepaint I joined the Anglo-Iranian Dramatic Society (a project of the British Council), which produced plays monthly, in English—and later in Persian. Performances were held at the Greenroom Theatre of the Anglo-Persian Institute in Tehran. The purpose of the society was to promote dramatic arts, which in Iran were still in their infancy.

During the seven years I was affiliated with the organization I served as producer, director, actor, stage manager—in fact served in all aspects of play production. Members of the society from which the cast and crew came were both Britishers and Iranians interested and talented in dramatics. We naturally did a number of Shakespearean plays (in English); but some of us felt that we were doing only half the job of the Society if all plays were done in English. The innovation of doing a play in Persian took place in

1945 when we presented James Elroy Flecker's *Hassan* in the Persian language.

This is a story about a confectioner in Baghdad who revolts against the cruelty of the court. Four of us (Elwell Sutton, the British Press Attaché and author of a number of books on Iran, a Mrs. Arfah, wife of General Arfah and one of the ladies in waiting for Queen Fawzieh, one other person and I) were charged by the Society to produce this play. It was a big production and we needed all the help we could get. One person felt we had made an unwise decision—to do this drama with our amateur resources in Persian—and withdrew. About this time rumors were floating around Tehran that Queen Fawzieh, who was departing for an extended stay in Egypt, perhaps might not return. Mrs. Arfah, a very enthusiastic member of our team, left us to accompany the queen. Mr. Sutton and I were left alone to hold the fort.

We spent the three hot summer months of Tehran sweating it out, producing *Hassan* in Persian with all odds against us. Perhaps it is difficult for the Western reader to comprehend the "odds." But at the time we were working with a group of completely inexperienced Persian amateur actors who were very talented and interested in dramatic arts but, for example, did not believe in memorizing their parts. "After all," some of them said, "what is the purpose of a prompter if you have to memorize your part?" We had to go through a lot of rehearsals because for the first time we were presenting a play on an open-air stage in Iran. There were seventy-five people in the cast, a large number of them doing only walk-on parts. Some of those who had the smaller parts could not see the necessity of sacrificing their afternoon nap in the middle of summer to come to a rehearsal at three P.M. just to be on the stage for only five minutes. "You can put anybody there for the rehearsal. I will be there for the opening night."

To top it off, one week before the play opened one of our leads fell ill with meningitis and I had to step into the part, leaving the heroic Mr. Sutton with full responsibility for the entire production. In spite of all, the performance was a success; we created a sensation when we brought a caravan of camels, including a baby one, and donkeys across the outdoor stage. We gave a number of command performances of plays at the royal court and our society became a prestigious center for developing dramatic arts in Iran.

Members of the court did not attend *Hassan*, the first Persian production of the society, but we were asked to present the play at the summer palace. We politely declined because of the complexity of staging it there. To round up seventy-five human beings and rehearse them on a new open-air stage would be challenging enough, but to find a new caravan of camels, mules and donkeys and make them do what we wanted was an experience I did not care to repeat.

After 1951, the pressure of activities in the area of motion pictures precluded my continuing actively with the society, but I accepted a position on the Board of the Friends of the Dramatic Arts, a newly formed all-Iranian society to promote dramatics in the country.

As my work as Films Officer in the joint British Embassy/British Council film department took me around the country, I became increasingly aware of a need for sports in which *groups* participate. Iranians have always been outstanding in individual physical feats such as wrestling, but group sports were almost nonexistent in the country. Before the time of Shah Abbas the Great (1587-1629), polo had been a very popular sport in Iran, but it died out at the beginning of the twentieth century.*

One evening in 1947, a couple of friends of mine, one of whom was the energetic head of a sports club in Tehran, went with me to the movies. I have forgotten what feature film was playing but I well remember the subject of the Movietone News. One part dealt with a sport that resembled soccer, but there was a difference: the players handled the ball as well as kicking it. This new game, we learned, was called rugby. The three of us were excited about it and discussed at length the possibility of introducing it in Iran.

The next day while chatting during our coffee break with the administrative officer at the Embassy I said, "You're a Britisher; what do you know about rugby?"

"I was a rugby coach at home," he answered.

"Great!" I said. "A couple of friends of mine would like to learn how to play the game. Would you show us the rules and tell us how to play it?"

He was delighted to help, and subsequently organized a team

---

*The game of polo is first heard of in Iran during the Sassanian Empire (A.D. 226-633).

made up of the Britishers in the Embassy and the Anglo-Iranian
Oil Company in Tehran. My friend, connected with the sports
club, put together a group of athletes, and thus we formed two
rugby teams, a young Iranian team with no knowledge of the
game but a lot of zest, and a middle-aged British team with excellent knowledge of the game but with very little zest.

The Shah is greatly interested in sports. At the first clash between the British and Iranian rugby teams, he ordered his brother,
Prince Abdul Reza, to kick the first ball—in the same tradition
as that of the President who throws the first ball at the opening
of the baseball season. Regrettably we lost to the British team
at our first attempt, but this did not discourage us and we became more determined than ever to develop the game nationally.
It was a cheap game to play (only one ball for more than two
dozen people) and it gave the players an exercise in group participation, teamwork and cooperation, all of which were badly
needed in the country.

A few weeks later the Shah ordered the Physical Training
Association of Iran to support our efforts. The Association consists
of many federations such as the Soccer Federation, Tennis Federation, Weight-Lifting Federation, and so forth, and Rugby became
officially a new Federation under the aegis of the Association. This
move gave us national, official status. A deputy of Parliament,
deeply interested in sports, although too elderly to participate,
acted as our first president. (I was appointed secretary, and later
advanced to the vice-presidency and presidency.)

As the Rugby Federation developed, our team became so good
that I found it wise to give my place on the team to someone else
and be satisfied with handling administrative work for the Federation. Soon the British resident team in Tehran was no longer a
challenge and we started inviting teams from abroad to compete
with us. We first met a team from the British Air Squadron in the
Middle East, and went down in ignominious defeat. A couple of
months later the Anglo-Iranian Oil Company invited us to play
against their team (made up of British employees of the company)
at Khuzestan. The competition was to take place during the No-
Ruz holidays* in Masjid-e-Suleiman of southwestern Iran where

---

*No-Ruz, an Iranian national holiday, falls on March 21, the first day of spring,
and continues for thirteen days.

the oil company had some of its rich oil reserves. At this match Prince Gholam Reza, another of the Shah's brothers, officiated in the presentation of the cup to the captain of the winning team (unfortunately, *theirs,* but we lost only by a very small margin).

We wanted very much to go on to Abadan, where the oil company operated one of the largest refineries in the world (a four- or five-hour drive from Masjid-e-Suleiman). We longed to play their team, but could not afford to do so—we had little or no money for travel or hotel accommodations. Besides, we were told that because of the No-Ruz holidays, oil company accommodations were impossible to find.

During the cocktail hour after the game at Masjid-e-Suleiman, I fell into conversation with a stout, unprepossessing-looking little Britisher who was interested in our problem. Finally he took me to the telephone and placed a call. Afterwards he said, "I think chances are that you will go to Abadan." Later I was paged to take a call, which proved to be from the general manager of the oil company at Abadan. Indeed we *were* going to Abadan!

The company sent their plane the next day to pick up our team, and accommodations were reserved for us. This time we won!

Who was the stout little Britisher? The visiting general manager of the oil company, with headquarters in London!

Eventually, about sixty rugby teams were affiliated with the Federation in Iran, a substantial increase over the number of soccer teams in the country, although soccer was played in Iran for many years.

In the early fifties, I became deeply concerned about something that happened almost every day outside my office on Avenue Naderi in Tehran: a parade of children carrying signs and banners that bore slogans like "Long live So and So!" or "Death to So and So!" Sometimes there were hundreds of these youngsters, aged about ten to fourteen, marching down the street—usually between nine and eleven in the morning before the sun was too hot. They were automatons carrying placards without the least knowledge of the cause or person they were supposed to be for or against. They were being used by politicians or whoever wanted to call attention to a pet issue. I presume the children were sold the importance of their participation in the demonstrations. But above all, this was a chance to "show off" while getting rid of pent-up energy.

When a child has not been recognized for an athletic feat or other display of skill, he may gain satisfaction by establishing his identity in relation to some person or cause.

A group of us thought that something wrong here should be righted. These children should have healthy and constructive outlets for their energy. But they had no playgrounds, no sports equipment, no arts and crafts centers to entice them when school was out at four in the afternoon or during vacation periods.

As early as 1949, we had organized a film showing and talent show by and for the students as a regular weekend program at the Anglo-Persian Institute, which continued for many years, but that was on a limited basis. By 1952 students and youth became increasingly involved in street demonstrations, striking for some change or another. To me this said that they needed an outlet to expend their energies in a constructive way.

I had been very much impressed with the 4-H clubs I had seen in operation on my visit to the United States in 1950. In these clubs children were motivated to raise pigs or cows, do handwork, or even learn photography. With this in mind, I proposed a plan to the government. In part it read:

> An organization will be formed in order to help and guide the youth of school age to become useful citizens for the future community of Iran and to provide suitable recreation for these youngsters. The organization will be called NATIONAL YOUTH ORGANIZATION OF IRAN (Saze-man-e-Melli-e-Javanan-e Iran) and will be a cultural and recreational establishment only.
>
> The organization shall be an independent organization and will have its own constitution and Board of Directors. However, the Ministry of Education and the Physical Training Association will both be active figures in running of this organization.
>
>   o o o
>
> The organization shall have the following activities: Sports—Field trips —Dramatic activities—Radio programs—Lectures, debates and story-telling sessions—Film shows—4-H Clubs—Photography Club—Music and Art.

As for financing the project, which would demand more than what the Ministry of Education and the Physical Training Association could afford at that time, it was suggested that American sources such as the Ford Foundation be approached. It was hoped that help might be forthcoming also from the United Nations.

Copies of the proposal were sent to the Shah and other high

officials in government, where the concept met with general approval.

The organization, however, did not reach many of the goals for which it was designed during the time I was in Iran (such as large stadiums in many of the cities), but it was a start toward a richer life for the youth of Iran. (During the summer of 1974, I was pleased to witness the Seventh Asian Games held in the magnificent 100,000-seat Aryamehr Sports Center in Tehran, as well as to see many sports and club facilities that have been built across the country for Iranian youth, under the patronage of His Majesty.)

One of the things that grew out of the project was the establishment of summer camps. The youth organization established a summer camp near Babolsar on the Caspian Sea for students of the University of Tehran. The Pahlavi Foundation sponsored international student camps near Ramsar, another resort area on the Caspian Sea. In these camps young people were offered two weeks of fun and enjoyment along with education. The first of these camps was organized by a number of enthusiastic young men under the leadership of Dr. Amir Birjandi. We were pleased when the Shah visited the camp and showed personal gratification for what was being done. In Iran today there are perhaps hundreds of summer camps—not only for students, but also for adult groups.

The Shah directly or indirectly supported such projects, established for the purpose of making life more meaningful for the people of Iran—from childhood through adulthood.

But, of course, the basic needs of everyday life—particularly in rural areas—were of major concern to His Majesty. The United States came to Iran's aid at this critical period in the country's history, chiefly through its Point Four program, initiated by President Truman in 1949. I was able to see the gratifying (although sometimes. not so gratifying) results of the program firsthand through my work in films with the United States Information Agency.

Former President Truman explains the motive behind the Point Four program in his memoirs:

> The Point Four program was a practical expression of our attitude toward the countries threatened by Communist domination. It was consistent with our policies of preventing the expression of Communism in the free world by helping to insure the proper development of these

countries with adequate food, clothing and living facilities. It was an effort to bring to such people, not the idealism of democracy alone, but the tangible benefits of better living through intelligent co-operation.[25]

Iran was the first country to benefit from the program, and so served as a sort of proving ground for the whole concept. (The program eventually served scores of newly developing countries, bringing both help and hope to millions of people.)

The original Point Four project in Iran concerned itself with improvement in the countryside, stressing assistance in areas of agriculture and public health—particularly in attempts to eradicate malaria, a disease prevalent in the Caspian region. In time, projects included help in constructing better irrigation systems, better transportation and communications systems, industrial development, and farm mechanization. American aid was responsible for sending hundreds of Persians abroad for study. Professional assistance reached into government agencies and tax administration.

One side benefit of the presence of hundreds of Point Four advisors was their show of willingness to perform all kinds of manual labor without loss of personal dignity—an excellent example for the youth of the country. As was stated in Chapter Three, many of the educated in Iran looked with disdain on the man who worked with his hands. I well remember that even though I was one of the top Iranian assistants to USIS in Tehran, some of my friends and acquaintances were shocked when I went out into the field with a motion picture camera in my hand, thereby stooping to the level of the manual laborer.

A humorous incident comes to mind. At this time, a friend of mine and I were a bit concerned about losing our hair—a terrible thing to happen to young men in their twenties. He decided to be the "guinea pig" for the two of us and experiment with hair restorers. He shampooed his hair, adding egg yolk to the water, tried a powdered herb in the water as suggested by a little old lady, and so on. This mutual project exemplifies our closeness as friends when he left for the United States to further his education. I fully expected our friendship to continue on the same basis on his return.

One afternoon, the Shah was scheduled to attend the graduation

[25]Harry S. Truman, *Memoirs of Harry S. Truman*, vol. 2, *Years of Trial and Hope*, Doubleday and Co., Inc., Garden City, N.Y., 1956, p. 232.

of cadets at a military college at which many of the ministers were present. As I walked in with my camera to cover the event for our weekly newsreel, many of the ministers greeted me in a friendly way. And then—to my surprise—I saw my friend of the hair restorer days, who had returned from the United States and had been appointed to the position of Director General of the Ministry. I wanted to drop my camera and embrace him after all these months. But on seeing the camera in my hand, he said a very cool *Hello*, looked away and started talking with the man next to him. Fortunately at this moment the Shah arrived and I started photographing. As His Majesty passed my snobbish friend, I failed to use my camera, waiting until the Shah had gone on beyond him. I did not want him in my coverage.

To implement its far-reaching projects, Point Four took over the production of technical assistance films in December, 1951, which was initiated by USIS, as mentioned in Chapter One. These films were produced particularly on subjects related to public health and agriculture, to help the villagers to help themselves. It was in this area that I served.

As has already been related, I went to work for John Hamilton at the United States Information Agency as Assistant Film Officer. My primary responsibility was to take care of all operational matters in the Film Section, which covered a rather wide range of service. I had charge of translating all Persian correspondence into English, receiving all Iranian visitors, interviewing all job applicants, maintaining contact with all agencies cooperating with the USIS Film Section, selecting and training field mobile unit supervisors, and orienting projectionist-drivers to their duties. In addition, I was expected to make periodic field inspection trips of our cinema mobile unit operation.

Many of the films were translated into Persian for a more effective and meaningful presentation. It was my duty to find and train able narrators, and on occasion I found it necessary to serve as narrator myself. I reviewed all newly received films with other staff members prior to cataloging, and decided on their audience suitability. Our pet projects at this time, however, were the cinema mobile unit operation and the local production of films.

As stated in Chapter One, a large majority of the motion pictures sent to Iran from Washington could not be used as they reflected an abysmal ignorance of the problems facing the villagers of Iran. One film, for example, entitled *Key to Convenient Kitchens*, was about as applicable to the needs of the Persian village homemaker as a film on aerospace would be to her farmer husband in his daily work. Another film on planting and harvesting, which showed a farmer riding his mammoth tractor over his tremendous acreage, and harvesting his crop with a combine, was like something out of science fiction to an Iranian farmer. Some villagers thought that what was coming out of the spout was dirt, rather than wheat.

At the time Herbert Edwards, Head of the International Motion Picture Division of USIA in Washington, sensed the situation, seeing the hopelessness of educating the villagers to help themselves with slick American films based on modern equipment and advanced agricultural technology. As the result of his concern (initiated in the first place by John Hamilton, as pointed out previously), he sent Dr. Don G. Williams, Director of the Audio-Visual Center of Syracuse University, to Iran to assess the needs.

On Dr. Williams' return to Washington, he supported Mr. Hamilton's recommendation that personnel be sent to Tehran to spearhead the production of films, to be made on the comprehension level of the rural Iranian audiences. In March, 1951, ten Syracuse University filmmakers arrived in Tehran to begin work on producing a number of films under contract with USIA. Their work proceeded in cooperation with The Fine Arts Administration of the Ministry of Education* under the direction of Mr. Mehrdad Pahlbod, and a pioneering and dedicated Iranian staff.

This contract was later transferred to the Point Four program and local production of films in Iran for Iranians continued until 1959. The result of this operation was 82 motion pictures, 49 filmstrips and a number of other audiovisual programs and materials, all designed and produced to help Iranian villagers achieve a better way of life.

Although I was not directly involved in the actual production of these films, except from the administrative standpoint, one of my assistants accompanied the American crew and later became a professional writer with them. Once films were completed, they were distributed through our cinema mobile unit operation which

---

*The Fine Arts Administration has now developed into a much larger organization, called the Ministry of Culture and Arts.

I personally supervised, and the results were most gratifying. We were now reaching the villagers on their home ground and communicating with them as equal partners rather than as total strangers.

It might be noted here that after these films had made the rounds by way of our mobile units a few times, in remote villages, they were used by the Ministry of Agriculture, and then by the Ministry of Education for adult audiences. Use of these films was not discontinued until twelve years or so after they had been produced.

The cinema mobile unit operation was sponsored jointly by USIS and the Iranian Department of Press and Propaganda under the general supervision of John Hamilton. It was understood that USIS would administer the operation, with the Department of Press and Propaganda (now the Ministry of Information and Tourism) providing for each mobile unit a supervisor whom we would train.

It was the duty of the supervisor who accompanied the driver-projectionist to select the films to be shown in each village, from the stock of films carried by the mobile unit. His responsibility was somewhat that of teacher, explaining the films when necessary, so that the public would gain the greatest possible knowledge from the material being presented.

Each supervisor submitted a daily report to me with a copy to his own department. These people were selected from the staff of the Department of Press and Propaganda, as well as other ministries, to serve for a period of six months, after which they were to return to their jobs to be replaced by others. This plan afforded an excellent opportunity for these supervisors, who dealt with programs in various media for the masses, to see and know the people on their home ground all over the country. A large number of those who served in this capacity became very prominent persons and still hold important offices in the Iranian government.

An overall plan was devised to prevent saturation of an area with film showings to the deprivation of others. Each province of Iran, according to its population, was assigned a given number of cinema mobile units to visit certain villages regularly for presentation of film programs.

Many problems had to be solved before the project was put into full swing. We had technical problems, administrative problems, and sometimes political problems. For example, when we first sent a mobile unit to the province of Azarbaijan (adjacent to the Soviet Union) the Governor General commented that although the showing of films was a very good means of education, if USIS were permitted to send a mobile unit to the villages showing American films, very soon the Russians would want to do the same, which neither he nor his government would care to allow. It was a sound point and in fact there was a danger that our film showing might trigger some political implications for both the Iranian and the American governments. However, the fact that the supervision of these mobile units was under the auspices of the Iranian government assured me that the Russians would not follow a similar plan. The aims of the Americans were not indeed to propagandize or brainwash the Iranians, but rather to help them help themselves.

We had all our cinema vans painted on each side (in Persian) with the sign, "Cinema Mobile Unit of the Imperial Government of Iran."

Apart from having the government supervisors of the units select their own films and run their own show, we sought cooperation from local authorities, from commanding army officers to mayors to local teachers, chiefs of police, and often religious leaders. With their blessings and under their supervision we proceeded with the first unit in the province of Azarbaijan in 1950.

After we completed our tour of Azarbaijan our conclusion was that the first cinema mobile unit operation was successful. We were received with tremendous enthusiasm and interest by almost everyone with whom we came in contact. Therefore we prepared to continue and expand our operation.

To give the reader a better idea as to what actually took place on these trips, I shall put down here a brief summary of a report that I gave to my supervisor on November 17, 1950, after I had initiated units into the northern provinces of Gilan and Mazanderan.

It was at this time that the full effects of Soviet propaganda were being felt in Iran, particularly in the northern provinces. The people were being bombarded by Communist radio broadcasts and by messages delivered over obnoxious loudspeakers across the frontier (as briefly mentioned in Chapter Three).

In many instances the people who saw our films had lived in the confines of their villages since birth and were unbelievably ignorant of what was happening in the world. Great numbers had never seen a motion picture and some thought we were magicians.

Our stock of films included the following:

The Funeral of Reza Shah
The Shah of Iran Visits the United States
The United Nations Aids the Republic of Korea
Infant Care
The Battle of Iwo Jima
The Liberation of Rome
The Human Body
Insects Are Carriers of Disease
Nurses in Training
New England Fisherman
Poultry Raising
Our Foster Mother the Cow

On Sunday, September 24, we showed three films to an audience of eight hundred people at Sangsar. During the film about the funeral of Reza Shah the people maintained a grieved silence. But the one depicting the visit of the Shah to the United States was greeted with a long cheer and loud clapping. (This was true wherever we showed the film.)

On Monday the twenty-fifth, as we moved on toward Astara, a small town on the Iran-Russian border, we were asked for a show wherever we stopped along the route. At one place, when the villagers saw the sign on our jeep, they all cheered, "Long live the government of Iran!" and "Long life to the mobile-cinema crew!" Five films were shown at Astara to an audience of twenty-five hundred people.

Early in the evening of Tuesday the twenty-sixth, we showed three films at Baghchesarary for eight hundred people, leaving at seven-thirty in order to return to Astara for an 8 o'clock showing. We found four thousand people waiting for us. Here we presented four more films.

We heard an amusing but touching story that afternoon from a Colonel Beylami, army representative in the area. A tribesman had excitedly reported that the night before there was a jeep in Astara with a few Tehranis. They had a machine and when one of them touched it they brought the Shah only a few meters away from him. "He was talking to *me!*" he exclaimed. "Believe me—he was talking to *me!*"

I gave a running commentary in Persian for each film presented (thus giving on-the-job training to the supervisor). Whenever possible I used local expressions and idiomatic phrases I had learned from the people in the few days I was in the area.

On this second night in Astara, at public demand, we repeated the showing of two films presented the night before: *The Funeral of Reza Shah* and *The Shah of Iran Visits the United States.*

Just as we finished the second film the skies opened. The rain continued throughout the night and morning (Wednesday, the twenty-seventh). We left Astara for Choobar, where we planned to give a show in the evening. The road is asphalted but crossed with several bridges that have the unfortunate habit of falling down when streams are swollen. About twenty-four kilometers out of Astara we reached the first bridge that had been a victim of the downpour; it had collapsed. The river is so deep in this area that no car can ford it. We had no alternative but to return to town.

In Astara we decided to reroute ourselves by way of Ardebil, a town in Azarbaijan province, and give some shows at villages along the way.

We found the road to be possibly the most difficult in all of Iran. It climbs into the mountains and is so narrow that two cars must maneuver carefully to pass each other. Fog hovered along the route, obscuring vision almost completely. Our yellow spotlight offered little help. A part of the time one of us would get out and walk ahead of the car, indicating the middle of the road.

About halfway from Astara to our destination, we came to the small village called Heyrea. It was midafternoon—about three o'clock. Here the frontier guard officer requested us to give a program for the villagers and the army stationed there. We set up the equipment in a teahouse (a place where villagers congregate, drink tea, and listen to the newspaper being read to them). The place was built to accommodate about a hundred people; but when we showed our films (four of them) a hundred and twenty villagers were packed in to see the presentation.

About five o'clock we moved on toward Hamin, passing through a village called Sonia. Here they begged us to return after our scheduled show in Hamin, agreeing to wait until midnight if we would promise to come back.

In Hamin we showed three films to two thousand people, most

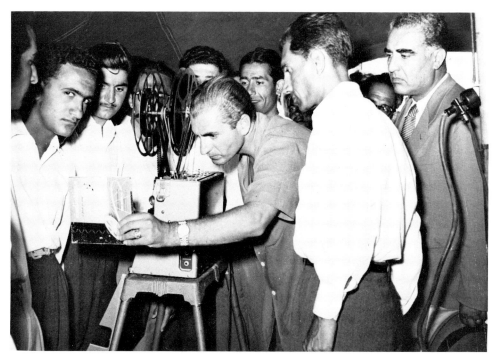

The Shah looking at a film in the audio-visual class at the first university summer camp at Babolsar, 1955

Prince Abdul-Reza Pahlavi shaking hands with members of the first rugby team in Tehran, 1948

Staff of USIS Film Section in Tehran, 1952

A cinema mobile unit

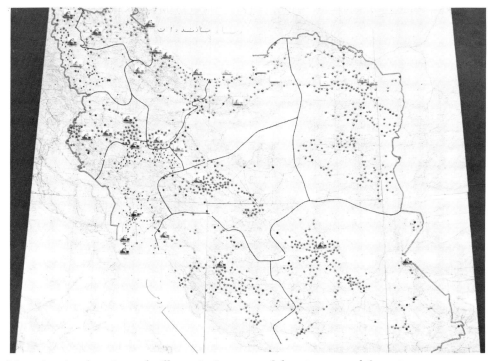

Map showing locations of villages in Iran served by cinema mobile units, between December 1952 and May 1953

A typical village in Iran of 1950s

Supervisor giving running commentary in the dialect of the local people during a film showing, 1952

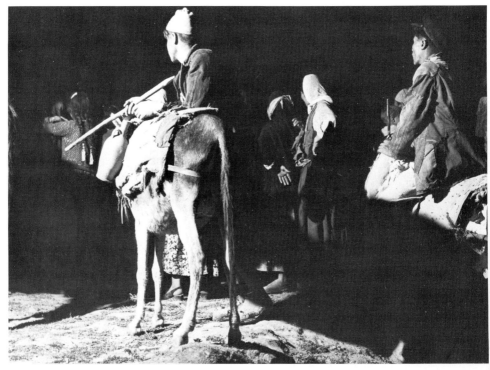

Part of the audience watching a film showing, 1952

Local musicians playing for the audience while the cinema mobile unit crew prepares for the film showing, 1952

Man dancing to entertain the audience waiting for the film showing to begin, 1952

Man enjoying the music and the dancing preceding the showing of the films, 1952

The author explaining a pictorial pamphlet on one of the films to a farmer 1951

A crowd of schoolboys surround a USIS mobile unit which has come t their school to show educational films, a program sponsored by the Irania ministry of education, 1952.

Caravan of camels in a desert region in Iran, 1952

Mr. Issari and his assistant taking a shortcut by camel to deliver spare parts to a stranded cinema mobile unit, 1952

A Qashghai tribal tent school, 1957

A Qashghai girl reading from her textbook in a tribal tent school, 1957

of whom had never seen a motion picture before. We returned to Sonia, arriving at about nine o'clock. Two hundred and fifty villagers had gathered for our presentation of three films. After the show my crew and I went to the teahouse and were followed by most of the audience, who congregated around us and eagerly asked questions about the films they had seen: "Do these insects really carry disease? How do they do it? Why have I not gotten sick after eating food that flies have sat on?" We finally left the grateful villagers to travel on to Ardebil, arriving about midnight.

On Thursday, the twenty-eighth, we learned from the commander in chief of the Ardebil army that the rains had stopped and it was possible for us to return to Astara. (Ardebil would be visited later by another mobile unit assigned to the province of Azarbaijan.)

On our return to Astara, we were told that, although the rain had ceased, bridges were still down and we could not proceed to Rasht, as hoped. And so, at the request of officials in Astara, we scheduled a show at seven P.M. Word had gone like wildfire throughout the area that the Tehrani "magicians" would again perform, and at "curtain time" ten thousand people had gathered to see our films. This time we showed seven films. For this group, the favorite was *Poultry Raising* and the two health cartoons, *Nurses in Training* and *Insects Are Carriers of Disease*.

At ten P.M., after finishing our day's work, we were feted at a dinner party given by one of the merchants of Astara.

We left Astara on Friday, the twenty-ninth, knowing that with bridges down we would have to ford some of the streams. Where the water was too deep for our vehicle, we chopped out a road through the forest alongside the stream, to a point where it was shallow enough for us to cross. It took us two hours to drive twelve miles to Choobar, the central village of the North Gargenrood tribesmen. We were met with the news that tribesmen from neighboring villages had arrived two days before for our film showing. Although our schedule had been disrupted by the rains, we agreed to stay for an evening's presentation. We set up our equipment at about four o'clock in the afternoon and played phonograph records for these people who had come so far and waited so long for us (some from a distance of forty kilometers), until seven o'clock. At that time we started the evening's event, during which we presented five films.

The Shah of Iran Visits the United States, the favorite film, was met with cheers and clapping throughout. Great excitement pervaded the crowd when the Shah was seen shaking hands with President Truman. Scenes in America were viewed with surprise and awe. Some said, "This place must be *the* Paradise!"

On Saturday, the thirtieth, we left Choobar for Rasht, but when we reached Lisar, we found another group of tribesmen impatiently awaiting our arrival. They had also come from far-off villages—some on foot and some on mules. We relented and made plans for two programs for the evening: one at Lisar at 6:30 P.M. and one at Salom (fifteen kilometers toward Rasht) at 8:30 P.M. We had to go to Salom in the afternoon to inform them that we would be there late in the evening. We returned to Lisar shortly before time for the showing there. About twenty-five hundred people viewed the four films presented and as soon as we had finished, we went back to Salom where a crowd of six hundred and fifty tribesmen and peasants were waiting. This show began at 9:25, for we had encountered difficulty getting there, crossing several rivers without benefit of bridges in the dark. But the people were patient, and very happy with the four films we presented for them. We pressed on to Rasht, arriving there—exhausted—at 3:30 in the morning.

After most film presentations, large numbers of pamphlets on infant care were distributed among the crowd. Most of the people could not read, but perhaps expected to find someone to read the material aloud to them. And, of course, there were illustrations for them to look at.

On Sunday, October 1, after I had introduced my crew to notables in the town, I left the mobile unit crew to continue with their good work and returned to Tehran. I experienced deep gratification when I calculated that, in about a week's time, we had shown our stock of films to almost twenty-five thousand people. Even if we had influenced or taught only two hundred and fifty of them to help themselves and be better members of their communities, it was all worthwhile.

Our cinema mobile unit operation expanded until there was at least one unit in every province of the country. I went out every two or three months with a driver in my Chevrolet Carry-All to inspect their work. I talked with the crews, checked on the condition of their jeeps and motion picture equipment, and sometimes gave them fresh films.

It was rewarding to see all these dedicated men living for months under very difficult conditions in remote areas without the comfort of their own homes, so that they might help their countrymen. During the many years this operation continued I never received a single complaint from any of these men, nor did any of them ask to be stationed permanently in Tehran. On the contrary, both supervisors and driver-projectionists, when returned to Tehran after six months in the field, could not wait to go back out again. To these men, whose names are beyond the scope of this book, goes my sincere gratitude for the valuable philanthropic work they did.

On occasion I received word in Tehran that a unit was grounded because of some problem or another. Rather than trust the uncertain local transportation facilities, I invariably jumped into my car and took whatever was needed to them. This gesture on my part had a favorable effect on the morale of the crews, for they knew that someone in Tehran was ready to help them when the need arose. Often to reduce both time and distance, which might involve several days of traveling on a dirt road, my driver and I would leave our carry-all near a tea house and mount a camel or donkey to cut across the countryside, carrying an axle or some other vital part, and supplies for these men. When we reached the stalled vehicle we handled the problem, whatever it might be, on the spot and the show went on again.

Through working with the cinema mobile units, I learned a great deal about the difficulties faced by the people in rural Iran. At one time or another I visited almost all of the fifty thousand villages in the country. I was made aware of four main problems: (1) lack of interest in the farmer by the landlord; (2) lack of education; (3) lack of medical care; and (4) lack of communication.

In those years (the early fifties) the farmers who worked the land had no share in its ownership. The system at that time was for the landlord to assign a certain portion of his land to a farmer who profited according to the individual situation. In all cases the landlord was due one-fifth of the crops for his land. If he furnished water for the fields, he took two-fifths. If the landlord furnished seed, he would get three-fifths; if he also furnished plow and draft animals, four-fifths. If the poor farmer did not have water on his land, had no seed and no money with which to buy it, and did not own oxen or plow, he might be able to retain only one-fifth of the crops he labored to raise, to support himself and his family. I became increasingly aware of the need for this feudal system in our agricultural areas to be changed, giving these farmers—many of them highly intelligent—a chance for a better standard of living.

One might think that these farmers who lived in almost primitive conditions in the very remote areas might be men of inferior intellect. However, this was not true. Some villagers, finding they could not make a living on the land, migrated to the cities, showing great promise in industry and business.

The daily life of these men of the soil followed a rather set pattern in the village. They arose before sunrise, prayed, had their breakfast and went to the fields, working there until late afternoon. On their return they went to the village teahouse (or coffeehouse), where they sat and visited with their friends, had their tea or smoked a bit of hubbly-bubbly, went home for a bite of supper and then to bed. In the gathering at the teahouse, one or two people might be able to read to the others—from the newspaper or other printed material such as pamphlets we distributed following our film showings. The pamphlets were designed to rely more on pictorial continuity than on printed instructions.

I often thought that if only these farmers could all have a chance for a rudimentary education, learning to read and write, they could help themselves so much more—even though they were destined to labor under the yoke imposed on them by the landlord. This opportunity did not come until the Shah's land distribution project and the Revolution of the Shah and the People in the late fifties and early sixties.

Educating the children of nomadic tribes, however, posed a problem unlike that in a village or an established town. In Iran there are many such tribes—perhaps ten to fifteen percent of the population belong to wandering tribes.

Two of the largest are the Bakhtiaris and Qashghais, who roam the area between Esfahan and the Persian Gulf. In winter they move south to the Gulf, where grass is abundant for their flocks of sheep, and as spring approaches they head north again toward Shiraz and Esfahan. (The government has, in recent years, made progress in influencing these people to settle down rather than follow the nomadic life.)

In the early fifties, one Qashghai chieftain with a vision, Bahman-Begi, who had been educated in the West, conceived a very imaginative plan for educating the children of his tribe. With the help of the Ministry of Education and the Point Four program, he established a mobile tent school that was set up wherever the tribe stopped for the sheep to graze. The tent was white rather than the usual black, with the flag of Iran fluttering above it. The color of the tent (or lack of it) and the presence of the flag designated that this was the tribe's educational center. The teacher moved with the school. Sometimes the white tent would stand in one place for only two or three days, but if it were known that the tribal leaders predicted a stay of as much as five days, the teacher would assign work and plan the program for that period of time.

School would close when the tent moved, and open when it went up again in its new location. No matter what the time of day, when the flag went up on the tent it was like ringing the old school bell. Time to start classes! I made a documentary film on this program entitled *Tribal Schools*, which became a motivational tool encouraging other tribes and rural communities to follow suit.

Foreigners who came to Iran, interested in education, always asked to visit a tent school. Sometimes it was hard to find. According to the individual tribe, the nomads traveled on camels, donkeys, mules, horses—and, of course, drove their sheep. We might drive to Shiraz (the northernmost point of the Qashghai tribal migration route) and inquire where they were, only to be told, "They were fifteen miles south a couple of days ago, but who knows where they are now?" We would have to seek them out.

One problem that arose once the novelty wore off was that non-Qashghai teachers could not keep up with the tribal life-style for long and consequently left their good work. And there were not enough educated tribesmen and women to go around. In order to guarantee the success of this program, the Ministry of Education established a teacher training school in Shiraz for the tribal boys and girls only. Young Qashghais who were interested in teaching received full scholarships and went through a two-year crash program to become tribal teachers. The establishment of this teacher training school saved the program from extinction.

Other educational programs for giving appropriate vocational training to the tribal children have been developed in recent years. One of them is a school in Shiraz where Qashghai girls can go (at no cost to them) for a period of two years, to learn the intricate art of tribal rug weaving.

There is a saying in Iran which comes to us through both religion and literature:

Pursue education from cradle to grave.

But the question in those years was: how could the average man achieve this?

In addition, the health problems out in the remote areas were staggering. On one inspection tour, I accompanied a mobile unit in the Khorassan area to the city of Mashad. About forty kilometers east of the city we stopped at a village just off the main road for the crew to arrange film shows there later. I was in a car a few miles ahead of the jeep and so was the first person to get out. (The roads were so dusty we always traveled well apart.) The dust stirred up by the two cars signaled to the villagers that we were coming and they poured out of their homes to see who we were and why we had come.

Suddenly I saw in front of me a beautiful girl—perhaps in her early twenties. She came forward, limping. When she reached me, she fell on the ground, then reached up and clutched my jacket, telling me something in Turkish. I could not understand her. Some of the villagers came forward and together told me what she was saying:

"I had a dream last night. I dreamed that Imam Reza [the eighth Imam of the Shi'ah religion, buried in the city of Mashad] told me that this afternoon a doctor would come to the village to treat me."

I picked her up from the ground and asked what her trouble was. She silently pulled up her skirt to show me that her leg— from ankle to thigh—was covered with boils. She was so sincere in her belief that I had been sent by Imam Reza that I had no choice but to support her.

However, I had to admit, in all honesty, that I was not a physician and that she must see a doctor. We always carried a small kit of first-aid supplies. I put some alcohol on cotton and bathed her wounds, applied some small bandages, and gave her aspirin to relieve her pain. Then I urged her to get to a doctor in Mashad (though I had no idea as to how she might get there).

It was an experience that haunted me. This beautiful girl was an example of thousands of Iranians in remote areas needing the services of competent physicians, drugs, and instruction in sanitation.

It occurred to me that one angle which might be pursued would be establishing a mobile health unit operation along with the cinema mobile units. However, American aid was not sufficient to cover the rather exorbitant costs of sending out qualified medical people and the expensive supplies that would be essential for a successful program. Consequently my proposal for establishing such an operation did not go far.

However, if we could not help them by providing doctors and medicine at this time, we could show them through the powerful medium of motion pictures how they could prevent certain diseases. And consequently more and more emphasis was put on simple films showing how a farmer could help himself with the means at his disposal. Typical titles of films produced from 1950 to 1959 for the rural audiences in Iran were:

Why Babies Die
Clean Water
Nutrition
Malaria
Anthrax
Milk and Milk Products—Sanitation
How to Bathe a Baby
Plant Trees for the Future
Improvement of Livestock
Sugar Beet Production
Rural Cooperatives
Rural Action in Building Schools

Some aid in agricultural areas came through improvement in livestock and methods of poultry raising. Large quantities of eggs were shipped to Iran from America along with incubators so that the chickens could be hatched locally. The chickens hatched from these imported eggs were then sold to the farmers to improve their breed of poultry.

Food, so closely related to good health, was improved, but great areas of need were neglected. The thought often came to me, when there was talk about expanding the poultry project, "What is the good of a farmer having a thousand fine chickens if his wife is sick or his family is dying?" I felt additional funds should be diverted to relieving the serious health problems of the rural population.

Another problem was the desperate need for good roads. The Allies had built roads from the Persian Gulf to the northern border for transportation of war supplies, and during Reza Shah's reign the big railway had been built across Iran—a masterpiece of engineering, particularly in the mountainous areas. (A point of interest is that the railway construction was financed completely by taxes paid by the consumer on tea and sugar.)

However, at the time I was working in the cinema mobile unit operation, we had few roads linking the fifty thousand villages. Iran needed connecting roads and bridges that were not at the mercy of heavy rainfall, to relieve isolation which breeds ignorance and a stagnant life.

The farmers' main mode of transportation was riding small donkeys. Someone in the Point Four program had the bright idea of bringing jackasses from Cyprus into the country to encourage breeding larger donkeys. The thought was that this might enable farmers to get from one place to another with their produce, even though better lanes for travel were not built. It was a joke for some time in Iran, and "wags" referred laughingly to jackasses bringing jackasses into Iran. The newspaper cartoonists had a field day with the concept.

Lack of modern communication media was indeed a serious problem for the country. Looking back one can say that television would have been an ideal way of connecting every village to the capital city as a means of educating, informing and entertaining people in all walks of life. But at the time, educational television had not even found a place in the United States. And there were more basic problems to be solved in the villages—such as the need for electricity.

Traveling in the country in those years impressed me with the fact that Iran was a rich country—rich in minerals, good land, good weather, beautiful scenery. Why should the people of this rich nation be so poor? There was not enough water in many areas, but there were big rivers and, with financial aid, dams could be built and the water controlled.

I was also impressed by the fact that Iran was a country rich in human resources. The people are intelligent, active, hardworking, with a great desire for learning and self-improvement.

To bring a better day, forces had to be marshaled under one banner. Governments came and went and personnel serving them changed. But the people of Iran looked to the Shah as the supreme power; his reign was continuous, ongoing—without interruption. He was a leader among men. And he was a good leader—educated, intelligent, highly motivated to carry through reform programs. Surely forces to elevate the life of the common man should be marshaled under the banner of the Shah!

6
Iran as Seen by
an American Filmmaker

Ignorance of one's own country is to be deplored! In the early fifties it was obvious to officials of the government and teachers in the schools that Iranian adults as well as children had little concept of regions of the country they had not seen. Those in the highlands found it difficult to visualize the Caspian Sea or the Persian Gulf, for they had never seen a large body of water. Likewise, those on the coast could not imagine life in the mountains.

Our office decided to utilize the team of filmmakers from Syracuse University to make five full-length travelogues, designed to be used in schools for the teaching of geography, and through the mobile unit operation to acquaint adults in the rural areas with the facts about their own country: the north of Iran; Tehran; Esfahan; Persepolis, and Abadan.

An unexpected benefit from the project was the insight some of us received into the life of Persian people. A foreign observer will note things which people of a nation do not because they have always lived with them and have become accustomed (or inured) to them. With his full permission, I give here some highlights from two reports turned into our office by John H. Humphrey, one of these American filmmakers, who produced and directed these films for us. The detailed word coverage describes the crew's trips into the countryside during the months of September and October, 1951.

Mr. Humphrey was accompanied by a very able technical

advisor, Dr. Taghi Mostafavi from the Archeological Museum, and
a skeleton crew, assisted by the Iranian army, making the trip in a
carry-all truck (and on occasion, army jeeps). The report is dotted
throughout with stories of the intense heat, flat tires and mechanical
breakdowns, because the group traversed miles and miles of rough,
primitively constructed roads.* But throughout runs a thread of
great appreciation for the stark beauty of vast stretches of country,
for the lush gardens and exquisite architecture of Iran, and a tremendous affection for the people, along with a cognizance of the
great problems facing them. The group started out on September
18 at six-thirty in the morning. The remainder of this chapter is
made up of excerpts from Mr. Humphrey's delightfully informal
report to my office:

One hundred and seventy-two kilometers northeast of Tehran
we hit Shah Abbas. There we saw the first of a series of caravanserais built on the road from Tehran to Mashad. This building was
built about three hundred and fifty years ago, of stone and mud.
It had been at one time a well-constructed building and many like
it are still in use. This particular one had started to fall apart and
one was able to see the huge piles of stones that had been used in
its construction. It is interesting to see the construction of the
roofs, which were a masterpiece for that day. They consisted of
domes, which were built over each separate room. These domes
then had two more layers of stone and mud built over them, with
air space in between. This formed a very good insulation from
the strong heat of the sun.

Never before had I been conscious of the exact color of the
earth itself. Dirt in small bunches is one thing, but when one sees
acres, miles, hundreds of miles stretching out before one, it becomes
a completely different color. We associate the color "brown" with
earth, but earth in large areas becomes like a dead brown; it has
all the warmth and life taken out of it. It then becomes like a corpse
of earth, instead of what we think of when we think of soil.

In the center area between Tehran and Mashad, we found a
new system of water supply from the jube.† The jube flows into a

---

*Those readers who may have visited Iran in the 1970s can appreciate the
phenomenal progress which has taken place in the country within only a couple of
decades. Iran is now a major center of business and tourism in the Middle East.

†A jube is a deep gutter or canal used to carry water to homes or fields.

central area between many fields, and here it breaks up into smaller jubes which go to the individual fields of the farmers. At this juncture there is built a small circular mud wall. Through this wall comes the main jube into a small pool. A villager sits inside the circular wall where the small pool is, and has a pan with him. In the bottom of the pan is a small hole, and the water comes up through this hole and eventually fills the pan. This is the time measure for the water supply for each separate villager and that is all of the water he gets at one time. Then the water is turned into another jube.

We drove on to Shahrud, where we met John and June Hamilton and Ali Issari. We had tea with the Director of Education and left a great deal of our extra luggage with him to help lighten the load. We would pick it up when we went back through there to Gorgan. At ten-thirty we stopped at Abbas Abad and had dinner. From there we drove on across the plateau, and the wind was blowing a strong gale. Everyone was filthy, dirty and tired. We finally arrived at Mashad at nine the next morning after being on the road twenty-seven and a half hours covering 1,585 kilometers (1,057 miles).

In Mashad

The Consulate is stuck way back in an almost inaccessible Kuche (alley-like street), but the building itself is very nice with very high rooms and the old type of cylindrical metal stoves built into the walls—typical of those in the old Russian mansions.

We went to the Sanctuary, the burial place of the eighth Imam (Imam Reza) of the Shi'ah sect of Islam. It is one of the most sacred places of the sect, and we were about the only Christians that have ever gotten into this Sanctuary. We went first into the garden of the Museum of the Sanctuary. This garden is very formal with trees and flowers laid out between the tile walks. There are two main walks running north and south with a long pool in between. The Museum is made of pink marble.

We photographed the golden dome from this garden, then went right through the Museum and out into one of the two large squares on two sides of the Sanctuary. We went quickly through the court because we were invading a religious sanctuary and could not blame the religious for resenting our intrusion, but nothing happened.

The Sanctuary was built by Shah Abbas. He traveled from Esfahan to Mashad on foot (a distance of about fourteen hundred miles) and when he got there he ordered the Sanctuary and the golden dome and golden entrance to be built. Although we did not get into the Sanctuary itself, we could glance through the window on the second-floor area and see that it was pink tile with inserts of mirrors all over it. The devout go to the golden crypt, which is surrounded by a golden fence, and pray and kiss the bars of the fence, and throw money and jewels into the inside area. This makes the Sanctuary one of the biggest money-making propositions in the country.

Farsi script, a form of Arabic, lends itself much better to architecture than does our Roman script. The vertical strokes with the wide sweeps in their script make beautiful designs in their architecture. For instance, the gold dome has an inscription by Shah Abbas, which makes a beautiful design even for those who cannot read it.

That afternoon we went to Ferdowsi's tomb. Ferdowsi is given a place of prominence among the Iranian people that would make Shakespeare pale in our culture. His poetry is not just poetry to them, but instead is actually a part of their daily living: it is more of their history, religion and mores than the Koran, the laws and historians all put together. Almost any Iranian can recite some of Ferdowsi to you, even if he is illiterate. The tomb is located about thirty kilometers (twenty miles) from Mashad, in the place where the ancient city of Tous once stood. Tous is where Ferdowsi was born and where he requested to be buried. The tomb itself is of yellow-white alabaster, with inscriptions of Ferdowsi's poetry. The room of the tomb is of mosaic tile and the crypt itself is of white alabaster.

We learned how they make the mosaic tiles. First an artist draws the design on paper; then the color of each piece is chosen. The paper is then cut to the desired pattern and pasted onto the tile. This is then chipped out and sanded to the exact size of the paper. These pieces are next put into a jig face down. The backs of the tiles are slanted slightly during the sanding process, so that there are cracks between the pieces. These are then filled with cement. When the work is completed a wire is inserted to secure the individual mosaic pieces, which are set into concrete.

In the Province of Gorgan

When we got to Pahlavi Dejh, north of the city of Gorgan, the two army captains with us were somewhat worried about our taking films there. They maintained that the Turkomans were fanatic Sunnite Moslems, and that if they thought we were photographing their women, they would kill us immediately. We finally hit on the idea of posing as engineers looking at their bridge, which ran through one end of the main bazaar street.

The attitude of the people was that of idle curiosity, until they finally decided that Joe (our cameraman, who was on top of the truck) was photographing. Then they immediately began to gather around the truck. To stall off the coming tide, two of us did some trading through Aziz, our interpreter, on two rugs and finally bought them. The crowd soon started to demand that we give them our film. When one of the captains told them we were engineers looking at the bridge, it didn't do much good. We jumped into the car and made a hasty retreat.

Across the Provinces of Gilan and Mazanderan

The breakfast here is always a battle. Americans are used to very different food (and a great deal more of it) for breakfast than the average Iranian. We finally got some eggs "nimroo" (which means fried), some Taftoun, a very, very delicious thin crackerlike bread, and coffee, which was strong enough to stand two dead men on their feet.

On the Road Along the Caspian Sea from Chalus to Rasht

We drove through this subtropical area. People carry most of the loads here on a pole across one shoulder with two huge reed baskets hung at each end. They grow mostly cotton, rice, tea and silkworms. The silk period was over, but they were harvesting their rice. I do so wish we could have taken some photographs in this area, but the light and rain would not permit it. We drove on to Lahijan. We ate dinner in the upstairs of a hotel, and had a fairly decent meal. The most extraordinary thing about the dinner was

that for the first time since I came to Iran, I sat down at the table
and ate where an Iranian woman also ate. She was the wife of the
Colonel, and is quite westernized, but still I have known other
westernized women in Iran but have never eaten with any.

In Rasht

The shops were all closed and there was a very big demonstration to show Dr. Mossadegh that the people of Iran were behind
his oil policy. While this demonstration was forming, I went to
place a call to Tehran. When I wished to leave the telephone
building, I found that I could not get out of the main entrance.
There were so many people around the front of the building that
the police had locked the doors and would not let us out. I finally
persuaded the police inside the building to let me out the back
way and I walked around the demonstration. I was sure that at
any moment the people would look at me and think I was English
and try to show more concretely how much they backed Dr. Mossadegh's policy. However, nothing happened and I proceeded back to
the hotel.

After leaving Rasht, we began a steady climb from about eighty
feet below sea level to about eight thousand feet above. This entire
valley through which we passed is farmed to the fullest extent.
The side hills are covered with trees of good size but many of
the trees have been cleared to make fields. Most Americans would
consider these hills too steep for farming. It is a beautiful sight
to see the light green of the fields and the dark green trees making a
patchwork out of the hills on either side of the valley. In contrast,
at one place we found terracing. In the valley the men were
threshing the grain.

In the Province of Azarbaijan

We soon got onto a fairly decent gravel road, and went up into
the mountains of Azarbaijan territory. The country got to look
better the farther we drove, with more green on the hills and more
gullies from spring and summer streams.

In Khorram Darre, which means "prosperous valley," the grape-
vines were all over. This is the best raisin area of Iran. We then
went by Selensyeh, an ancient city which has now been destroyed.

"Gate of All Nations," at the house of Xerxes, Persepolis (*Photo courtesy of Audio Visual Department, Ministry of Information and Tourism, Iran*)

Tomb of Cyrus the Great, founder of the Persian Empire, at Pasargade

General view of Persepolis

Tomb of Esther, Queen of Xerxes (King Ahaseurus, 5th century B.C.) in
Hamadan

Khajou Bridge in Esfahan, built during the Safavid dynasty, 1499-1736 A.D. *(Photo courtesy Audio Visual Department, Ministry of Information and Tourism, Iran)*

Tomb of Avicenna, great Iranian physician, in Hamadan *(Photo courtesy of Audio Visual Department, Ministry of Information and Tourism, Iran)*

The Shrine of Imam Reza (the 8th Imam of the Shi'ah sect), at Mashad
(*Photo courtesy Audio Visual Department, Ministry of Information and Tourism, Iran*)

'omb of Ferdowsi, great epic poet of Iran in Tous, near Mashad

The Shrine of Shah Nematollah Vali at Mahan, Kerman *(Photo courte Audio Visual Department, Ministry of Information and Tourism, Iran)*

The Armenian Church in Julfa, Esfahan, built during the reign of Shah
Abbas the Great

main street in Kermanshah

Veresk Railway Bridge, built during the reign of Reza Shah the Great 1925-1941 (*Photo courtesy Audio Visual Department, Ministry of Information and Tourism, Iran*)

It was at this location that most of the ancient Shahs of Iran grouped their armies for battle. This was also the capital of Iran during the Mongolian dynasties and there is a huge tomb still standing which was built for one of the Mongolian Shahs. However, he was killed in the east for his clothes and rolled into a bag and made into a pulp.

On the afternoon of our drive to Tabriz, we drove up to a very old bridge of which the central part had been destroyed. This is Pole Dokhtar, which means Daughter's Bridge. This Bridge was destroyed by the Democrats during the Azarbaijan revolt in 1946. It had been built over eight hundred years ago. It has very interesting construction, with the roadbed laid on three tubes which go from one pillar to another, the pillars being made of bricks. These three tubes apparently form a lighter and stronger bed than solid brickwork would form. It is an amazing piece of architecture.

In Tabriz

In the afternoon we went to what is popularly called the Arg. This is actually the mosque and fortress built during the Mongolian dynasties. The dome has now collapsed and only three of the walls stand. When one considers the amount of man-hours spent to build such a structure out of bricks with the tools they had in those days—eight hundred years ago—it is frightening. It was built by Ali Shah, who was Minister of State of Guasan Khan, one of the later Khans after Genghis. In the U formed by the three sides, the citizens of Tabriz have erected a monument to the soldiers, officers and people killed during the Azarbaijan revolt of 1946.

The northeastern section of the city is known as Sorkhab, which means Red Water, because it lies directly at the foot of a large mountain of red clay. When it rains, all the jubes in this section of the city run red.

In Tabriz and Rezaiyeh you can see the influence of the European cultures more than in any other place in Iran. Their streets, their buildings, their ways of living are more European, or Russian at least.

In Tabriz I found the first really large Christian church I have seen in northern Iran. Tabriz and Rezaiyeh are the centers of the Christian community in Iran. Here is the center of the Armenian Russian group.

The Golestan Gardens in Tabriz cover a full city block with fountains, trees, Reza Shah's statue and flowers, and many beautiful walks through the gardens.

In Maragheh

From Tabriz, we went south along Lake Rezaiyeh to a small town named Maragheh. We saw a tomb built for the mother of Halaku Khan. It was built about the year 700 of the lunar calendar. This Halaku Khan was a Mongolian king, the one who was killed in the eastern part of Iran by being rolled into a bag "until the seven skies fall or he is dead." The skies did not fall and he was turned to pulp.

In Rezaiyeh

In Rezaiyeh we got shots of the new sugar factory. It is a very modern establishment from Czechoslovakia. It has houses for some of the employees, and a 12-year school, a hospital and cafeteria. Some statistics: it covers a 300,000 square meter area and the buildings themselves cover 30,000 square meters. It uses an average of 750 tons of sugar beets a day and 130,000 tons a year. The average good beet of that area is 15 percent sugar, the top grade is 18 percent. The factory produces 15,000 pounds of sugar a year. The pulp is used for fodder; however, it can be used for production of alcohol in the future when they get some more equipment.

We also went to the Lake itself and photographed the "boat" which goes across the lake to Tabriz and some of the other ports nearby. The "boat" consists of a barge which is towed by two small steamships. They tow with heavy chains. The day we were there, many of the peasants who had been working in Rezaiyeh and the surrounding area were going back home. They were crowded onto the deck and into the hold until you weren't sure it would stay afloat. It reminded me a great deal of the stories of the boats that first brought the immigrants to the United States during the Industrial Revolution. The lake itself is much like Salt Lake and the countryside around it is very much like Utah. The lake has 4.5 grams of potassium sulfate for each gram of water. The mud of the lake is dug up and used by the Russian hospital in Tehran for the treatment of rheumatism. The entire bottom of the lake is a solid deposit of salt. As we drove along we saw where workers had dug channels from the lake to drying pits on the shore. The pits were full of what would become good fertilizer for the fields of some of the villages around there.

We stopped on our way into town and picked up some shots of some of the women and boys picking tobacco. Their tobacco, at least what we saw, is very small in comparison with ours. The two girls we used for this sequence were each given ten rials (twenty-five cents) when we were done, and you have never seen such happy faces in your life. They were probably ten to twelve years old, and their faces lit up when they thought of the extras they could buy with this money.

In town we went to the Girls' School. This school was built in 1926 by an American Presbyterian Mission. It was taken over by the Iranian government in 1938, along with all other foreign schools in Iran. We photographed there. Both the principal, a woman, and one of the teachers, had gone to the school when it was run by the Americans. One woman spoke very good English, and we had a nice conversation about the school, her relatives in the United States, and the curriculum.

We had an opportunity to go through the bazaar at Rezaiyeh. I picked up some hats and turban cloths, then went to watch the making of the felt rugs which are so common to the poorer houses in Iran.

The wool of the sheep and goats is brought in and graded as to color: black, brown or white. It then is fluffed. This is a very interesting process. A man sits on the ground with a large pile of raw coarse wool in front of him. He has a bow which looks very much like a huge bow for arrows, except that it is heavier, and has a weighted end. The bow has a string drawn tight across it. He pounds this string with a wooden mallet. This causes the string to vibrate at a very high rate, and when he lowers it rhythmically into the raw wool, the fast movement of the string fluffs up the wool. It billows up into the air much like fluff candy. This is then taken and placed in the proper quantity on a strip of canvas. The wool is placed so that it will come out a certain desired thickness and also a certain square dimension. This is then rolled into a tight roll with the canvas as backing. The canvas roll with the wool inside is then tied together and rolled. And when I say rolled, I mean rolled. Three men stamp on it with a beat of one, two, three.

One is the stamp, *two* is a rolling push forward, and *three* is a step with the other foot. It is perfectly timed to the sound of their breathing, which comes out in small explosions and echoes beautifully around the enclosure. They never lose a beat, and when they get to the end of the rolling area, they step to the other side, change feet and are on the beat without a loss of a second. It is one of the most fascinating and interesting processes I have ever seen.

We slept extremely well and awoke in the morning and washed. Very seldom in the outlying towns and villages do you find a wash basin. Instead everyone washes at a pump by a pool in the yard. The pump also supplies water for drinking as well as for washing pots and pans. In this particular governor's house—Governor Ardalan—we washed while the Kurdish women kept coming to the pool to get their morning water. They are really colorful and beautiful. They wear shoes made of soft cloth or leather, with pantaloons that blouse out and have a tight band around each ankle. The pantaloons are usually rose, pink, orange, gold, and so forth, with a slight design. Over these they wear a skirt, usually of a contrasting brilliant color, that comes to midcalf on their legs. The top of the costume is either a blouse with a heavy padded jacket when it is cold, or a light vest-type jacket when it is warm. These are covered with coins of gold, silver or brass, or just spangles. The women wear huge earrings, and some still have the pierced nose with the coin or spangle in it. On top of the head they wear a stiff cap of velveteen with spangles, covered with a plain white cloth kerchief tied across the chin. They do not wear the *chador* (veil). We were grateful that they didn't so that we could enjoy their beauty as well as their beautiful costumes. The women who came to get water were regal in their bearing and even when they were carrying two five-gallon cans of water on their shoulders, they gave you the impression that you should bow if you spoke to them.

Dr. Mostafavi explained the reason for polygamy (now outlawed), especially among such tribes as the Kurds. It is not purely a sexual matter, but rather a matter of economics. The Kurdish women do most of the work. Therefore, when a man begins to get land or sheep, he must have more wives to take care of his bigger holdings. The wealthier he becomes the more wives he must have until his children can help out.

After breakfast, which consisted of soft-boiled eggs, bread, cheese and honey, with the ever-present tea, we met the governor, a very interesting man. He is Kurdish and the people of the community respect him greatly because he is one of themselves. After looking at the dismal clouds, we decided to take a stroll through the bazaar and see if there was anything we desired. The people stood when the governor came by their booths, and we were treated like visiting royalty. We bought some caps, both men's and women's, and I also got a beautiful piece of brocade, which the Kurdish men use for their Friday shirts. It is one of the finest pieces of Damascus brocade I have ever seen. Some of the people who have been in Damascus say it is of the best quality made there. It has a black background with silver dogs, birds and trees on it—real silver thread. Each animal and tree is outlined with red thread. It is a beautiful piece of craftsmanship.

I also bought a turban. These turbans are not at all the way I had imagined them to be. They are made of a piece of silk or artificial silk about six feet square with fringe on two sides. They are usually black with a slight silver-gray stripe through them or sometimes with a red or green stripe. Tying the turban is really a work of art and deft manipulation.

The turban is a very practical piece of clothing. You can use it as a prayer rug, as a sheet in the summer, as a rope to tie your horse if necessary, or as a shopping bag. With a little soap and water it is quickly cleaned. But, used as a head covering, the time consumed in tying it each morning for me would be killing.

We decided to get to Sanandaj before dark. We started climbing almost immediately to about six or seven thousand feet and then came to a tableland. This high table is well watered. The rains are brought in by the winds from the Mediterranean Sea, across Syria to hit the high Kurdish mountains. The land really looks like a lowland plain with rolling hills. Then when you see the clouds down below you, you realize that these hills are mountain peaks in the distance.

In Iran Shahr

We got into Iran Shahr for lunch. This was just a small whistle-stop town and we stopped at the one teahouse. There was a very ugly man who played a very nice instrument called an *oud*. It is very much like an Italian street singer's guitar. The body or sounding box is a lopsided, half-round wooden structure of inlaid woods. The neck or fingering board is longer than those in the United States. There are more strings on it. This man played and sang a couple of songs for us. Their music is more rhythmic than the average Iranian music.

While we were eating, a Kurd rode up in great haste and jumped off his horse. Their horses are some of the most beautiful animals I have ever seen; clearly they are of Arabian stock. The trappings and the saddle are made of leather which has been stitched with brilliantly dyed string. They also put a felt saddle mat on the saddle. This is made to fit over the horn and also over the back of the saddle seat, leaving a padded section on which to sit. About a one-yard square felt pad comes down on the side of the saddle, which is also richly embroidered. The horse and rider really made a very beautiful appearance.

This Kurd got the local law enforcement official and they both went riding off in great haste, with rifles strung over their backs. The night before, one of a band of raiding Kurds had been killed when he had tried to get into a house. And so the two men were out to look for the rest of the group. Needless to say, I was glad I was not on the other end of those rifles because the two men looked as if they would know quite well how to use them.

In Sanandaj

After lunch, we departed and drove on to Sanandaj, arriving there at 9:30 P.M. On the way down we had stopped to shoot some scenes of the Kurdish villagers who had all "turned to winnow their grain." They were very friendly and courteous and I think I can safely say that of all the Iranian groups I have met so far I like the Kurds the best.

In Kermanshah

We finally got into Kermanshah, or just out of it at Taghe Bostan at one P.M. This is the ancient site of three monuments carved into the side of the hill. The oldest, built in the year A.D. 209, shows two kings of the Sassanian period holding the ever-present wreath of kingdom. One king is standing on the head of the vanquished foe. The second, which is in bad repair, was carved in A.D. 295 and is of Ghobad Khosro Parviz. The third dates back to about A.D. 605, and is the largest. They are very interesting as they show a great deal of the dress and the culture of that period. On each side of the largest niche are carvings of hunting scenes showing the king hunting on the plains, in the mountains and from a boat.

Here we left our military guard and proceeded to Hamadan, arriving there at seven-fifteen. On the road from Kermanshah to Hamadan we passed the Bisotoun Mountain, which is where Darius I carved his famous sculpture of the nine vanquished foes, all bound, lined up in front of him; he has his foot on the tenth. This sculpture was pictured in the *National Geographic* just before I left the States. It was, however, the biggest disappointment I had in Iran. I had imagined the figures to be enormous even when viewed from the ground—as they are carved way up on the side of the mountain. However, they are very small, and it was impossible to make anything definite out of the carvings from the road. I imagine that if one could get up close to them, they would be impressive, but to me they were most disappointing.

In Hamadan

In Hamadan, we stayed at the Hotel Iran, which is directly across the street from the new monument they are building to Avicenna. He was an ancient (nearly a thousand years ago) philosopher and doctor. This monument is built out of solid granite and contains two large rooms, one a library for his works and the other a reception and office room. Then behind the front two rooms is a circular room which will contain the tomb of Avicenna. Above this circular room are eight concrete pillars about seventy-five feet high. These pillars are rectangular, and slope in from a large circular base to a narrow circular top on which sits a cap of concrete much like a dunce cap. It is a very handsome building and one with the best workmanship I saw in Iran.

In Tehran

We just made it back the night before two important religious holidays (ninth and tenth of Moharram)° and we watched many of the parades from the shadows of the balconies of our hotel.

°Imam Hossein, the third Imam of the Shi'ah sect of the Moslem religion, was killed, along with seventy-two of his followers on the tenth of Moharram, sixty-two years after Hijrat, in Karbala, Iraq. The story of his life and his pursuit of justice and right against all odds forms one of the most fascinating examples of a man devoted to the cause of human dignity in the annals of history.

After five days of reorganization and repair, I left Tehran for the southern part of the trip. This time I took the two new members of the Syracuse University Project with me.

In Ghom

We arrived at Ghom and went directly to the Sanctuary. This Sanctuary is second only to that in Mashad in religious importance. It is the burial place of Fatima, the daughter of Mohammad. It, too, has the golden dome, but the *Eivan* (porch) is mirrored instead of gold. The Sanctuary is not quite as beautiful as that of Mashad, but the greater simplicity adds to its beauty, in my opinion. I enjoyed seeing it as much as that of Mashad.

The Museum is filled with many of the ancient gifts. Particularly interesting were the jewels given from the garments and crowns of the different Shahs and placed in the Sanctuary. There were rubies, emeralds and gold in beautiful design. The interesting thing about all of the Iranian jewels I have seen so far is that they are not cut or polished like those with which we are familiar. Instead, they are of semipolished uncut baroque forms.

There were also two tombs of two old kings. They are made of bronze or copper and are large boxes about eight feet long, four feet wide and about four feet high. They were very interesting from the standpoint of comparison with the tombs of ancient times or the Middle Ages of Europe.

We proceeded on our trip to Kashan, noted for its fine carpets, all of which are produced as piecework in the homes of the townspeople. While in Kashan, we were able to photograph the making of a carpet. The workers had kindly brought a huge loom (four and a half meters high and three and a half meters wide) from the house and set it up outside. The carpets they were weaving, which would cost about a hundred and twenty toomans (twenty-four dollars) per square meter, had a background of red.

The designs are first drawn on graph paper, and then a painter selects the colors and paints two pieces: one piece is just one-fourth of the middle section of the carpet and the other a corner of the border. These are then studied by the workers and transferred practically from memory into the carpet.

We also saw thread making, or yarn making, for the carpet, which is still done on the primitive hand implements, centuries old.

We then went to visit the garden, named Fin, which is truly an interesting place—in Iran, where water is so scarce. Here is a natural spring. The water flows from the spring into a large pool; from there it goes into another large pool; and from there it flows into four or five jubes. One of these jubes goes down through the garden itself, finally appearing in the form of low fountains. There must have been nearly fifty in one line, and about twelve around one pool.

The garden was originally built by Shah Salman, three hundred and thirty years ago. Later (about a hundred and fifty years ago) Fath-Ali Shah arranged the rest of the garden. It was he who put the fountains in the garden. The spring itself issues about six hundred and sixty cubic meters of water per hour. The water is not good for drinking because of the high mercury and lime content. However, some claim it is good for bathing, which I cannot imagine, considering the lime content.

Nassereddin Shah's Prime Minister was exiled from Tehran to this garden about a hundred years ago. After he had lived there about two years, he was taken one day to the private Hammam, a bathhouse, and murdered by a group from Tehran. Previous to his exile he had been in great favor with the court, but his enemies, being afraid of his possible power, talked the Shah into the murder.

Here I saw fish and soft-shelled crab for the first time in Iran. The pools and streams were filled with them.

Kashan is noted for its *anar* (pomegranates) and for its scorpions. I was told they have three types of scorpions: one a small white one about the size of the end of the little finger, a green one about the size of the little finger, and a black one much larger. The former two are deadly poisonous, while the latter is much less dangerous.

We left Kashan and drove across some of the most barren country I have ever seen. I do not know if the glacial action got as far south as Iran, but the mountains and the territory next to the mountains looked as if the glaciers had brought huge boulders and deposited them when they receded northwards.*

The area, which is the beginning of the great central desert of Iran, is almost completely uninhabited. The mountains form a stop for the clouds, which must empty their loads of torrential

---

*Mr. Humphrey is correctly describing the last ice age.

rains. From the appearance of the water-dredged areas around the mountains, huge sections, as much as a hundred to two hundred yards across, are obviously washed quite regularly with heavy waters. The water pushes what little topsoil remains onto the plains below. From a distance, this border of the plain looked as though it was farmed, but I could not be sure.

We drove on slowly until just after we hit the junction of the other road from Ghom to Esfahan. Here we stopped at a small village and had dinner. I shall not forget getting what I thought to be hard-boiled eggs, and breaking one in typical Humphrey fashion over my head, only to find it was not hard-boiled at all. I needed an egg shampoo anyway.

In Esfahan

Esfahan has so many monuments that it is very difficult for me to know exactly where to start discussing them.

The large building on the west side of the square is known as Ali Qapou, which means "large gate." This five-story building which looks out over the square was used by Shah Abbas for viewing the polo games played there. This field has now been removed, and a large garden with a pool has been built in its place, but the goalposts of stone still remain.

At the southern side of the polo ground stands the huge blue tile domed mosque called the "Masjid-e-Shah." The court of the mosque has—as usual—a large pool in the center, with the three *eivans* (porches) on three sides and the mosque on the fourth. This mosque has a double dome like many of the larger mosques, the inside dome being round, while the outside dome is of the shape we always picture mosques to be. This construction is done purely for beauty, and not for any practical reasons.

On the east side of the field is the mosque of Sheykh Lotfollah, which has a very beautiful pastel yellow dome with a nice flower design in the tile. To me, this is the most beautiful mosque in Iran. At the northern end of the field is what is now the bazaar. This is a very different bazaar from that of Tehran, as it is a factory-bazaar. That is, most of the goods are made right in the bazaar and not purchased somewhere else and then brought to the bazaar for sale. Esfahan is known for its silver, saddle bags and copper. I bought some saddle bags, which will make beautiful cushions for seats against the wall or on a chair. (Usually they are used against the wall and that is the way I believe they should be used.) They are really made for throwing over a donkey and the two sides are filled with melons, straw, vegetables, stones, wood, or what have you.

Another very interesting monument is the Chehel Sotoun, or Forty Pillars. One of the old palaces of the Shah, it has a huge porch held up by twenty pillars. Everyone, on seeing it, asks why it is called Forty Pillars—that is, until he gets to the far end of the pool in front of the palace and then can see the twenty pillars reflected in the pool.

There are also two bridges which are interesting. One of them, the Sio-Se-Pol (Thirty-three Bridges) is made up of thirty-three pillars, giving it its name. The other bridge, Khaju Bridge, is interesting because it is both a bridge and a dam.

Just up the river from these two bridges, a new one is being constructed which will be about five spans, built of concrete and steel. It was fascinating to watch the workers make the forms, which were rounded smoothly as if for a work of art. One thing I have noticed about Iranian construction is that it is usually all finished as though for an artistic purpose. The only thing that prevents all such structures from being very fine is the material out of which they are made.

Sunday morning we went to Jolfa.° This is an Armenian village, which Shah Abbas moved from the Armenian center near Rezaiyeh. He was impressed by the fact that the Armenians are very good workers, and therefore moved them near his capital, which at the time was Esfahan. We went into the church, which, incidentally, has a dome like a mosque. It was decorated inside in a way I have never seen before. There were no pews or seats, as in the churches of America. The walls are covered with hundreds of paintings of the different stories of the Bible. This is all done in a flat two-dimensional painting and with much gilt and brilliant colors. The altar is solid silver, with draperies of brocaded velvet, and is one that every tourist should see, as I am sure there are few like it in the world.

In Yazd

Yazd is one of the two strongholds of the Zoroastrian religion in Iran. I had been greatly mistaken in my preconceived idea of

---

°A small village near Esfahan.

Zoroastrian temples. I had always imagined them to be built with
a circular wall, in which a permanent fire was burning. However,
we found a regular building, with a porchway around three sides,
and a doorway on the fourth. We were not permitted into the
inner room, which contained the fire. The simplicity of the place,
and the overpowering smell of the almost sickening sweet smoke
made me wonder what type of service the worshipers could hold
in this place, and how long they could possibly stand the heavy
pungent odor.

We left Yazd and drove across the most barren desert I have
seen in years. It reminded me of the uninhabited areas of Arizona
and New Mexico. However, it was so extensive, and you could see
so far, that one realized more and more that water is the greatest
problem of Iran. We saw only one small village until we hit Anar.
Anar is the name for pomegranate and is truly a good name for
this village. The pomegranates are larger and sweeter than any I
have ever had in the U.S.; they are about the size of a medium
grapefruit. Here they do not break them and eat the seeds as we
do in the States, but instead they soften them as we do an orange,
and then bite the skin and suck the juice. This is a very ticklish
job, as it must be done just right. If you break the outer skin you
have a permanently dyed shirt. Also, when one bites into the skin,
the juice gushes out like Old Faithful.

We drove across this great desert, stopping a couple of times to
give the road workers some water. It must be a terrible task to be
out in the middle of this desert without any water, and seeing only
a very few vehicles go by.

In Kerman

Kerman is noted for its carpets throughout the world. It is surprising to see these people work for hours, days, weeks, months on
one carpet and see how they are able to complete a design with very
little reference to the pattern. One of the most interesting things
about Kerman carpets is that they are not trimmed on the looms as
other carpets are, but are trimmed after the entire carpet is completed. The carpets for American markets are left with a much
longer nap than those for Iran. I prefer the Iranian carpets because
they show the design better, and also because they look richer.

We went to an athletic contest which was more or less like

our field days—there was a great variety of different exercises and games. The Iranians are great for weight lifting, much more so than the Americans. While there we saw a very interesting display of ancient Iranian exercises—exercises that have been handed down for centuries. They are done to the beat of an ancient type of drum, and the singing of the drummer. I enjoyed this very much, and watching the young children do some of the exercises was really marvelous. They far outstrip most of the American children in their athletic prowess.

That evening at the governor's home proved to be very interesting indeed. It is surprising to see how the Iranians think of the U.S. at times. During the evening they spoke of a certain American professor who had been in Iran for many years, and who had been a great friend of the Iranians until the 1946 Azarbaijan revolt. At that time he began to write a series of very uncomplimentary articles about Iran in the New York papers. He is, I believe, the head of what is now called the Oriental Institute. Because of this one man, you could see that their trust for Americans was anything but one hundred percent.

One interesting thing we saw while in the Kerman area was an ancient type of oxen well. This is the type that one always thinks of as being in Egypt. It consisted of an ox, driven round and round, moving a large wheel. This wheel is connected to a vertical wheel. A series of small pottery jugs tied onto a couple of ropes run over the vertical wheel. These pots drop down fifteen meters to the water level, fill themselves, and then are pulled up and dumped when they are pulled over the vertical wheel at the top.

In Persepolis

Persepolis, called by the Iranians "Takhte-Jamshid," which means "Terrace of Kings," is built in a valley right at the side of a mountain which is of gray limestone. This mountain has a slight natural projection sticking out into the valley. On this projection Darius started a terrace, which is four hundred and fifty meters long and three hundred meters wide. The terrace is completely faced with the gray limestone. On the north side of the western face of the terrace is a huge switchback staircase. This is double, with a common beginning, going north and south and then switching back to a common end just in front of the huge gateway. There are a hundred and ten steps in this staircase and they all have about a four-inch rise. All of the stairs of Persepolis are of a small rise because the kings were not supposed to take big steps, and in fact, some of the sculptures show them with their legs tied together at the ankles with a ribbon. Another more prevalent explanation for the small rise of the steps is that horsemen could go up the steps without dismounting.

One walks from the western side of the palace of a hundred pillars toward the huge palace called Apadana to see another set of thirty-one steps. The sculptures of these steps are all of bas relief, representing people from the many countries which Darius had conquered. In the center of the face of the steps are carved scenes that one observes all over Persepolis—that is, of the rearing bull, with the lion biting the bull in the back, and tearing at its back with its claws. This symbolizes the power of the heavenly gods over the earthly things. One also sees in many places the symbolic picturization of the Zoroastrian religion, Ahura Mazda (from which comes the name "Mazda" lights).

Ahura Mazda symbolized the great single god of Zoroaster, and although his followers worship light (fire), water, air and earth they are all part of Ahura Mazda. Darius was a Zoroastrian.

Most people know Persepolis as the home of Darius, which is correct, but few people know that Xerxes—Darius' son—actually did most of the construction and commissioned the better sculpture that is there.

The word "Persepolis" itself is interesting. This region originally was called "Pars" by the Greeks, who mispronounced the word "Fars" (the Iranian name). However, one Greek writer called it "Persepotolis," which means "the destroyer of cities," and the word has been adapted and used until it is now "Persepolis."

As is known, Persepolis fell to Alexander the Great and while he was there, his mistress, Thaïs, wanted to burn it and Alexander let her. What a holocaust that must have been. The rocks still show where the burnt timbers fell.

In Shiraz

Shiraz is the burial place of two of Iran's greatest poets—Hafez and Sa'di. These poets are by far the two most loved people in the country, and their beautiful tombs show it.

The tomb of Hafez is in the northern part of the city. It consists of a long pillared porch, facing onto two pooled gardens. Behind this is a circular pillared dome, under which is the tomb. The place smells of flowers, birds sing and one hears the play of the fountains of which Hafez wrote so beautifully. Following is a quotation from the works of Hafez, the greatest master of Persian lyric poetry and the literary giant of the fourteenth century.

> Do not condemn your neighbor out of hand. Be generous.
> Forgive. Pardon. Think of your own failings.
> If each knew everything about the other, he would forgive
>   gladly and easily; there would be no more pride,
>   no more arrogance![25a]

Sa'di's tomb is farther to the east, and in a very small gully between two of the mountains that surround Shiraz. This is a white marble building with a blue-tiled dome. Here one feels the purity and the slender beauty of the poetic line on the columns and filigree doors. Inscribed on the gate leading into the garden surrounding the mausoleum, a place of pilgrimage to lovers of poetry and literature, is a line of poetry by Sa'di which says: "The tomb of Sa'di of Shiraz will still scent of love—even a thousand years after his death."

In the Province of Fars

We sent the army jeep up ahead (after leaving Shiraz) to contact the Ghashghai Khan to get his cooperation in filming the group that was staying on his property.

The Khan was a young man of about twenty-four or twenty-five. His father's tent was about forty-five feet long and about twenty feet deep. This tent was a large three-sided affair made out of woven cloth—black goat's hair. The tent was held up by three sets of poles, one set on each edge and one across the center of the long side. This divided the tent into two sections, one for the women and one for the men and for entertainment. Around the entire inside lower part of three walls was what we would call a woven runner of brilliant colors. It was all of eighty-five feet long and about four feet high. This kept the main amount of wind off the lower area of the tent, where the inhabitants sat or slept. The floor of one side was covered with carpets, and around the walls of

---

[25a]*Springs of Persian Wisdom*, op. cit. (pages not numbered).

the entertainment side there were many brilliantly colored bolsters for use as armrests or cushions when one sat.

The horses of this area were truly beautiful—reminding me of the Kurdish horses. The horses wear blankets which are usually made of woven material with tufts of different colored yarn making a raised design in the fabric.

The women's costume was similar to the Kurdish costume, with brilliant colors and many spangles and coins used as decoration on their dresses and headpieces. Many of the women had pierced noses with large jeweled rings on one or the other side of the nose. Their costumes were better made and more brilliant than any of the Kurdish costumes we had seen previously. However, I am sure that if we had been able to get the Kurdish women dressed for a festive occasion, we would then have seen some of their beautiful costumes.

The bread making in this area was quite different from any I had seen before. Because they are a nomadic tribe, they cannot bake their bread in pits like most villagers do. Instead, the fire for baking is covered with a slightly rounded piece of sheet metal placed on stilts. The pieces of very thin, waferlike dough are laid out on top of the metal sheet and periodically turned. They do not take each piece off after it is baked, but leave it on and merely add another piece of dough on the top, which then bakes when the pile is turned over. It is very interesting to see the deftness with which the old women handle the rounded sticks that they use to transfer the paper-thin dough from the rolling board to the griddle.

That evening we made arrangements to get some Lorish men to do a warrior dance. We went to a large field near the village and the musicians soon brought the people streaming to the area to take part in and to watch the warrior dance. This dance is ancient, coming down from the time when the warriors used to fight hand-to-hand in combat with spears and swords. One dancer takes a pole about five feet long which he uses to defend himself. The other takes a shorter stick, about a yard long and about half an inch in diameter, which he uses as a sword to try to hit his opponent.

The dancers prance around in a circle to the growing rhythm of the instruments and finally one of them calls out. The man with the pole stops and places the pole in front of himself, using it to ward off the coming attack from the swordsman. The swordsman prances up and down in front of the defender, placing the stick against his forehead as if contemplating where and how to attack.

The swordsman comes slowly in toward his opponent until suddenly with terrific vigor and what one might almost call sadistic desire, he thrashes out with the stick to try to hit the legs of the defender. The idea is that he must touch the defender with the stick and the defender should try to jump away or to use the pole to ward off the stick. Many times when contact is made the stick is broken either against the pole or against the legs of the defender. It is a performance which certainly gives one an idea of what war must have been like centuries ago, and also gives one the sinking sensation of the welts and the black-and-blue marks on the legs of the dancers.

The costumes of the dancers were nearly as interesting as the dance itself. The coat is worn by both the Lors and the Ghashghai, and varies a great deal as to the quality of cloth, but the cut of the costume is almost exactly the same. In general appearance it looks like a very long lounging coat. It is unbuttoned, but kept together in front with a long sash wound around the stomach. The shoes are the *giveh*, or woven cloth shoe, with either leather or rubber (old tires) soles. The hat of the Ghashghai group looks much like an inverted pot sitting on the head. The pot has two wings on it coming from the bottom edge of the pot. These two flaps go up on either side, are semicircular, and come to the same height as the hat. Normally the Ghashghais wear the hat so that both flaps are up against the crown. When they are out in the bright sun, the hat is given a half turn on the head so that the flaps are in front and in the rear. The front flap is then brought down to shade the eyes. When it rains the back and front flaps are lowered, so that the rain does not run down the neck, but off the flap of the hat. The Lors merely use the pot with no flaps. Theirs is of black instead of brown felt.

In the Province of Khuzestan

The drive from Ahwaz to Abadan is across more desert, but you always have the feeling that there is something out across those barren, sandy fields that you should be able to see but can't. Then when you come closer, you are able to make out the fingers of the stacks sticking up into the sky. This is the first indication of Abadan. It seemed to us like a mirage, as the town appears to be floating on water. Actually this wasn't too far wrong since Abadan is actually an island. The river from Ahwaz comes south to Abadan, where it joins the Shatt-el Arab (the "River of Arabia," made up of the joining of the Tigris and Euphrates) and then goes on to the island of Abadan, between Khorramshahr in Iran and Basrah in Iraq.

In Abadan

Abadan may be characterized as an immense refinery—the largest in the world.

The prime consideration among the people I spoke to in Abadan was not oil, but the fact that there had been some twelve hundred English there, and not more than a hundred were needed for the operation of the plant. The rest, of course, were believed to be spies or engaged in some sort of *sub rosa* activity. They also objected strongly to the master-servant attitude of the English.

I would like to make one observation here about the general attitude of all the English I have ever met in Iran. No Englishman believes that the Iranian can ever be taught to be modern by Western standards, and therefore sees no reason why he should even try. The attitude of the English is one of complete indifference, and, in fact hostility toward anyone who would like to try. I believe this is a very significant factor in the Iranian attitude toward the English.

In Khorramshahr

More than any other part of the country, Khorramshahr is actually what I have always imagined the Middle East to be like. It had the palms, the single sail barges which carried the goods up and down the river, the houses and the Arabic costumes. These brought out the flavor of the Middle East as I had conceived it, and which I missed in most of the country.

Summary

A lieutenant in Persepolis told me many of the problems of the young men and women in this country. He spoke of the frustration among them because of their social order, which will not allow them to show their emotions. He also spoke of the difficulty a young man has when he wishes to express his ideas and how some of his friends have been jailed for expressing theirs. He spoke of young people who are watched closely by the Iranian police for fear that there will be a political social revolutionary party.

I would say that the future of the country lies in those people who are now between the ages of sixteen and twenty-five, and it will depend almost completely on what happens to and for them as to whether the country will become Communist or whether it will actually blossom out into the politically and economically strong nation it could become.

The Mullahs I have met have been extremely interesting and kindly men, on the whole. However, from the conversation of many people, I realize that Mullahs are using religion to control the people for their own ends. They seldom use the religion to help the nation.

Iran is on the whole a very poor country, primarily because it is mostly agricultural without water. The landowners are often extremely rich but their money does not stay in Iran. Much of it is invested in foreign countries.

The health of the nation is one of the worst imaginable. There are signs everywhere of the terrible diseases that stalk through the country because of bad sanitation and poor diets caused by poor incomes.

Most of the Iranians are illiterate, but certainly not ignorant. Many of the uneducated people have a type of intelligence which shows through, no matter what their reading ability may be. It seems to me that herein lies one of the most important factors that can be changed in Iran. All people should have the opportunity to go to school no matter what their financial situation might be.

I have enjoyed the trip beyond all measure and consider it an opportunity of a lifetime.*

---

*This concludes Mr. Humphrey's report.

7

Baptism of Fire

Visual education is, I believe, one of the greatest instruments for social change known to man. In the West, where the post-teen generation has been born and raised within the sight and sound of television sets, the persuasive power of visual communication is considered unchallenged by any other medium. But in the East the novelty of visuals is a power in itself which captivates people, especially those with little or no education. Proper use of it can change their lives by highly motivating them, raising new hopes and persuading them with very little resistance to accept the author's message. It virtually opens a window to another life.

Iran did not have television in the early 1950s but it *did* have movie theaters in the towns and cities. Going to movies was a way of life for almost everybody, very much as in the period before the advent of television in the United States.

Most of the Persian people have always found something to entertain themselves during the long weekends. In the early 1900s most urban people used to go on a *gaerdesh*, which simply means an outing, on Thursday or Friday afternoon. They often visited historical places, or went for a promenade along the famous avenues and around the big squares in their towns. In such places they found jugglers, dervishes, magicians and others who entertained the public. And there were always a few Shahre-Faerangs (literally "foreign towns").

A Shahre-Faerang is a peephole box, measuring approximately

107

three by three by two feet, set on four legs about four feet in height. The owner carried it around on his back, setting it on the ground when he found a customer. Each box usually had three peepholes with big magnifying glasses. Inside, a roll of related pictures was wound on two wheels, and the owner, who generally had a pleasing voice, explained these pictures as he wound them through the box one after another. The people paid a *shahi*, smallest coin of the period, to watch through the peepholes. The entire set of pictures took about ten to fifteen minutes for showing, and then new customers took the places of those who had seen them. Most shows were made up of series of pictures of foreign towns and famous historical personages who had lived there, or pictures of tales from folklore or fables popular with the public. (The major subject of these shows, foreign towns, was of course the source of the name by which the contraption was known.)

One of the popular shows was the adventures of Amir Arsalan,* a Persian tale about a young king of Rome who is a Moslem but falls in love with the daughter of a Christian king in Europe. To reach his beloved princess he fights all powers in Europe and not only gets the girl but spreads Islam throughout the European countries.

These Shahre-Faerangs can still be found in some small towns, but with the expansion of motion picture theaters and the Iranian TV network reaching most cities and villages they are rapidly going out of business.

Motion pictures were first introduced to Iranians during the late 1920s in the form of silent movies. The theater was a long hall, its floor covered with *ziloos* (a cheap Persian cotton rug) upon which people sat as they did in the mosques. In this fashion they watched the "cinema," as it was and still is called. The films were projected on a white sheet or wall near which a man stood explaining the film in much the same way that storytellers and dervishes had been relating stories for centuries in teahouses or with the Shahre-Faerang. Later on a couple of musicians were added to the commentary so that when the narrator got tired of talking, they could take over to keep the audience from getting bored.

---

*This story is the creation of Naghib-al-Mamalek, official storyteller of Nasser-eddin-Shah Qajar, who used to tell the story to the Shah every night at his bedside until the monarch went to sleep. One of the Shah's daughters, Fakhroldowleh, sat outside the bedroom and wrote down the story for posterity.

When the "talkies" came to Iran the commentators and musicians lost their jobs to cut-in translations. Important sections of the film were translated with a local touch, and these translations were photographed and inserted in the body of the film. People who could not read were at first dissatisfied with this exchange; but soon it became habit for all the literate members of the audience to read these translations aloud so that the unfortunate illiterates could understand, and everybody was happy.

The new medium of entertainment, however, was severely attacked by the Moslem religious leaders, who considered it degenerate and immoral. At first the illiterate segment of the public agreed, objecting in particular to women being shown with their faces uncovered, and even worse with bare heads, short sleeves and part of the legs showing. But as Reza Shah's powers increased, the Mullahs' powers decreased, and cinema, which could easily have been banned as a political weapon by the Mullahs (as happened in some other Middle Eastern countries), was saved from religious interference.

Public disapproval was slowly overcome as people became accustomed to the new form of entertainment and to seeing women's faces after Reza Shah passed a law in 1936 banning the chador, or veil. As time went on cinema became the primary entertainment of the general public, taking the place of the old storytellers, jugglers, magicians and Shahre-Faerang. There was a lack of other inexpensive recreational facilities, and soon most families dwelling in cities and towns having cinemas were going to see a motion picture at least once a month.

Unlike in the U.S., even the coming of television in 1958 did not affect cinema adversely. By the mid-1950s there were some seventy-six movie theaters in the country—twenty-seven of them in the capital city of Tehran. These theaters were attended by several million Iranians on a regular basis, representing not only a good segment of the population but an important one. These were the people with some degree of power who, unlike the villagers, could influence the future of the country.

It became apparent to me that we should not waste the opportunity to reach this audience, showing them the development programs started in the country, and creating public support and enthusiasm for them. During a meeting in my office I proposed production of a newsreel on a regular basis, to be distributed to Iranian cinemas without charge. My boss, Edward Wells, Public

Affairs Officer of the Embassy, jokingly banged on the conference table and said, "Damn it, I have been wanting a vehicle like this for three years now, but no one came up with an idea." I said that if he would provide the funds I would produce the newsreels.

By the end of 1953 we began monthly production of *Iran News*. For the first time Iran had its own newsreel in which local events were highlighted. The favorable reception of audiences all over the nation encouraged us to increase releases to twice a month, and then to once a week. People found new pride in themselves when they saw the latest news happenings of their country on the screen. It gave them the feeling of participation in events. Important portions of the newsreels were reduced to 16mm every two or three months for showing to rural audiences through our cinema mobile unit operation.

This new project of ours took me to the oil fields of Masjid-e-Suleiman (as discussed in Chapter One), where I impulsively took the cinematographer's camera from his hands and filmed the poignant sequence of the Shah in deep conversation with the radiant common laborer in the fields—the final incident that paved the way for me to be selected as the official cinematographer, to go to India with His Majesty, the Shahanshah of Iran.

In my necessarily close association with the monarch in this new assignment, I was even more deeply confident that here was the real source of leadership for desired change. On state visits, I found the Shah at all times to be alert as to what he might learn that could be applied to the modernization of his country. For instance: advanced banking in Turkey, the irrigation systems in Japan, dam building in India, and so forth. Perhaps the main purpose of his frequent state visits was to establish friendly relations with other nations, or to promote *friendlier* relations, but inspection of modern ways of living and the utilization of the new technology was nevertheless just as important. On these trips the Shah seemed avid to learn about everything that he might apply in principle to his own country.

As stated in Chapter One, on a Thursday morning in February of 1956 I was informed that I had been chosen to go to India as the Shah's official cameraman. I went to my boss, the new Public Affairs Officer of the United States Information Service in Tehran, and told him that I would be leaving for New Delhi early Saturday morning as a member of His Majesty's entourage. His unexpected response was, "You're taking a vacation?"

I asked, "You're not interested in my making a documentary of the Shah's state visit, for release in Iran?"

"Oh—we might use a little footage in the newsreel . . . but not coverage of the whole trip."

Taken aback a little, I said humbly, "I will need equipment—camera, films, and so forth," and to this he said, "That's up to you."

I hardly knew what to do, but said, "Okay. I will take a vacation. May I take a camera?"

He maintained his attitude of indifference and replied, "No, it would be an infraction of the rules for you to take an official camera for personal use." Taken completely by surprise I left his office and went to seek assistance elsewhere.

The cameras we used at that time were Bell and Howell "Imos" with three lenses, but the only one available to me was that of a friend who was kind enough to let me borrow his. Unfortunately his camera had one lens—a 50mm normal. I knew that without a telephoto and a wide-angle lens my coverage of the news events would be extremely difficult. But I had to "make do" with what I could get. My first experience as cameraman for the Shah promised to be a true "baptism of fire."

I bought four thousand feet of 35mm negative film, paying for it out of my own pocket (although I was promised by the Director of Information and Radio Department that I would be reimbursed). I was ready to go.

When I arrived in New Delhi and saw the Indian crews with all their equipment, I was ready to return home. I knew that these professional men with all their fine equipment and adequate crews would make a documentary of the visit and present it to the Shah as a goodwill gesture, and there I was with my single-lens camera, my lack of experience, and only four thousand feet of film. (I should have had five times that much so that I could choose only the best and discard the rest!) Suppose I got back home (I thought) and found the whole coverage of technically inferior quality, and the Shah saw the documentary made by the Indians, perfect in all details and then looked at mine. It might resemble an amateur's "home movie." This was the first time the Shah had taken an official cinematographer with him! I finally concluded that I just had to do the best I could with what I had. I started photographing.

India and Iran have had a close relationship ever since the Aryan tribes settled in the subcontinent and the plateau of Iran, and have continued on a mutually friendly basis through the years.

Mr. Jawaharlal Nehru, Prime Minister of India, wrote in his book, *Discovery of India:*

> Among the many people and races who have come in contact with and influenced India's life and culture, the oldest and the most persistent have been the Iranians. Indeed the relationship preceded even the beginning of Indo-Aryan civilizations . . . racially connected, their old religions and languages also had a common background. The Vedic religion had much in common with Zoroastrianism, and Vedic Sanskrit and the language of the Avesta closely resemble each other.[26]

It was because of this close and historic relationship that the Shah and Queen chose India as one of the first states to visit. Indian officials and the Iranians in our Embassy there had done a magnificent job of preparation for the visit. Events of the three-week stay were planned to the minute and executed carefully throughout.

To give the reader an idea of how state visits are handled by the host nation, and reciprocal gestures made by the guest dignitary, I shall report the visit of the Shah to India in some detail.

On February 16, 1959, we arrived in New Delhi, where the Shah and Queen were greeted at the airport by the President of India, who reminded the gathering of the relationship between the two countries, spanning a period of two thousand years.

It is usually customary for the Ambassador to the country to have prepared a response ready for his head of government to read. Such was the case in New Delhi that day, but the Shah found himself in a bewildering situation when he looked at the prepared script and found it was in French. What to do? He spoke the language fluently, but this was not the language for the occasion. The brief speech should be given in Persian or English. Quickly the Shah asked, "Is there a translator here who speaks English?" Fortunately an Iranian reporter, a Mr. Khusro Medhat, from the Department of Broadcasting and Radio, who could speak excellent English, stepped into the breach. The Shah translated the text from French to Persian and the interpreter relayed it to the audience in English. It was a three-language event.

Particularly in those days, the head of a country dared not depart from a carefully worded statement on such an occasion. Although the Shah speaks fluent English, he could not chance translating the French text into English on the spot for fear of

---

[26]Quoted in Vachla, *op. cit.,* p. 21.

using a phrase that might be misinterpreted, whereas a slip on the part of an interpreter would not constitute a diplomatic breach.

After the exchange of greetings and the gun salute that followed, the company drove to Rashtrapati Bhaven, the government house that was to be the residence of the Shah and Empress Soraya during their stay in the capital city. The Shah and President rode in the first car and Queen Soraya, Nehru and Indira Gandhi rode in the second.

After lunch at the residence, and tea with the President, their Imperial Majesties were visited by Prime Minister Nehru. A state dinner took place in the evening. The following day the royal couple visited Rajghat, where Gandhi is buried. They placed a wreath on the tomb, and then drove to the Red Fort. Old Delhi, formerly known as Shahjahanabad, has in its limits many masterpieces of architecture, some rich in history. The Red Fort dominates as a symbol of Moghul magnificence.

Protocol has established a procedure usually rigidly followed by heads of state on visits such as this one to India. However, sometimes incidents may happen that shatter the best-laid plans. One such incident occurred during the first week of our visit to India.

It is expected that the head of the host country should call on his guests soon after they arrive at their residence. This tradition was followed on February 16 at four-forty when the President of India came to the Rashtrapati Bhaven to call on Their Majesties and have tea with them.

It was proper in this case for the Shah to be close to the door (in the foyer) when the President's car arrived in front of the building. Before he stepped forward to greet the President, the Indian national anthem was to be played, followed immediately by the Iranian anthem. The two would shake hands and enter the building together.

To replace a live band of instrumentalists, records were to be used. The whole proceeding had been rehearsed and everyone knew exactly what to do. However, when the President's car arrived, a member of the protocol office, overexcited by the whole affair, gave a miscue to the man handling the record player. The recording of the Indian national anthem blared forth as the Shah and Queen were descending the stairway and the President was just entering the doorway. It would have been most rude for the Shah to continue coming down the steps during the playing of his host's national anthem. (He might have proceeded had it been the Iranian anthem.) The President stood in the doorway and the Shah stood frozen on the stairway with the Queen behind him. No one could move, with the exception of the photographers. We were always free to move at any time if we were discreet in choosing where to position ourselves.

But who wanted to take a picture of the Shah in the middle of the stairs, the Queen two steps behind him, and the President twenty yards away?

When the recording of the Indian anthem had finished, the Shah came down the steps as fast as he could without sacrificing his dignity, and the President came forward at the same quick pace. But the Iranian anthem stopped both of them in their tracks, and again they stood some distance apart during the playing of the second recording. The greeting was again paralyzed. It was a most unfortunate incident!

On February 18 we went to the Shrine of Nezam-u-din Aulia (a Moslem shrine). Later we visited Kutab Minar, a pillar supposedly endowed with a sort of legendary superpower. It is said that if one stands on the base of it, his deepest wish will be fulfilled. We watched the Shah and Empress as they climbed the base and it occurred to me, as it must have to the others in the company, that the royal couple were fervently wishing for a son.

On February 19 after a visit to a community project, Their Majesties witnessed a soccer match between the Indian and Iranian armed forces teams. (The Iranians won.)

That evening we boarded a special train which was to serve as our headquarters for fifteen days. We arrived the next day in Nangal, where we visited the Bhakra Dam, one of the largest in all of Asia—at least at the time. Nehru said of it, "Bhakra Dam is something tremendous, something stupendous, and something which shakes you up when you see it. It is the symbol of India's progress." The dam was built to harness the waters of the River Sutlej. A lake fifty-five miles in length impounds seventy-four million acre-feet of water. (One acre-foot equals 43,560 cubic feet.)

In 1956 there were no dams of any significance in Iran, and the Shah showed deep interest in the construction. He talked earnestly with ministers in his entourage, urging them to study the plans, with an eye to building dams in arid Iran.

On the twenty-first, the party visited a military institution called Chetwood College in Dehra Dun. I was interested in their "Parade step" which resembled a waltz step, and I gave it good coverage.

An interesting incident occurred on the twenty-second, when we arrived at Bharatpur as guests of the Maharajah at his summer palace grounds. The Shah and Empress took most of their meals in their private quarters and so I am not sure about the kind of food served them. For most of the entourage, however, the hot Indian food was almost our undoing. Even the bread and water tasted heavily spiced to us. The only thing served that wasn't spiced was fruit (bananas, oranges, apples) placed in an elaborate arrangement down the middle of a long table. All the Iranians reached for fruit as a relief from the hot spices. None of us felt he dared tell our host that the food was too highly spiced for us to eat. We pretended not to be particularly hungry, and reached for another apple or banana.

A recreational event planned for the party here was a duck shoot at a man-made lake, covering several acres. The Shah has a very keen eye and is a "good shot." On that day he was the champion of the duck shoot. The photographers did little shooting, although we were supplied with guns of our own choosing. Most of us shot pictures rather than duck.

In the afternoon, the villagers put on a colorful folk dance for our entertainment.

On the twenty-third our train took us to Bareta, where we went out for a tiger shoot. The royal party climbed up into little lookouts in the trees, and as tigers came into view (pursued by beaters who had rounded them up) the Shah shot two and his aide, Mr. Ardeshir Zahedi, felled another.

The following day we arrived in Agra to visit the famous Taj Mahal, which we saw both by day and by moonlight. This beautiful building, one of the seven wonders of the world, was built by Iranian architects and masons. Those of us from Iran noted the strong similarity between this famous monument (built by the Shah Jahan between 1630 and 1648 for his beloved wife Mumtaz Mahal) and the mosques in Esfahan. A French savant, M. Grousset, in discussing the influence of Persian architecture and art in India says of the Taj Mahal, it is "the soul of Iran incarnate in the body of India."

On the twenty-fifth, an honorary Doctor of Law degree was

conferred on the Shah at Aligarh University, a large Islamic institution. Sir Sahyid Khan founded the Aligarh Institute of Scientific
Society in 1864, and in 1895 established the Mohammedan Anglo-
Oriental College. In 1920 the college became a teaching and residential university named Aligarh University.

In his response to the honor conferred on him, the Shah suggested the possibilities for an exchange plan of students and professors between Aligarh University and Tehran University—a very
progressive idea for that time.

The visit to Shahnajaf in Lucknow, the center of Urdu culture
in India, on the twenty-sixth was very significant. Indian Moslems
believe that Ali, son-in-law of the Prophet Mohammad, is buried
here.

On the twenty-seventh in Benares, the Shah and Empress rode
elephants to the bank of the Ganges River, then took a boat ride—
past the shores where pilgrims bathe in the sacred water and the
cremation ghats smolder, viewing the ancient Hindu city on both
sides of the river.

The next day we left our "train home" and emplaned for
Hyderabad, capital of the province. The head of this state, Nezam-
e-Heyderabad, originally Iranian, and one of the richest men in
the world, served as our host.

More than a thousand years before our visit large numbers of
Iranians had immigrated to India to enjoy religious freedom. As
was mentioned in Chapter Two, the Arabs conquered Iran, forcing
the Persian people to accept the Islamic faith, burning all their
religious books and demanding that all read the holy Koran only.
Some of the Parsees, who are followers of the ancient Zoroaster,
fled to India, where they continued to live after their homeland
was no longer under Arab domination. (*Parsee* is now more or less
a religious term. Originally it referred to any person who came
from Fars and the Aryan tribe of Parsees. But the Parsees came to
be known as followers of the Zoroastrian faith.)

During those early years, the Parsees built many beautiful
gardens at Hyderabad. When the Shah visited the city, it was
natural that he should be welcomed by many people of Persian
origin. A great garden party proved to be the highlight of our
visit there.

On March 1 we arrived in Mysore. The Maharajah of Mysore,
during a visit of Their Majesties to the zoo, presented a small ele-

phant to the Shah in a very amusing ceremony. The animal had been trained to give a lei to the Empress, which he did with great aplomb; the Shah then accepted the gift. The elephant was later shipped to Iran by cargo plane.

On March 2, the royal party went to a forest lodge for a *shikar* (wild game hunt). Strange as it may seem, elephant hunters ride elephants to the hunt! We were told the reason is that the elephant you are hunting won't run away from another of its kind.

The hunter must be a "crack shot." He must shoot the elephant directly between the eyes in the middle of his forehead to kill him. If the hunter misses and only injures the animal, the wounded elephant will charge—a procedure not in the interest of the hunter.

Two elephants were furnished for the Shah and Empress and their host. Two of us photographers accompanied the hunting party but no elephants were furnished for us. We had to walk—or run—alongside the elephants. Having had enough of this exercise after the shooting of one elephant, we proceeded with all speed out of the jungle (for we had no protection from wild animals) to the safety and comfort of the jeeps waiting for us at the edge of the forest.

We stayed at Mysore until March 4, when we departed for Bangalore, capital of the State of Mysore. It is a city of imposing buildings and public gardens. One such garden, tremendous in size, is called Lal Bagh. The Maharajah's palace was very impressive, blending Hindu and Moslem architectural styles. Here in Bangalore we watched the famous Indian dances performed by girls between the ages of seven and twelve.

After Bangalore we flew to Poona and then to Bombay, where a banquet was held in honor of the Shah and Empress. The following day receptions were given by various groups, including members of the Iranian community.

The social calendar on March 7 included lunch with the Iran League at the Taj Mahal Hotel, and a reception and dinner given by the Chairman and Directors of the Tata Industries—also at the hotel. The party left for Tehran on the following day, March 8.

On the surface it might appear that the visit was one grand, carefree vacation for the Shah. Actually the schedule was far more rigorous than the highlights mentioned here. It would appear that the Shah had little time or occasion to discuss affairs of state, with a calendar packed with social events: teas, receptions, dinners,

shikars, garden parties and other soirees. But he was accompanied
at all times by official representatives, if not the President or Prime
Minister. Who knows what was discussed on the boat on the
Ganges River, in the lookouts at the tiger shoot, en route by train
from one point to another, or at the dam site? A polished table
between two heads of state or the rigid, correct atmosphere of
diplomatic exchanges is not always a necessary adjunct for the
expression of ideas, words of counsel or oral agreements.

So that all events would proceed smoothly, detailed instructions
had been issued to advise all guests as to protocol. As an example,
the following information sheet was distributed to guests preceding
a soiree (given in honor of the Shah and Queen) by Makarajkumar
Dr. Dijaya of Vizeanagran, LI. D., M.L.C. at Vijayayanagaram
Bhawan Banaras, Feb. 27, 1956:

> Guests are requested to assemble at 8:10 P.M. sharp in a line in the
> Drawing Room. When Their Imperial Majesties enter the Drawing Room,
> the National Anthems of Iran and India will be played, after which, the
> host and the hostess will conduct Their Imperial Majesties round the
> guests. You are requested to mention your name to facilitate presentation.
>
> Members of Their Imperial Majesties' Party are requested to stand
> together in one line on the right-hand side on entering the Drawing Room,
> so that the other guests may stand in another line on the left-hand side
> to make their presentation to Their Imperial Majesties easy.
>
> Immediately after presentation, the Dinner gong will be sounded and
> you are requested to proceed immediately to the Dining Room and occupy
> your respective seats according to the Table Plan. When the guests are
> seated, Their Imperial Majesties will be conducted to the Dining Room
> and you are requested to rise in your seats, when Their Imperial Majesties
> enter the Dining Room.
>
> After the Banquet Their Imperial Majesties will leave the Dining
> Room first and then the guests will follow to the Drawing Room to witness
> the Variety Entertainment.

The plans made were carried out with precision.

Looking back over those three weeks in India, I am reminded
of one very humorous incident. We had excellent service on the
train across India. A porter was assigned to each compartment to
keep it clean and to keep the occupants supplied with their needs.
Our porter, following the British tradition, always brought us
early morning tea with cream and biscuits. At about six o'clock he
would rap on the door, come in, set up a little table, and announce,
"Sir, tea!" We'd get out of our bunks and enjoy our refreshing tea.

My roommate, Ali Khadem, an official photographer in the

entourage, knew very little English, and so on our trip I tutored him. He learned to count and to say a limited number of words in English such as *water, tea,* and so forth.

Persians drink a great deal of tea, and sometimes we wanted more than the porter brought. One day, after morning tea, I was shaving in the washroom when I called out to Khadem, "Why don't you get us some more tea?" He called the porter and I heard him give the order. But the tea never came and we had to leave the train to join the Shah's entourage for the day's activities, without it. I said, "Khadem, what did you tell the porter?" and he answered, "We would like *two teas.*"

When we returned to our compartment in the evening, we found a very beautiful little parrot in a small cage. Often when we visited a town, the mayor would send us each a commemorative gift; so we concluded the bird was a souvenir present from the local official. But why one and not two parrots? No name or card was attached to the cage, and so of course we could not identify the donor.

When we went to the dining car for the evening meal, we asked other members of the party if they had also received parrots, but no one had! The mystery was solved later when the porter came to make up our beds for the night. He gave us a Moslem greeting and after we responded, he pointed to the cage and asked, "Good Sir?" Khadem nodded politely, and then I said, "Do you know where this parrot came from?" He answered, "Oh yes. Your friend here asked me for a parrot this morning—*a tuti.*"

The porter's English was poor (as was Khadem's) but he surprisingly knew a little Persian, and thought we wanted a *tuti* (the Persian word for *parrot*) rather than *two teas.* It seems that he went immediately to his superior after the early morning request and reported, "One of the members of the entourage wants a parrot," and the answer was, "Very well, go and get one for him." The parrots were everywhere and easy to capture, but finding the cage had posed a problem.

The porter's determination to fill this request is an excellent example of the treatment we received everywhere in India. The people across the land appeared eager to please us and make our visit to their country a memorable one.

The Shah and his entourage returned to Tehran by way of Pakistan, stopping there for a two-day visit. The reception was warm, partly due to the fact that the wife of President Iskandar Mirza was an Iranian woman. On our second day in the country, the United States Secretary of State, John Foster Dulles, met with the Shah and I photographed them together. The footage was included in the newsreel for Iranian cinemas soon thereafter.

On my return to Tehran I took my four thousand feet of film to the laboratory and urged the technicians to process the footage at once and with utmost care. It was my first assignment as the Shah's official cinematographer and I did not know at the time whether or not I had any pictures at all worth keeping. I was told that the film couldn't be processed that day because they didn't have enough footage to make using the laboratory facilities worthwhile. But, noting my anxiety and my sense of the need for immediacy, they agreed to process my film at once. The man in charge said, "Mr. Issari, you look very, very tired. Why don't you go on home and relax while we're running this film through the processors?" But I *couldn't* go home and relax until I knew I had gotten *something*. I waited a couple of hours for the film to come through and was exuberant to see that I had some kind of image on it. Not until then could I sense any relief from inner tension, and go home to rest. After all, I was the only cinematographer on the trip; this was the only Iranian film made; the responsibility of getting movie coverage was *entirely* up to me. Newspapers had sent a few "still" cameramen, but mine was the only record of the trip in motion pictures.

I was reminded of this situation when I read an account of President Nixon's visit to China, in the magazine *American Cinematographer*, written by Jim Kartes, CBS News cameraman. I quote:

> The press had made more than two thousand applications to cover the President's journey to China. But only eighty-seven were press personnel, approved through negotiations between China and the United States. . . . There were only nine cameramen and two soundmen, and each network basically was allowed three people to film with. Actually I was told that during negotiations the Chinese could not understand why only *one* cameraman couldn't represent *all* the American networks.[27]

He goes on to explain that they finally had to have eight cameramen chosen to operate on the "one-man band" principle, each

[27]Article by Jim Kartes. *American Cinematographer*, June, 1972, pp. 623, 625 and 702.

handling his own lighting and sound, plus one cameraman and soundman to accompany the President, and pool material shot. But each of these men was well supplied.

It was estimated that each cameraman shot about eighteen thousand feet of film . . .

> Each network could have used at least five more crews and producers, but since this was impossible we licked the problem by using a little Yankee ingenuity: Most of us just didn't get much sleep.[28]

Of course the President's visit to China was one of the historic events of the age, while the Shah's trip to India was one of much less import. Then, too, three hungry television networks were crying for footage in 1972, while in 1956 (when we took the trip to India) Iran had no television at all.

But the President's visit lasted eight days; the Shah's lasted twenty-one. The President had nine cinematographers with eighteen thousand feet of film *each;* the Shah had *one* cinematographer with only four thousand feet of film! Because of the circumstances under which I made this film, the reader can appreciate my anxiety.

Within twenty-four hours, I had a print of the film on the Shah's visit to India—a film that ran about thirty-seven minutes. I found it necessary to discard only footage lasting about three minutes.

I edited the film, put sound, narration and music with it. When it was finished, I took the product to the Minister of Court and said, "I have the film I made in India, and I would like to have you arrange for His Majesty to see it."

I was nonplussed when he asked, "Didn't you send your film over yesterday? I gave it to the projectionist to show to the Shah."

"No," I replied. "It just came out of the lab. It couldn't have come to you yesterday."

The Minister reached for the telephone and called the Shah's projectionist: "Did you show the Shah the film on his trip to India?" The immediate answer was, "Yes. His Majesty saw it last night."

I expostulated, "He *couldn't* have seen it last night. It just came out of the laboratory!" And then it dawned on me that the Indians had undoubtedly gotten their film completed and delivered to the palace before I had finished mine. Of course, this *was* the case.

---

[28]*Ibid.*, p. 702.

The projectionist walked into the room to find the cause of the confusion. When he told me that the Indian film was sixty minutes in length my heart sank. I thought about the professional outfit with their superb equipment, and then of my one-man, one-lens effort—a film only thirty-seven minutes long. I decided thereupon the only thing to do was to walk out of the Minister's office with my film and forget about the whole thing. But the Minister of Court insisted that I leave the film with him, and I complied.

When I returned to my office, I found there an invitation to view the Indian film, to be shown that evening from 7:30 to 8:30 in their cultural institute—to a select audience. Although I had a dinner engagement at eight o'clock, I decided to go to see as much as I could. I was the first person to arrive at the institute.

The film showing was delayed and did not begin until 7:45. I stayed for half of the film before regretfully leaving. But I felt much relieved as I compared the Indian film with mine. It was technically excellent, but the point of reference differed greatly from mine. It had been made strictly from an Indian point of view. The cameramen had obviously been intrigued with such things as the Shah's uniforms and the Queen's beautiful gowns. On the other hand, I had made my film for local consumption (in Iran). I tried to show through my camera what the Shah and Queen were seeing! I wanted to take my countrymen *with* their Shah and Queen on this trip.

Two days later I received a call from the Minister of Court and he instructed, "Come on over. I want to talk with you."

On my arrival he said, "Here is your film. His Majesty saw it last night and said you had done an excellent job! He has issued orders that you be rewarded. What can we do for you?" My answer was, "His Majesty's satisfaction and appreciation are all I ask. However, I would be happy if the film were to have wide distribution."

The Minister said, "Very well, I will call the man in the government responsible for this type of project and ask him to order prints of the film to be shown all over the country and at Iranian embassies abroad."

Unfortunately it took a couple of years for the order to cut through government red tape, and prints of the film for Iranian embassies abroad were never made. My only print was shown in a few cinemas in Iran (where it was enthusiastically received), but that was all.

About this time rumors persisted regarding the imminent separation of the Shah and Queen Soraya. With the pending separation "in the air," government officials deemed it unwise to buy a film that had so much of Queen Soraya in it—an understandable decision, but a rather sad one for me. And so my first film never got the distribution I was hoping for, and therefore was a financial disaster. Nevertheless, the whole experience had been a gratifying one.

8
From Director
to Photographer

Having successfully emerged from the baptism of fire in India, I was asked to accompany Their Majesties to Turkey a few weeks later. By now my office supervisors had seen the Indian documentary and realized my unique position as official cinematographer to the Shah. Thereafter they agreed that I was to accompany him on State visits as part of my duties whenever so assigned by the Royal Court; they realized the footage I obtained was very useful for our own film production work. They sanctioned and cooperated with subsequent trips to eighteen different countries, though my travel expenses were provided by the Court.

On May 15, 1956, the Royal plane left Tehran for Ankara, capital of Turkey, and I was on board. Having described the State visit to India in some detail, I feel sure the reader has an idea of the traditional ceremonies that revolve around such journeys. Of course there are certain variations in different countries leading out of local protocol or historical background.

On this occasion, a number of government officials and foreign envoys gathered at Mehradad Airport by invitation to wish the Shah and Queen a happy trip, as part of a formal departure ceremony for the head of state. Near the plane, Imam Jomeh of Tehran offered a prayer for a safe journey and this practice has been part of official ceremonies ever since.

Turkish President Celal Bayar, Prime Minister Menderes and

other government officials welcomed Their Majesties as they disembarked in Ankara. The usual exchange of greetings followed,
and the national anthems of both countries were played by the
military band. Other traditional welcoming ceremonies were observed and thus we started our official visit to Turkey.

Every evening I sent the films I had photographed during the
day to Tehran, with necessary instructions and background information, to be processed and put into our weekly newsreel for
theatrical distribution across the country. Upon my return the
entire footage was reedited and made into a documentary for distribution via our cinema mobile operation as well as other outlets
throughout Iran.

Just to give an example of the kind of documentaries I made
for these visits, following are excerpts (translated from Persian)
from the script of the documentary on the visit to Turkey:

> The warm and sincere welcome, which punctuated every phase of
> the royal trip is perhaps unprecedented in the annals of Turkish history.
> Ankara was once before a witness to such an enthusiastic welcome and
> that was twenty-two years ago when the late Reza Shah the Great visited
> this city upon an invitation by the late President of Turkey Kemal
> Atatürk.
> In the afternoon of this day, His Imperial Majesty the Shah placed a
> beautiful wreath on the tomb of the founder of the new Turkey—Kemal
> Atatürk. The great Turkish leader Kemal Atatürk on 19th May, 1919,
> with the assistance of a group of brave Turkish young men, entered the
> city of Sasoon to begin his historical fight for the independence of the
> country. Since then the Turkish youth, throughout the country, celebrate
> this day and observe lavish festivities.
> This year, due to the presence of the Royal couple in Ankara, a grand
> parade took place in the "19th of May" stadium in their honor. . . .
> Twenty-two years ago, Reza Shah and Kemal Atatürk, two outstand-
> ing leaders of the East, opened a new era in the friendly relations be-
> tween Iran and Turkey. With the visit of President Bayar to Iran last
> year, the ties of this friendship strengthened even more, and now with
> the visit of Their Imperial Majesties to this country, the unbreakable
> Turko-Iranian friendship and brotherhood will be solidified even more
> than ever. In this reference His Imperial Majesty the Shah said at a
> banquet in Ankara: "The Baghdad Pact is a culmination of the ties of
> unity and understanding existing between Turkey and Iran, so that the
> present generation, and the next, will benefit from the result of this
> alliance."
> President Bayar, in reply, said: "With time, the importance and value
> of Iran's adherence to the Baghdad Pact will be better understood. To-
> day's world events show how much courage and determination are neces-
> sary for working toward a real peace." . . .
> After a five-day sojourn in Ankara, Their Majesties, accompanied by

President Bayar, took off on a special train to Zangouldak, a seaport of the Black Sea. . . . Here Their Majesties boarded the royal yacht amidst the loud cheering of Zangouldak inhabitants.

Savarona, the beautiful yacht (which was Atatürk's personal property, and was later dedicated to the navy), after passing along the shores of the Black Sea, docked in the historic city of Istanbul. The descent of Their Majesties and President Bayar was marked by a naval salute, performed by the docked ships and those of the Turkish navy. . . . Following this, Their Majesties departed for Dolmeh Baghcheh, which was designated as their residential quarters. . . .

On the second day of their visit to Istanbul, large-scale military maneuvers took place in the presence of Their Majesties, President Bayar and Prime Minister Menderes, as well as various important military officials. . . . The bravery of the Turkish soldiers and the fine tactics employed were praised by His Imperial Majesty the Shahanshah, the Commander in Chief of the Iranian forces.

In the evening of that same day, His Imperial Majesty the Shah visited the Istanbul University amidst the loud cheering of the students, and in an impressive ceremony he was presented with an honorary doctorate degree. . . .

The next day, the Royal couple left for Izmir aboard the *Savarona*. On the way the Shah inspected a naval base located on an island in the Marmara Sea. In the afternoon the *Savarona*, escorted by battleships, took Their Majesties and President Bayar to Izmir.

The inhabitants of Izmir had been preparing themselves for a warm reception of Their Majesties, and the streets were decorated with Turkish and Iranian banners and with triumphal arches: "Long live the Shah and Empress of Iran—Today is our New Year's Day—Greetings to the Iranian people. If a thousand enemies aim my death—when I have you on my side, I'm afraid of no one."

Thousands of similar signs and slogans covered the city of Izmir. . . . The Turkish planes circled in the air, signifying welcome to the distinguished guests (as the royal yacht neared the docks). Many of the inhabitants came out several kilometers into the sea in their little boats to welcome the visitors. . . .

With the visit to Izmir, Their Imperial Majesties concluded their visit to the brotherly country of Turkey and after a fifteen-day journey, returned to Tehran.

The Shah seemed to be particularly interested in all army and navy installations and the staged maneuvers, probably evaluating inwardly Turkey's military capabilities—in case members of the Baghdad Pact* were forced to carry out defense measures.

In Ankara, the Shah was very much interested in the many houses that, like those in the United States, were open to view

---

*A pact among Iran, Turkey, Iraq, Pakistan and Great Britain for cooperative defense of member nations. It was in effect a collective security organization with the United States as an observer in the Pact.

without enclosures. (In Iran almost all private homes are hidden away behind walls.) He became much impressed with this style of attractive fences and flowers around houses, and wished we could do the same in Iran, in an effort to beautify our towns and cities. Upon our return to Tehran attempts were made to encourage such a change. The new idea was put into practice at the Shah's marble palace; soon the British Embassy and some government ministries followed suit. But the concept did not take hold. The Iranians are too fond of their seclusion—and seclusion is assured by walls.

Another thing which attracted the Shah on this trip was the number of banking establishments in Turkey. At the time in Iran we had only a few banks, the most important being Bank-e-Melli Iran, the official banking house of the country. The idea of establishing different banks in Iran was initiated shortly afterwards and today there are many banks in Iran, both privately owned and sponsored by the government, specializing in various areas. The result has been great improvements in banking, trade and economy.

But the most important outcome of this visit was further strengthening of Irano-Turkish relations, two important members of the Baghdad Pact, and the cementing of a personal friendship between the Shah and President Bayar as well as with other high officials of Turkey. I believe their friendship saved the concept of this pact from shattering after the coup d'etat in Iraq which resulted in the assassination of King Faisal, certain members of the royal family, and his strong-willed premier Nouri Said. After the coup d'etat in Iraq the new regime withdrew from the Baghdad Pact, but the other countries (Iran, Turkey, Pakistan and Great Britain) reorganized under the same concept and formed a new treaty named CENTO which has lasted ever since. Many good things, particularly in economic developments, have evolved from this treaty for member nations.

Later in the same year the Shah planned an important visit to Moscow, and I was invited to go as official cameraman. In this instance, I asked to be excused due to a rather delicate situation.

While I was working for the British Council in 1949, I set up the first film festival in Tehran. Within a month, the Russians followed suit with a film festival of their own. I was head of the joint British Embassy/British Council Film Division, but I was not invited to attend their functions during the festival although all others in my office received invitations. One can say that the failure to include me was merely an oversight on their part; on the other hand, the Russians might have been irked at me because I had "beaten them to it" the previous month. Relations were a bit cool.

By 1956 I had transferred to the American Embassy, which made the situation even more sensitive. Russian officials might classify me as pro-American, or as an underground representative of the country—photographing areas of the Soviet Union as a spy for the United States. Although Khrushchev, the Prime Minister at the time, had eased the tension between the USSR and other countries of the world, I felt it wise for me to forego the visit. The officials arranging the itinerary could see my point. On this trip His Majesty took only still photographers with him—no cinematographer.

The Iranians, because of historical conflicts, were very suspicious of the Russians at the time. Although the behavior of members of the occupying Russian army during World War II was for the most part civilized, Iranians still feared them. Such an attitude was understandable.

On occasion during the war, certain Iranians mysteriously disappeared from the scene and were never heard from again. With my own eyes I saw people picked up on the street, put in Russian jeeps, and driven away against their will. These Iranians might have been white Russians who had defected from the Soviet Union after the Communist revolution in Russia.

And then, as has been outlined in Chapter Three, the Russians were difficult to displace after World War II, leaving only after pressure had been applied by the United Nations urging their immediate withdrawal.

The Shah and Queen Soraya, although treading on shaky ground, found their reception to be hospitable. According to information given in the book *Mission for My Country* by Mohammed Reza Shah Pahlavi, and other reliable sources, the Shah was able to exchange frank views with Mr. Khrushchev and his colleagues, including Bulganin, Mikoyan, Voroshilov and Shepilov.

In conference the Russians insisted that their policy of international relations was that of peaceful coexistence and noninterference in the affairs of other countries. After an attempt to establish this fact in the mind of the Shah, they asked him why he had joined the Baghdad Pact.

But what the ruling Russian authorities of the day failed to see was that for centuries Russia had attempted to advance to the warm waters of the south through Persia; that they had been guilty of aggression during World War I; and that in the face of treaties of friendship they had invaded the country in World War II, and in 1946 established a puppet government in Azarbaijan.

Khrushchev nevertheless saw the Pact as aggressive and militant in nature. The Shah insisted that Iran had no intentions whatever against the Soviet Union, and informed him that in meetings of members of the Pact, discussions of defense concerned the Zagros and Alborz lines that were in Iran, not in the Soviet Union.

Khrushchev apparently was convinced that Iran had no aggressive intentions toward his country, but voiced the fear that the Pact might compel Iran to submit to demands of a big power (indirectly referring to the USA), and allow Persian territory to be used as a base for attack on the Soviet Union. The Shah and his accompanying advisers denied that such a danger was present. A joint communiqué was then issued, declaring strengthened relations between the two countries, and in effect the political atmosphere grew friendlier.

In August of 1956, a devastating flood caused extensive damage in the southern provinces of Iran. In accordance with his usual custom in cases of such a national disaster, the Shah flew over the area to get firsthand information about the extent of damage so that he could counsel with government officials as to what might be done.

In Iran, as I suppose is true in any other country, it is difficult to navigate through government bureaucracy and red tape. The Shah as head of state was the only person who could bypass the government regulations and accomplish things fast. To help the victims the Shah took a number of ministers and other officials with him to the devastated area.

This was an important activity of the Shah which I felt was highly significant for the people of the country to see at firsthand, so I decided to accompany him myself and make a film of this visit.

The size of his party grew so big that we needed two large planes to transport us. In each area the Shah talked to the people, assessed their needs, and gave instructions to the appropriate government official for action. He emphasized that he wanted action *now*. Things started to happen sometimes even before his party left the area. Naturally people were pleased with His Majesty's visit and came to realize more than ever that he is deeply concerned about their welfare, and is doing something about it. Highlights of the visit were photographed and later shown all over the country.

On the return trip from the disaster area, we stopped for lunch and an overnight stay at Zahedan, a town near the Iran-Pakistan border. As was my custom when away from home, I visited the bazaar to try to find souvenir gifts for friends and members of my family. In Zahedan I chose a beautiful little Pakistani table bell, nicely decorated, for my two-year-old daughter Scheherezade, and tucked it in my pocket. The cost was only fifty-four rials (a little over fifty cents).

On this trip we had found it difficult to get all the ministers accompanying His Majesty on board for a prompt departure. Protocol dictated that all officials in the Shah's entourage had to be in their respective places at the airport before the Shah's motorcade arrived.

After a brief departure ceremony the Shah and some ministers (most likely the ones who had to confer with him in the plane) would board the first plane and take off for the next stop on our itinerary. Immediately afterwards the rest of the party including the members of the press, would board the second plane and take off.

Upon reaching our destination the Shah's plane would stay airborne until the second plane landed. Thus we were able to be ready to perform our respective tasks at the new location while observing the rules of protocol.

During this visit it became increasingly difficult to collect everybody in the right place at the right time. The Minister of Health was in deep conversation with the local Director of Health in a far corner of the airport, or the Minister of Roads would be located somewhere talking to a councilman in the area. Local officials who otherwise might find it most difficult to get an audience with ministers were making as much as possible out of these unusual opportunities for conferences about their problems.

Being a filmmaker my main concern was to capture on film the important events of the trip. To be "on top of the news" I was selfishly interested in getting the "show on the road," and I had to chase these officials and round them up from various business discussions and into the second plane so that we could leave immediately after the Shah.

When His Majesty's plane left Zahedan airport, I pulled Scheherezade's bell from my pocket, rang it sharply, and called out, "All aboard, please!" The musical effort to get these busy men on board was surprisingly effective. Everybody wanted to see my bell.

We had one more stop before Tehran—at Kerman. Again I used the bell to call members of the party to the plane. After we boarded, a number of people wanted to buy my little Pakistani bell. "How much did you pay for it? Will you sell it? How much do you want for it?" they asked. Someone offered five hundred rials; another a thousand. I silenced them all by saying, "It's for my daughter! It is not for sale!" Interest in possession of my bell increased, and I finally had an idea as to what to do in the situation. Iranian newspapers later carried the story:

> Ali Issari, assistant motion picture officer, U.S.I.S. Tehran, went with HIM the Shahanshah of Iran on August 4th to cover for a newsreel the royal visit to the flooded areas of the south. Their party went to Esfahan, Yazd, Kerman, Zahedan, and returned to Tehran August 8th. When the party stopped for lunch at Zahedan Ali Issari and other members of the party went to the local bazaar to pick up a few souvenirs. A small table bell made in Pakistan attracted his attention and he bought it for 54 rials to take back to his two-year old daughter Scheherezade. The party left for Tehran the next day early in the morning. It was about four hours flying time to Tehran. In the plane were Dr. Jahanshah Saleh, the Minister of Health, General Ansari, the Minister of Roads, Engineer Taleghani, Minister without Portfolio, Dr. Khanlari, Under secretary to the Ministry of the Interior, Dr. Khatibi, the Director of the Red Lion and Sun (Red Cross), General Riahi, the Fifth Army commander, correspondents, photographers, officers and soldiers of the Imperial Guard Division, the Shah's special valet, Mr. Sharifi, Mr. Peyman of USIS Radio Section and Ali Issari.
>
> In the plane, when members of the party saw the bell and came to know that only 54 rials was paid for it, Mr. Issari was offered twice and three times as much as he paid for it, but he refused to sell it as it was a souvenir he picked up in Zahedan for his daughter. When the offers went up and the requests became serious, he declared he would put the bell up for auction for the benefit of the flood victims. Peyman was asked to call the auction and Issari to collect the money. The auction was done in the American style and before the plane reached Esfahan, halfway to Tehran, the sum of 10,320 rials was collected. And Peyman pronounced

Dr. Saleh the winner. Everyone in the plane contributed and the auction really ended when almost all the wallets were empty.

The collected money was turned over to Dr. Khatibi, the Director of the Red Lion and Sun and the bell was named the Scheherezade Bell. The interesting point in the case was that Saleh gave the bell to his seven-year-old son Shahrad in the Tehran airport when he asked his father what he had brought him from the trip.

The newspaper *Etelaat* carried this headline for the story: "Finally Scheherezade's Bell Became the Property of Shahrad."

The story was released through United Press and Associated Press all over the world.

Before accompanying the Shah to India, I had sometimes sent cameramen to cover the activities of the Shah for our newsreels without my supervision. Although I gave specific instructions as to what I wanted in the coverage, the results were all too often not what I had hoped for.

After the visit to India, I changed my policy and thereafter went with His Majesty whenever he was involved in major events I felt merited national coverage in motion pictures.

As stated previously, manual labor has, through the years, been considered beneath the dignity of the educated man—even one with only a high school diploma. It would have been very easy for me to continue to sit behind my desk as an administrator and give orders to my crews, not stooping to handle a camera myself— an act of manual labor. But at times I preferred to "demote" myself to photographer, from the position of director, in order to get the kind of footage I desired and to make the kind of film I wanted. At the time the motion picture industry in Iran was in its infancy and we were not blessed with large numbers of skilled cameramen to assign to important jobs.

And so it was that I became more and more deeply involved in filmmaking, dedicated to the idea expressed at the beginning of Chapter Seven that visual education is one of the greatest instruments for social change known to man. I did not limit my filming activities to those directly associated with the Shah, but rather included all those related to the country as a whole. My ambition was to help inform and educate the people of Iran.

My next assignment was to accompany His Majesty to Saudi Arabia. A tragic incident that occurred two or three years previous to the time the Shah chose to visit this country had disrupted relations between Iran and the Kingdom of Saudi Arabia.

Although thousands of Moslems travel to the holy city of Mecca during all seasons of the year, one period is designated as the special time for a sacred pilgrimage (the tenth of the Arabic month of Zi-haj). It varies according to the lunar calendar, and may come as early as the end of January or as late as December. During the year in which the tragic incident occurred, the Haj period fell in the month of August. It is very hot in Mecca during this time.

For a true Moslem to be drunk at all is hardly probable; for him to be drunk in the holy city is unthinkable. It is said that one Iranian from the city of Yazd making his pilgrimage to Mecca, and going around the Kaaba (the holy house of God), became ill because of the excessive heat of that year. When he vomited, a guard, thinking him drunk, straightway beheaded him.

The security organization at Mecca is independent of the government of Saudi Arabia; the king and other high officials are not responsible for measures carried out by guards at this holy place. A committee has sole jurisdiction. Although blame for the shocking reaction of the guard could not be placed on the king and his government, drastic action was called for. Iran's response to this unforgivably cruel act was the breaking of relations with Saudi Arabia. The Shah's visit (in March 1957) was the first step toward reconciliation between the two Moslem countries.

It must be made clear at this point that the kingdom of Saudi Arabia has progressed considerably since our visit nineteen years ago. Under the wise leadership of the late King Faisal, who was Crown Prince at the time of our trip to this country, and his able successor King Khaled, it is steadily moving forward.

The laws of the land are based on *Sharia*, the Islamic religious law, and enforced to the letter. It is probably for this reason that Saudi Arabia has the lowest crime rate in the world, according to a United Nations survey.

Until the 1930s people lived just as their ancestors had lived over a thousand years ago when Mohammad rose in Mecca and introduced the religion of Islam. Then oil was discovered and brought wealth, and with it prosperity and new ways of life. The country is now a land of contrasts; one sees Cadillacs side by side with camels, and oil wells pump out millions of barrels of oil where nomads erect their tents. With an increasing revenue from oil the government has started many programs in all areas of social development.

In a country where picture-taking was still taboo in 1957, today the majority of its urban dwellers have a television set on which they watch programs locally produced.

On Tuesday, the twenty-first of Esfand (according to the Persian calendar), H.I.M. the Shahanshah, who is an experienced pilot, flew his own plane to Riyadh, capital of Saudi Arabia. I was a member of the entourage on board. At the border, a group of Saudi Arabian fighter planes met the royal plane and escorted us to the capital city.

When we arrived in Riyadh, the entire entourage was housed at Alhambra Palace, one of King Saud's palaces in the capital. When we checked in, our Saudi hosts made a sincere attempt to welcome us and to make us feel at home, which is perhaps what caused us to experience a great deal of confusion and commotion. But after the Shah was shown to his quarters things quieted down and the rest of us finally were assigned to our rooms. The palace was large enough so that everyone was given a separate apartment with one or two bedrooms, a sitting room and small kitchen facilities.

The still photographer who shared my train compartment in India, Ali Khadem, suggested that I let him room with me—partly because I could speak English and a little Arabic and French. However, our host insisted that Khadem must stay in No. 36 (I was assigned to No. 11). Because of the excitement and disorganization at the desk, I suggested to Khadem that he go on to his room and we would try to make the change later when everything had settled down.

When I went to my room I found that I was on one side of the palace with other members of the press party but Khadem was on the other—where I could observe a great deal of action with a number of guards on duty. After a few minutes Khadem came dashing to my room and exclaimed, "That man has sent me to the Shah's valet's room! There has to be some mistake."

I went down with Khadem and carefully explained, "Excuse me, Sir, but there seems to be some confusion as to room assignments. Which is Mr. Khadem's room please?" The answer was "Thirty-six."

"But No. 36 belongs to the Shah's valet and is next door to the Shah's apartment," I said.

"Yes, we know," was the reply, "That is the reason we assigned him to that room."

"But Mr. Khadem is a photographer, and he should be near the members of the press," I countered.

"Photographer? We had put him in the servants' quarters."

Fortunately, at this moment, another member of the party who spoke excellent English, as well as Arabic, came along; speaking in the bewildered man's native tongue, he again explained the situation and the matter was cleared up. The error had occurred because of my friend's name, *Khadem,* which in Arabic means *servant* or one who serves. Our host had thought he was listed only as *servant* rather than in his family name.

Khadem was thereupon assigned (with me) to No. 11, which was a nice apartment with two bedrooms and adequate accommodations for the two of us.

To protect him we decided to call him by his first name, Ali, and add Alseyed to it at official parties; this means *Master* in the Arabic language.

In the afternoon of our arrival in Riyadh, the Shah visited a military college, escorted by Prince Fahd Ben Saud, Minister of Defense and Air Forces, and in the evening he was feted at an elaborate dinner at the Nassarieh Palace. It was a magnificent affair, but the added glamour and social balance afforded by the presence of women were missing.

At dawn the next day the Shah, accompanied by Prince Amir Salman Ben Abdol Aziz, Prince of Riyadh, was shown the new capital city of Saudi Arabia, Riyadh. Only a year before, following instructions issued by the King, the reconstruction of Riyadh had started. Modern buildings were in the process of construction all over the city.

A visit to a school, which seemed to have been established particularly for the education of the king's many sons, and an exhibition of military maneuvers filled the day's calendar.

One event on the Thursday program was perhaps of the greatest interest to me—a colorful exhibition held at the Malaz Stadium. Before the program started, two of King Saud's favorite children were presented to H.I.M. the Shah, one of whom was Prince Mashour, whom many will remember as the child the King brought to the United States, where he was successfully treated for leg paralysis by American doctors.

The event started with an impressive parade of military units, and was followed by a spectacular exhibition put on by horsemen riding the famous Arabian thoroughbred stallions.

The segment of the program most interesting from a cinematographer's point of view was a sword dance, executed with pomp by members of the special armed royal guard, tribesmen and tribes' chieftains. Leading this group was Prince Amir Salman Ben Abdol Aziz, and other members of the royal family.

The sword dance, which is one of the most exciting traditions in Arabia, is a symbol of zeal and warriorship. The dancers, while singing rousing songs about the Almighty Lord, the King and the country, slowly approach the royal personage with stamping feet. In this case, as the dance reached its climax, Amir Salman presented his golden sword to King Saud.

The whole exhibition lasted from about one o'clock to half-past four. I had, by this time, photographed the military parade, the Arabian horses, and had gotten all the angles—high and low—of the sword dance. I felt I had gotten enough footage and was relaxing, when suddenly I saw the leader (who was the King's brother) approach the King and the Shah, dancing with his sword. Here was the climax! And then to the amazement of all present, the King not only accepted the sword, but rose from his chair. All of us photographers jumped to our feet when a local photographer exclaimed, "My God! The King is going to dance! This is the first time any photographer has ever seen King Saud dance!"

Without a second to check focus or *f* stop or to see if I had any film left in my camera (at that time I was using a Bell & Howell Imo Camera, which takes spools of only a hundred feet, a little more than a minute in length in 35mm), I aimed the camera directly at the King, looked through the viewer and pressed the trigger. King Saud came a few steps forward, dancing with the golden sword. First he put it on his left, and then on his right, executing the traditional steps, and then returned the sword to the Prince and sat down amid general acclaim.

My camera was hand-wound, and the very moment the King sat down my camera stopped. The footage counter showed seven feet after zero. To my dismay I realized that it was quite possible that I had photographed the King without any film passing through the camera and had missed an opportunity of a lifetime. By dancing for the Shah, the King had—in his way—given a very great tribute to his royal guest, and I may have missed filming this highlight of the entire visit!

When we returned to the palace, I went into the darkest place I could find, the bathroom, and opened my camera to see if there were a couple frames left on the spool, but there weren't any. I took the film out of the camera, sealed it in a can, marked it and put it in my camera case. I could hardly sleep at night during the rest of the stay in Saudi Arabia, worrying about that sequence. (When I returned to Tehran, I went straight to the laboratory, supervised every phase of the processing of that hundred feet— letting the remaining five or six thousand feet of footage wait. Right at the end of the roll, I was elated to find six feet of pictures of King Saud's five seconds of dancing!)

On Friday, the twenty-fourth of Esfand, we flew to Jeddah, where the Shah was greeted by a number of the town officials, including Amir Abdollah Al-Faisal, and the Minister of the Interior. Present at the airport were also the members of the diplomatic corps in Saudi Arabia, who were introduced to His Majesty by the Iranian Ambassador. The Shah then was escorted to the royal palace of Rouyas, which had been designated as his residential quarters during his stay here. It should be noted that in the kingdom of Saudi Arabia, the King and his cabinet reside in Riyadh, with the exception of the Foreign Minister, who is in Jeddah with his entire Ministry. For this reason all foreign embassies are in Jeddah rather than in the capital of the Kingdom, Riyadh.

The special reason for the Shah's coming to this area of Saudi Arabia was to make a pilgrimage to the holy city of Mecca, about thirty miles east of Jeddah. Every Moslem who has the financial means and is in reasonably good health is required by Islamic law to make one pilgrimage during his lifetime at the specific time of year referred to earlier in the chapter. If a Moslem, meeting these requirements of wealth and health, has relatives—or even neighbors— for whom he feels responsibility, his first obligation is to them. If he is still financially able to go, he must do so and perform the rituals called *Haj*. A man may make a pilgrimage for his wife, or a wife may make a pilgrimage for an incapacitated husband; however, if only one of a couple goes, the rituals must be performed twice.

About one million Moslems from all over the world, including the United States, go to Mecca once a year in the month of Zi-haj. If a Moslem is in the vicinity of Mecca at any time other than the special designated date for Haj, he must make a pilgrimage to the holy place. His ritual, which is simpler at this time, is called *Omrah.*

Going through the entire ceremony is very demanding physically, very rigorous for the elderly, for pregnant women, or for those with debilitating handicaps or diseases. However, necessary facilities such as wheelchairs are available now to make the pilgrimage feasible for these people.

The historical background of the rites is interesting to Jews, Christians and Moslems, as it goes back to Father Abraham. As Biblical scholars know, it appeared that Abraham's wife was unable to bear children. Knowing her husband's deep yearning for a son, Sarah urged Abraham to mate with her Egyptian handmaiden, Hagar. And so "it came to pass" that Hagar bore Abraham a son, Ishmael.

Following the birth of Ishmael, Sarah miraculously conceived and gave birth to a son, Isaac. As might be expected, a deep jealousy grew up between the two women. Sarah fearing that Ishmael, being the older of the two sons, might find favor over Isaac, demanded that Hagar and her son be banished from the household.

Abraham, distressed by the situation, prayed for guidance, and was told that the mother and son would survive and eventually be well cared for if he would send them into the desert with a skin of water and a loaf of bread.

Hagar and Ishmael were subsequently sent out into the desert with the water and bread, but soon the supplies were gone. They expected to die from thirst and hunger. Hagar, unable to endure seeing her son suffer, put him under a bush and gave way to weeping. However, she half expected Abraham to relent and come to get her. She ran to the top of a small hill and looked in the direction of what had been her home. Seeing no one coming, she ran to another mound which she considered a good vantage point from which to see a great distance. Seven times she ran between these two dunelike hills (a distance of a little less than a mile) and climbed to the top, looking for someone to help her and her son in their distress. Hagar thus established a part of the ritual of the pilgrimage to Mecca.

The Jews trace their beginning to Abraham through Isaac; the

Arabs also trace their beginning to Abraham, but through Ishmael. One wonders why these two peoples, being cousins in origin, have always been fighting each other!

The rituals followed by pilgrims to Mecca are very complex. They must, first of all, be dressed properly for the pilgrimage. No non-Moslem may proceed toward Mecca after reaching a place about halfway between Jeddah and the holy city called Ahram. Here the pilgrim takes off his regular clothing and dons holy robes made up of two towellike lengths of white cloth. The pieces must be twisted for security (the bottom is like a sarong) and must be neither tied nor knotted. No fasteners of any kind are permitted.

Upon entering the shrine the pilgrim first walks to the holy Kaaba, a cube-shaped stone building with a flat roof in the center of the Great Mosque. Moslems believe that Kaaba, inside of which is a tiny little room, carved from it, was built by Abraham after God told him to build a house for Him there. This sacred stone is said to have turned black from the tears of repentant pilgrims, but according to another tradition, by the sins of those who have touched it.

In this room the Arabs kept their idols—idols that Mohammad broke, declaring: "These are not gods! There is but one God! God is everywhere and needs no statues!"

After he has said certain prayers, the pilgrim walks around the holy Kaaba seven times, drinks water from the Zamzam well— a place said to be a source of water discovered by Abraham for his thirsty wife and son, Hagar and Ishmael. The pilgrim again prays, then goes outside of the shrine and climbs to the top of one of the two mounds (Marveh) from which Hagar is said to have shaded her eyes and looked for rescuers. He then runs to the second mound (Saffa), climbs to the top, then returns to the first hill, going back and forth seven times. (The little hills are about ten feet high.)

Having reenacted Hagar's agonizing actions, the pilgrim returns to the Kaaba for more rituals, after which he leaves a part of himself (a lock of hair or a snip of fingernail) and the major part of his pilgrimage is thus completed.

After this initial ceremony, the pilgrim goes to the city of Mina (about ten miles outside Mecca), where he throws stones at an upright column, an action which symbolizes torturing the Devil. Other rituals are followed, the whole ceremony covering a period of three or four days. Afterwards the pilgrim offers a sheep, cow or calf in sacrifice; if he is wealthy enough he may even offer a camel.

This rite is founded on God's command that Abraham offer a sacrifice to Him. According to Moslem belief, Abraham took his son Ishmael to the mountain to sacrifice him for God. He placed a knife to the boy's throat but the Angel Gabriel stayed his hand, providing Abraham a sheep to offer in place of Ishmael, his son. Today after the conclusion of Haj rituals about one million animals are sacrificed to God by the pilgrims in Mecca. The original idea was to give the meat to the poor, but if there are a million pilgrims, there are a million animals sacrificed and of course there is no way to distribute this vast quantity of meat to the poor of the area. The livestock, after slaughter, are now buried.

The pilgrim, on completion of the ritual, immediately takes on the title of Haji; thereafter he may assume this designation, which commands the respect of his peers. He is now a nobleman in spirit.

In Moslem Africa, it is the custom for those who have made the trip to Mecca to wear a distinctive white head covering. Only a Moslem or a convert to the Moslem religion is admitted to Mecca or any other sacred shrine such as that at Medina. A non-Moslem may go to a mosque, but not to a shrine.

On the tenth day of Zi-haj (the last month in the Arabic lunar year), which marks the culmination of the Haj rituals, the King of Saudi Arabia, accompanied by Moslem leaders and ambassadors in Mecca, comes to the Kaaba; the door to Abraham's House of God is opened, and he and some of his followers enter to sweep and scrub the interior of the holiest place in Islam. At this time the cloth covering of Kaaba, which is handmade and decorated in Egypt, is changed.

(Although the Shah's visit was not scheduled to coincide with Haj, a great exception was made for this Moslem king, on his first visit to Mecca. The door of the room in Kaaba was opened so that the Shah and his entourage could visit this most sacred place.)

The Shah and his party donned the pilgrimage robes in Jeddah and rode in convertible cars to Mecca so that we would not be under cover during this short journey—according to Shi'ah tradition. On the way, as is the custom, we recited verses from the Koran, carrying these meanings: God, I am coming to you; God is great. There is only one God!

Only a few of those who accompanied the Shah from Jeddah,

plus all the members of his entourage, went into the Great Mosque to do the pilgrimage ritual. The others (including King Saud's brothers and the Governor of Mecca) stayed outside to chat and have coffee while they were waiting.

On his arrival at Mecca, the Shah removed his glasses, for the pilgrim must remove everything excepting his two towellike pieces of clothing, and a pair of wooden or rubber slippers. He can wear nothing that ties, such as shoes with strings, nor can he wear jewelry of any kind.

I wore the traditional garments, finding it necessary at times to hold up my sarong with my elbows tight against my body, as I stole pictures. I had no free hands, holding the camera, and I did not trust the way I had twisted my sarong to secure it.

I use the term "stole" advisedly. Saudi Arabian Moslems did not believe in the reproduction of images, and taking pictures at Mecca was strictly prohibited, at that time.

As the still photographers walked into the Great Mosque with me, they checked their flashbulbs and all their cameras at the gate, with the exception of their miniature cameras, which they secreted under their top towels. Inside the shrine I saw them surreptitiously sneak shots of the scene and then slip their cameras under their clothing and proceed with great nonchalance and innocence.

However, the minute I put my finger on the trigger of my movie camera anyone close could hear that giveaway sound: *rrrrrrrrrrr*. I tried it anyway and almost immediately felt a hand on my shoulder and heard a voice, "No, no, no!" I said, "Fine . . . thank you," and strolled on. At another location I tried again with the same results. Guards were everywhere.

I was determined to get some kind of sequence. Here was the Moslem King in Mecca making his first pilgrimage; I was his official cameraman and was not permitted to record this important visit.

I tried this tactic three times and the fourth time I was surrounded by guards. It was a wonder that they did not carry me out bodily. Probably they were deterred by the fact that they knew I was in the Shah's entourage, and they probably remembered the rift between Saudi Arabia and Iran due to the rash action of a guard in this place.

By this time it was about four o'clock and I knew the sun would set within an hour or so. At the guards' bidding, I walked out of the shrine, pondering what to do next. I noted that a great deal of construction was in progress which would eventually afford beautiful long corridors around the holy place. It occurred to me that I might climb up on the outside and find a high vantage point for filming the Shah near the Kaaba. I saw a little boy standing there, and urgently needing some help, I inquired, "Do you speak English?" (English is the second language taught in the schools of Saudi Arabia.) He didn't seem to have anything at all to do, so when he answered, "Yes," I said, "Come on."

I had a camera box full of film, for I had no pockets in which to carry it. It was difficult to carry that box and take pictures, at the same time holding up my sarong. I said, "If you'll carry this box for me I'll give you a rial" (about thirty-five cents). Then I asked him if he knew a high place from which I could take pictures. He said he did and started running ahead of me carrying my heavy box of film. He guided me up some winding stairs and we finally got up on the roof. What I saw was unbelievable! There was all of the holy shrine lying before me. It was beautiful! I was all alone up there with the exception of the little boy, and so was able to lay everything down and handle my camera with freedom. I turned on my telephoto lens and started photographing, thoroughly pleased with myself.

My joy was short-lived, for suddenly up loomed a soldier with bayonet. He was speaking in urgent Arabic and giving me the sign to get out. I stepped back to ask my little companion to translate for me what the man was saying, but he had disappeared. Feeling quite sure the soldier was saying, "Come with me!" I gathered up my things and followed him.

He led me down to a tiny dark room where I confronted in the dim light a small man wearing Arabic pants, an American army coat, and the Arabic white cloth with circlet on his head. He said something to the soldier, who went out, closing the door behind him. I had a moment of panic when I realized I was in this dark place with an official who might not know a word of English, and I was guilty of breaking their sacred rules. I decided to let him have the first word. The man paced back and forth for a while and then asked in perfect Oxford English, "Did you photograph the holy Kaaba?"

"Yes," I answered quietly.

"Why?"

"I am the official cameraman for the Shah of Iran," I replied. "His Majesty is performing the rituals in the holy Kaaba. I must have pictures of this very sacred ceremony. If I go back to Iran and cannot show the people of my country where their Shah went on his pilgrimage, they will be disappointed. Any sequence I get here will be the most important part of the film covering the Shah's visit to Saudi Arabia. It will strengthen the ties between the people of my country and the people of your country. I feel it is my job to photograph the Shah here and I did it."

"Did you know that photographing the Kaaba is forbidden?" he asked.

"Yes," I replied, "some guards told me I couldn't photograph inside, so I came out and looked for a high place. A little boy showed me how I could get up to the roof. Nobody told me I could not take pictures from the roof. From that high place I knew I would not interfere with the people who were praying. I couldn't bother anybody on the roof."

The little man looked at me intently and then started pacing up and down again. I knew my fate was in his hands and I thought with an inward shudder of that other Iranian who had lost his head at Mecca a couple of years previously.

Finally he asked, "Do you know who I am?"

"No, sir."

"I am the Chief of Security for the Holy Shrine."

"I am very pleased to meet you, sir," I managed to say. "I am Ali Issari."

"Very well, Mr. Issari," he said, "take your film, I will not confiscate it. Don't think that the reason I will not take action against you is because you are a guest of the government and the official cameraman for the Shah. My leniency is due to the fact that you answered my questions truthfully. You may go. You are the first person to make any motion pictures of Mecca.* Do not make any more!" I promised I would do as he said, thanked him, and hurried outside, thankful to be a free man.

I found that the Shah had made his seven rounds of the Kaaba and was running between the mounds. I was free to take a little footage of him doing this part of the ritual. This was the last

---

*I have since learned that I was the second—an Egyptian team filmed Mecca in 1935.

activity of the day I could photograph, however, and so I started getting all my equipment together. Each of us had been given a Cadillac with driver for the trip over from Jeddah. As I was putting my equipment in the car assigned to me, I saw the little boy who had left me just when I needed him most.

"Why did you leave me?" I asked. "I needed you! What happened?"

"Well," he said, "I'm sorry, but I didn't want to talk to that soldier. I don't like soldiers."

"I think you should have stayed with me," I insisted. "I can't speak Arabic well and you could have translated for me what the soldier was saying."

At that moment, the Iranian Ambassador approached, bowing as he did so. I thought, "Why in the world is he bowing to me?" We were good friends and I decided he was joking, and so I returned his bow.

And then I was startled to hear him address the little boy standing beside me, "Your Highness, how nice to see you!" He shook hands with the child, who replied with great poise, "Thank you! Thank you very much! Are you going to the Palace, Your Excellency?"

"Not at the moment, but I will be going in a few minutes," the Ambassador answered.

"Well then," remarked the boy, "I'll see you at the party tonight." He looked at me, said nothing, and ran off to one of the cars.

"Wait a minute . . ." I gasped to the Ambassador. "Who is that little boy?"

"Oh, don't you know? He is one of King Saud's sons."

I was stunned! "If that is the case, you'd better send me back to Tehran, and now!" I groaned, and told him exactly what had happened.

"They all look the same, and are dressed the same," I explained. " 'Prince' was not written on his forehead. I offered him a rial to help me, and he seemed to enjoy doing it." We both knew that this was perhaps the first bit of work the little prince had ever done in all his life.

We could both understand why he had said he did not want to talk to the soldier—that he did not like soldiers. He knew that the Committee at the shrine was all-powerful and to have to chastise a member of the King's family would have presented a very delicate situation. He may also have thought that were his father to find out he had degraded himself by taking the role of a laborer, carrying a cameraman's equipment, he would be greatly displeased.

The Ambassador promised to make inquiries and if damage had been done he would try to take care of the matter. I went back to Jeddah and stayed in my room at the hotel until he called and told me that all was well and that I could attend the banquet.

I arrived for the event early enough to photograph the Shah and King when they entered, and there I saw the little prince. I approached him in all humility, making the deepest bow I had ever made for any monarch. I apologized and tried to explain my actions of the afternoon. "I hope I can do something to compensate," I added.

He quickly responded, "You can! Take my picture tonight." I did as he had requested. I acted as his personal photographer, and he somewhat dominates my coverage of that elegant party at the Palace of Rouyas.

I told the still photographers about the incident, warning them against being too familiar with any of the guests present, without definite identification. We did not want to be caught asking a member of the royal family to bring us coffee!

The Shah's next stop was Medina, where the holy verses of the Koran were first offered to Mohammad by the "one and only God" and spread among the people.

His Majesty visited, among other revered places, the Alnabavi Mosque or Mosque of the Prophet, where Mohammad is buried. The Mosque has a beautiful black dome.

When we arrived in the city, I applied to the Governor of Medina for a permit that would allow me to photograph this place. His reply was that since no one could photograph inside the shrine, there was really no reason for me to go there. When I insisted that the purpose of my accompanying the Shah was to photograph this sort of thing to show the twenty-five million people in Iran, he relented and promised to make arrangements for me. Subsequently he assigned an officer, second in command to the Chief of Police, to escort me.

I found that this officer could really do very little except protect me. He would walk with me to a good position for a "shot" and say, "Go on. Take your pictures." When I saw people gathering to watch, I would put my camera down. But when they saw a policeman was with me they would wander away. I did get through one of the gates inside the shrine and was able to steal a few shots.

After the Shah's pilgrimage to the Holy Shrine, he stopped at the burial ground next to the shrine where Mohammad's daughter and several of his other descendants and important figures in the Shi'ah sect are buried. Although Saudi Arabian custom frowns on the erection of a dome or monument over a saint's tomb, the Shah requested that a monument be placed here in memory of these leaders of the faith. King Saud acceded to this wish and promised such an installation.

I have one very special personal memory of my trip to Saudi Arabia. While we were in Medina, I took out a little time one morning for shopping for souvenirs to take home. When noon came and the muezzin gave a call to prayer from the mosque next door to the shop, all the shopkeepers and Moslem customers dropped whatever they were doing and walked out of the shop. I said to the clerk, who was showing me some gold earrings I was considering for my wife, "Where are you going?" He answered over his shoulder, "We go to pray. We'll be back in ten minutes." There was no one left to "mind the store" for the entire time he was gone. When the clerk returned he acted as though we had not been interrupted and asked, "Which one do you like? You favor this one?" and the discussion continued just where it had left off.

It is said that you can leave your jewels or your wallet in the street or on the curb there in Saudi Arabia, and come back an hour or more later and find them undisturbed. According to the strict Moslem law, a thief, if apprehended, loses the hand with which he stole!

When the first editing of my film was done, I found it to be more than forty minutes in length. I had used almost every foot of the film I had taken with me. A few of my colleagues and friends with experience in Saudi Arabia advised me to make the film as long as possible. In my final editing, I tightened the film by only a few minutes, and in spite of my cinematic judgment, which told me to keep the scenes short and to the point, I let them run long. We sent a print of the film to King Saud, and through the Saudi Arabian Ambassador to Iran we found that he liked it very much. However, the King had one criticism: "Why is the film so short? Where is the rest of it?"

Perhaps I was a bit sarcastic when I said, "How could I make it longer when I was refused permission to do any photographing in many places of importance?"

This rejoinder was transmitted to the capital Riyadh, it seems, for the next time I saw the Ambassador he said, "King Saud would like for you to return to take pictures of anything you wish." I should have liked very much to accept the King's invitation, particularly to have made a film on the fascinating rituals of the pilgrimage to Mecca, but I had no one to finance such a project. (Later a friend of mine, who was the owner of a film company in Tehran, obtained permission to do so, returning with a beautiful full-length film of a pilgrimage to Mecca and other holy places—a film that became one of the best sellers among feature documentary films in the Moslem countries.)

My documentary of the Shah's visit to Saudi Arabia was very popular and much in demand in Iran, where it was shown in all the cinemas across the nation. I was advised that in some towns, the Mullahs (most of whom are opposed to the showing of motion pictures) requested theater managers to arrange private showings for them in the post-midnight hours after the movie houses had supposedly closed for the night.

9
Divine Destiny

In Iranian movie houses, it was customary for the audience to stand during the playing of the national anthem before and following the movie. Back in 1956 a portrait of the Shah was flashed on the screen during the anthem, which, incidentally, is a very long one. It seemed strange to me that the theater managers never changed that slide. It portrayed the Shah in his mid-twenties although he had at that time reached his late thirties.

As we had a great deal of footage of the Shah in various events within the country, as well as on state visits, I decided to make a moving picture of His Majesty to be shown during the playing of the anthem, replacing that outdated slide. It was really quite easy to put together sequences of events, such as the Shah reviewing the army, going to Parliament, inspecting villages, or cutting the ribbon for a new railway.

Theater owners were very happy to make the change, for they found the motion picture of the Shah to be very popular with their patrons. I still have in my files a Persian newspaper clipping, dated January 1, 1957, written by a man named Mirzano, Acting Director of Cinema Park Company, and the president of the Theater Owners Union. Following is a translation:

> The Cinema Park Company wishes to express its utmost gratitude to Mr. Issari, the Director of the Film Section of the American Information Office, for producing the motion picture of the national anthem and flag

of Iran. He has produced this most interesting film in an exceptionally
pleasing way and has made it available to all the cinemas in the capital
and the provinces without charge.

We had enough material from our newsreel coverages to make
a new one every month, had it been desired, but I did not produce
them that often. We made one every six months or so, and distributed prints to the movie houses in the country along with our
newsreels. One that I had hoped to do as an official visual accom-
paniment to the national anthem was to show the Shah as the head
of the country and Commander-in-Chief of the Iranian Armed
Forces. I visualized showing him in his various uniforms (sometimes with the Iranian flag as a background): his Parliament uniform and his official decorations; his army uniform; his navy uniform, and his air force uniform. This national anthem film would
also include shots of Persepolis, symbolizing the continuous monarchy in Iran over a period of twenty-five hundred years, shots of
the Shah with different classes of people, and depicting His Majesty
as a leader of his nation, pointing the way toward a greater civilization. The Shah reacted favorably to the idea, but unfortunately his
busy schedule precluded the making of the film.

It was during this year that the Shah expressed his appreciation
for my services in the field of motion pictures and audiovisual
education by bestowing upon me the Order of Pas:

UNDER THE AUTHORITY OF GOD ALMIGHTY
WE, MOHAMMAD REZA SHAH PAHLAVI,
SHAHANSHAH OF IRAN,
IN RECOGNITION OF OUTSTANDING SERVICES
OF MOHAMMAD ALI ISSARI,
IN ACCORDANCE WITH THE REQUEST
OF THE MINISTRY OF INTERIOR,
WITH THIS ORDER BESTOW UPON HIM
THE ORDER OF PAS OF SECOND CLASS
DATED 23rd DAY OF ABAN IN THE YEAR OF 1336.

In the early 1960s I made a film entitled *Biography of the Shah
of Iran* for the Pahlavi Foundation. Using both still and motion
pictures, I tried to show not only the continuity of events in his
life, but also some of his thinking, his philosophy and his ideals.
Not being able to show the reader this documentary, here I will
utilize the printed medium to present certain information about
the Shah's background and beliefs.

He was born in Tehran on October 26, 1919, and lived with his mother, brothers and sisters during his early years in one of the older residential districts of the capital city. When his father was crowned Reza Shah Pahlavi, Emperor of Iran, Mohammad Reza Pahlavi, aged six, became Crown Prince in a dual ceremony of pomp and grandeur in the mirror hall of Golestan Palace in Tehran. Upon becoming the Crown Prince of Iran, he was sent to an elementary military school. A French governess was engaged to take care of the young Prince while he was out of school. It was due to her influence that the Shah now speaks French as fluently as the Persian language.

After graduating from the elementary military school (in May 1931) the Crown Prince was sent to Switzerland to continue his education. He remained there until his graduation in the spring of 1936. Upon his return to Tehran he entered the Military College in the capital city, where he remained for two years. His personal life from this point on has been outlined in preceding chapters: his marriage to Princess Fawzieh in 1938, his divorce ten years later, his accession to the throne in 1941, his marriage to Soraya Esfandiari in 1951, his subsequent divorce in 1958, the turbulent years, following World War II, during which his sovereignty was threatened, and finally his marriage to Farah Diba in 1959.

The Shah's personal convictions are, however, not generally known, particularly to the Western reader. His Majesty is truly a man with lofty ideals and strong religious beliefs. In his book *Mission for My Country* he refers with admirable frankness to incidents that occurred during his early years that served to establish in him this deep religious faith.

Soon after his investiture as Crown Prince, he fell seriously ill with typhoid fever, and for a time it was feared he would not recover. He recalls that during his illness, Ali (Mohammad's chief lieutenant and son-in-law, and the first Imam of the Shi'ah sect) appeared to him in a dream, with his two pronged sword. He sat on his heels on the floor and offered the sick little boy a bowl containing a liquid. At his bidding, the prince drank from it, and the next day his fever broke and he embarked on the road to recovery.

The other events to which the Shah now attaches great significance occurred during his seventh year. That summer he took an excursion with his family up to Emamzadeh-Davood (a Shi'ite shrine) in the mountains just outside Tehran. An army officer (and relative) placed him on the saddle in front of him to ride up the steep trail. The horse slipped and the little prince was hurled against a jagged rock head first. He later told his father that, as he fell, he saw Abbas, one of the Shi'ite saints, who held him, protecting him and cushioning the blow as he struck the rock. Although Reza Shah did not believe the child's story, he was amazed that his son had escaped without even a scratch.

The Shah remembers well an event that occurred while he was walking with his guardian near the royal palace in Shemran. Their path lay along a picturesque cobbled street. Suddenly a man with a halo around his head, greatly resembling Jesus as depicted by some of the great painters of the West, appeared before him. The little boy recognized him as the Imam who, according to the Shi'ite faith, disappeared, but is expected to come again to save the world.

The Shah writes concerning this encounter:

> I asked my guardian, "Did you see him?"
> "But whom?" he inquired. "No one was here. How could I see someone who was not here?"
> I felt so certain of what I had seen that his reply did not bother me in the least. I was self-confident enough not to be bothered by what my guardian, older and wiser though he was, might think.[29]

He defends the reality of his experience, knowing that Western readers might consider it an illusion. He says, "But remember that a faith in non-material things has always been characteristic of the peoples of the East."[30]

The Shah has felt since childhood, because of these experiences, that there is surely a supreme being protecting and guiding him. He says:

> I know that some supposedly sophisticated people would be much irritated by such a notion, but it seems to me that God has saved me from dangers and perils. Englishmen are not ashamed to say, "God save the Queen!" and Americans inscribe on their coins, "In God We Trust."[31]

Since the Shah has grown to adulthood, he has experienced several close brushes with death, but he has survived. One wonders if it *has* been because of divine intervention.

[29]Mohammed Reza Shah Pahlavi, *op. cit.*, pp. 54, 55.
[30]*Ibid.*, p. 55.
[31]*Ibid.*, p. 56.

In 1948 he went to Kuhrang, near Esfahan, to inspect an irrigation dam. After the visit, he and the general in command of the area, took off in a light single-engine plane, with the Shah at the controls. About ten minutes after being airborne, the two men were shocked when the engine went dead. The Shah had to make a forced landing in a ravine full of rocks and boulders. He was able to raise the nose of the plane and avert striking one huge rock, but could not avoid collision with another boulder in his path. The impact tore out the undercarriage of the little plane and it cavorted some distance on its belly. When a propeller struck a large stone, the plane executed a slow somersault, landing upside down. The two passengers were suspended by their seat belts in the cockpit, but both escaped without serious injury. The Shah comments in his book that this miraculous reprieve from death could be charged to good luck, but he prefers to give thanks to the Almighty for saving his life.

In February of the following year, he was about to enter the Law Building at the University of Tehran to attend the annual ceremony commemorating the founding of the institution. Suddenly a man, posing as a photographer, aimed at him at close range. Three bullets passed through his military cap without striking his head, but the fourth penetrated the right cheekbone and came out through his nose.

The Shah saw that the would-be assassin was aiming for his heart, so he jumped back and forth in order to avoid being hit. The man fired once more, wounding His Majesty in the shoulder; his last shot failed to fire—it was found to be stuck in the gun.

The murderous young man threw down his weapon and tried to flee, but was gunned down by a security officer. On this episode the Shah writes:

> Perhaps I may be forgiven for thinking that this incident seemed to fit into the pattern, which had so early taken shape in my mind, of God's support . . .
> I have known since early childhood that it was my destiny to become a king, and to preside over a land whose ancient and often magnificent culture I venerate. I want to improve the lot of my people, especially the common folk, and feel that my faith supports me in this difficult task. Indeed, I should consider it arrogant to believe that I could accomplish my life-work without God's help.[32]

---

[32]*Ibid.*, pp. 57, 58.

Other attempts on his life have been made, but miraculously
he has escaped them all. In 1964 one of his guards started shooting
at him with a tommy gun when he was entering his office at the
Marble Palace but not one bullet hit him! One cannot but agree
with him that it is God's hand that has protected him from all
dangers, permitting him to perform the mission for which he was
chosen.

That "mission" might be defined simply as the betterment of
the life of the people of his country. As a monarch of action as
well as vision, he set about the gargantuan task of alleviating the
sad state of the farmers in Persia (as described in Chapter Five).
Early in his reign he issued a decree turning over all his inherited
farm lands to the Government to be administered in such a way
as to be beneficial to the peasants. All revenue from the lands was
to go back to them in general improvements.

Unhappily, the plan did not work out as the Shah had en-
visioned. He discovered that profits from the farms were being
retained by the Government to meet financial demands.

In 1951, the Shah issued another decree calling for the division
of his lands (more than two thousand villages) into plots to be
owned by the peasants themselves. Knowing that the villagers
would not have the capital necessary to buy equipment and supplies he created a Bank of Development and Rural Co-operatives.

His plan met with strong opposition by Dr. Mossadegh, the
Premier, and a number of big landlords and he was unable to
continue with his development program. (However, on Mossadegh's
overthrow, the Shah resumed his efforts in behalf of the farmer,
and by the mid-sixties more than 500,000 acres of agricultural land
had been transferred to the hands of 25,000 villagers.)

To fulfill his mission in other areas, the Shah established the
Pahlavi Foundation in 1958—a nonprofit organization to coordinate
certain community services. Capital was in the form of shares or
interests in factories, ships for commerce, hotels, a bank and other
such business and industrial projects.

Income from the Foundation has been used through the years
to make life better for the Persian people by financing projects
such as the construction of low-cost housing, establishment of
restaurants with low-cost menus in poor districts, building bridges,
operating orphanages, and contributing to the welfare of the poor
by furnishing assistance in areas of shelter, food, health and education.

The Foundation's Institute for Publication and Translation of Books has published classics of both East and West, and awarded prizes for manuscripts of exceptional literary merit.

The Shahnaz Youth Clubs have looked to the Foundation for support in establishing summer camps and related activities.

Like his father, the Shah has, through the years, pursued the business of the modernization of Iran in encouraging the building of factories, irrigation systems, highways and dams. He has been particularly interested in dams, for the country needs to save every drop of water it can.

Iran is a dry country and has always needed more water than it has had for the growing of large crops and vegetables. Most of the rain flows to the sea, either to the Caspian Sea in the north or to the Persian Gulf in the south. The construction of both large and small dams has alleviated to a great extent the need for water control, for irrigation and hydroelectric power. The Shah speaks of his childhood days in Shemran, suburb of Tehran, where mountain-fed streams flowed through the grounds of the summer palace. Here he and his companions spent hours constructing miniature barriers, not realizing that he might some day be influential in the building of great dams such as the one on the Dez River, near the town of Andimeshk, named after him Mohammad Reza Shah Dam. It is a gigantic structure more than six hundred feet high. The sides of the canyon at the dam-site are parallel and straight. This dam (highest in the Middle East) feeds 550 megawatts into a rapidly developing national electricity grid. The stored water irrigates perhaps 160,000 hectares. Water control, through the construction of dams such as this, prevents devastating flooding of great areas of Iran.

To perform one's mission (improving the lot of his people) a monarch must look beyond the horizons of his own country, strengthening its links within the family of nations, considering the international scene as well as the domestic one.

Visits with heads of states in their own lands have through the years been the accepted method for forging friendships among nations. The Shah, deeply interested in all activities of the Persians, whether they were in industry, agriculture, government or recreation, accepted an invitation to visit Japan officially at a time that coincided with dates set for the Asian Games in Tokyo. As patron of all sports activities of Iranian youth, he particularly wished to be in Tokyo at this time, where he would witness many

Iranian athletes in international competition. This was during the year 1958.

I flew to Tokyo a few days earlier than the Shah to make shots of the capital and historic structures such as the Golden Pavilion, and footage of the Japanese people in their daily routine, so that the Iranians would have some idea of what their Shah had seen.

I was, of course, at the airport with camera in hand when Emperor Hirohito greeted the Shah on his arrival. The day following, Crown Prince Mikasa came to take the Shah in his royal coach for a visit to the Palace—a picturesque bit of pomp and ceremony.

One of the Japanese newspapers had arranged a special exhibit of more than four hundred pieces of Iranian art in the National Museum of Japan on the occasion of the Shah's visit. The display was inaugurated by Emperor Hirohito and the Shahanshah and was open to the public for two months following.

A visit to a camera factory and a television factory preceded attendance at the opening of the Games. The Iranian athletes, who took part in eleven different events, were presented to the Shah before the activities started.

About fourteen hundred men and women participated in the Asian Games, the third in a series. Crown Prince Mikasa, Honorary President of the events, launched the grand parade that marched before the royal party in colorful array. As might be expected the Japanese had the largest number of representatives. It was a windy day, and the members of the Malayan team who wore straw hats were divested of them by the strong breeze, as they marched along struggling to maintain their dignity.

After the parade, Emperor Hirohito inaugurated the Games, at which time five thousand pigeons were released into the air. It was a most impressive sight!

National Japanese dancers performed for the royal party and spectators, presenting a breathtaking exhibition of precision, rhythmic movement by hundreds of figures who almost covered a great field.

During the games, the Iranian teams won seven gold medals, fourteen silver medals and eleven bronze medals.

After five days in Tokyo, we took a train to visit other parts of Japan. In Kyoto, the Shah was amused by an exhibition game of *kemari*—a version of football that has been played in Japan for seven hundred years. The team was not made up of rugged youths in uniforms with shoulder pads and protective helmets. The players, of middle age and older, wore elegant costumes with tall head-dresses. Only the feet were utilized in moving the ball, and needless to say, the wild pitch of excitement reached by the spectators at a Big Ten or "pro" game in the United States was totally absent. It was more or less a display of decorous traditional movement, but it was most interesting.

Actors and actresses, making a film on location outside Kyoto were presented to the Shah, after which he watched some of the filming procedures. Like all tourists to Japan, we visited the ancient Todaiji Shrine and the deer park at Nara, and then returned to Tokyo.

One of the most memorable parts of our tour was an overnight stay at a typically Japanese mansion in Kyoto. Here we lived, dined and wined in the old Japanese style. It was at this place that I had a rather disturbing experience.

It is an old Persian custom that when someone admires some-thing, the owner feels obligated to offer it to him. The natural result is that Persian people are shy about overexpressing appreciation or admiration for fear of being misunderstood or setting up an embarrassing situation. (Of course, customs are now becoming more and more westernized—particularly in the cities.)

At dinner, we were seated at little low tables, Japanese fashion, with charming Japanese girls acting as our hostesses. My particular hostess admired a ring I was wearing; it happened to be one that had come down to me from my great, great, great-grandfather, who had once been a governor of Esfahan. Writing from the Koran is inscribed in minute characters in the setting, and an alexandrite had been placed over the inscription.

My hostess spoke only a little English, but when she said, "Ah . . . it's very nice," what could I do? I hesitated and one of our party asked, "What's going on?" I said, "She likes my ring."

"Be a Persian," he said.

"That's for you," I said, taking off the ring and handing it to the girl.

"Oh, no . . . no," she said, but I insisted, "It's for you."

In turn, she gave me a little purse, in it a picture of a scene from Japan on a postcard, and a small photo of herself. She insisted that the ring was too much for her to take, and when she indicated that it was the alexandrite that she particularly admired, I saw my way out of the dilemma. With a penknife, I dug the stone out of the gold setting and gave it to her. She was very happy, but I'm sure I was even happier, getting my family heirloom back, at the same time "being a Persian." Later I had another stone put in place of the alexandrite. Ever since that time I do not wear that ring when I feel I have to behave in a typically Persian way.

Nothing of great significance occurred during the remainder of our visit before our return to Tokyo. In Tokyo, we were informed that the Shah did not plan to return to Iran at once, but would go to Hawaii and eventually to Washington, flying on one of the commercial airlines.

All members of the press had flown into Japan forty-eight hours before the Shah's arrival, and we had been wondering when we would be able to return home, for all international flights were booked for two weeks because of the Asian Games. His Majesty graciously permitted us to return to Iran in his private plane. This permitted the press party to release their still and motion pictures and feature articles on time, not having to wait a week or more, when such material would have been dated.

A few months later I accompanied the Shah to Italy.

My boss at the time, Burnett Anderson, received the following letter from Hossein Ala, the Minister of Court, on September 18, 1958.

Dear Mr. Anderson,

Your suggestion about making Mr. Ali Issari available for His Imperial Majesty's forthcoming visit to Italy and Morocco is much appreciated.

The Shahanshah has been graciously pleased to allow Mr. Issari to be included in the suite as cameraman.

Yours sincerely,

Hossein Ala

Mr. Burnett Anderson
Counselor for Public Affairs
American Embassy

Although the Shah visited Italy, the trip to Morocco had to be canceled because of unexpected events in Italy.

Three still photographers and I went ahead of the Shah to Rome to obtain background material and to become oriented. We arrived rather late in Rome on October 8 and were met by a representative of the foreign office who took us in his small Fiat car to the Park Hotel (which I have learned was Dulles's favorite hostelry in Rome.)

The next morning, October 9, we noticed that newspapers at the kiosk were all bordered in black, and then we saw the headlines: POPE MORTO. We were nonplussed as to what to do. Then we received the information from Iran that the Shah was postponing his visit to Italy until after a new pope was elected, and consequently the visit to Morocco, which was to have been made immediately after the one to Italy, had to be canceled.

There we were in the hub of the Catholic world at the time of the death of their great leader; so I felt the only thing for me to do was to photograph the funeral of the pope (before returning home) for general release in Iran.

One of the still photographers and I went out to the Castel Gondolfo, where the Pope had died, and took some pictures. When the body was brought out to be taken to St. Peter's through the streets of the ancient city, we joined the procession. Being Iranian (and definitely *looking* it) we were mistaken for Italians. No one questioned our presence.

We noted that the men in the procession had removed their ties, so we removed ours. Occasionally I would drop out of the group, take some footage, and then rejoin the procession. We found ourselves directly behind the cortege following the Pope's immediate family, affording us excellent opportunities for getting a very personal coverage of the sad event.

After the funeral we were approached by Dott. Ing. Enrico Mattei, President of the National Hydrocarbon Industry of Italy, who invited us to stay in the country for a brief visit. He offered us the use of his private plane and for ten days we were his guests— in Naples, Capri, Milan, Bologna, Venice, and of course, Rome.

Subsequently Mr. Mattei and the National Iranian Oil Company signed an agreement that the National Hydrocarbon Industry would exploit Iranian oil, with seventy-five percent of the income remaining in Iran. It was one of the most revolutionary oil agreements in the history of the Middle East. (Later Pan American Petroleum Corporation, a subsidiary of Standard Oil of Indiana, signed a similar agreement.)

In late November, the new pope was elected and the Shah and his party flew to Italy on November 24 for the promised State visit.

Planes from the Italian air force escorted the Shah's plane to Rome from the country's border.

Signor Giovanni Gronchi, President of Italy, members of the Italian cabinet, along with the Iranian Ambassador, members of the Embassy, and other officials met the Shah and escorted him to the Quirinal Palace.

It may be of interest here to note that the Quirinal Palace was built for the Pope during the latter part of the sixteenth century, and was used for almost three hundred years as the Popes' summer residence. However, after the fall of the Church from temporal power and the rise of Victor Emanuel to the throne in 1870, the Quirinal served as the residence of the kings of Italy, and then in turn became the residence of the Presidents of the Italian Republic. Its name derives from the fact that it stands on the highest peak of Quirinal Hill, where in ancient days stood the Temple of Quirinus and of the Sun. The Palace consists of several buildings set in a spacious park surrounded by walls.

The schedule of the Shah's visit included the usual dinners, luncheons, receptions and visits to industry, with a few events of special interest added. One day he received members of the Iran-Italy Cultural Institutes, and on another day, dedicated the statue of Ferdowsi, the epic poet of Persia who lived more than a thousand years ago. The statue of Ferdowsi is located on the grounds of the Iran-Italy Cultural Institute in Rome.

Keeping up with the social calendar, being appropriately dressed for all occasions—often in white tie and tails—preceding the Shah in order to be present to photograph his arrival, and staying for all events until after his departure, was a grueling, demanding duty. We were often up by six o'clock in the morning, dropping in bed exhausted at one or two A.M.

One night we had been detained at a formal party until the small hours, but were expected to be at the airport early in the morning to fly out to Pisa, and from there drive to Livorno Port to inspect the naval academy, where a number of Iranians were study-ing.

I arose with the sun and tried to stir the other photographers and news reporters out of their sleep, urging them to get ready to go. To my surprise, every single one of these press people decided he would skip the trip to the naval academy to catch up on his rest. I went alone.

At the academy, His Majesty received the Iranian students and chatted informally with them. After a while one of them asked, "Could we have our pictures taken with you?" and of course the Shah agreed. There stood the Shah with the eager, excited Iranian students, and there was no still photographer present. These young men wanted a picture they could show to their families and friends, and all I had was a movie camera.

The Shah inquired, "Where are all the photographers?" I managed to mumble something about their being exhausted, but hastened to say I could make still pictures from frames taken from my movie film, and promised to send copies to the students. The day was saved.

When I returned I struck terror in the hearts of the lazy photographers when I said, "His Majesty was asking for you." "Why? What for? What happened? What did he want us for?" they chorused in a verbal bombardment. I explained and then told them I had had to lie to protect them.

On December 1, the Shah bade farewell to a large party of dignitaries led by President Gronchi and Prime Minister Fanfani, and flew back to Tehran.

During this visit, I was honored by the government of Italy, receiving the Order of Cavalier of the Republic of Italy.

To receive a citation from the President of the Republic of Italy was a very high honor; however, being cited by Pope John XXIII, one of the most revered and deeply loved of all those who have served the Catholic world from the Vatican, was perhaps the greatest honor I have received in my lifetime.

With deep gratitude I quote here the translation of the citation from Latin: *

POPE JOHN XXIII

ACCEDING WITH PLEASURE TO REQUESTS MADE TO US THAT WE MAKE PUBLIC TESTIMONY OF OUR GRATEFUL GOOD WILL, SINCE WE HAVE LEARNED FROM THESE REPRESENTATIONS THAT YOU HAVE DESERVED WELL OF THE BLESSING AND FAVOR OF THE CATHOLIC CHURCH AND STATE, WE DO CHOOSE, APPOINT, AND DECLARE YOU,

MOHAMMAD ALI ISSARI, OF THE NATION OF IRAN, CAV-

---

*Translated by William M. Seaman, Professor of Romance Languages, Michigan State University, September, 1973.

ALIERE COMMENDATORE OF THE SACRED ORDER OF POPE SYLVESTER AND GRANT TO YOU THE RIGHT TO ALL PRIVI-LEGES WHICH ARE ASSOCIATED WITH THIS HONOR.

GIVEN AT ROME, AT ST. PETER'S, THE THIRD DAY OF THE MONTH OF JANUARY, 1959.

CARDINAL TARDINI

The Shah's visits to Japan and Italy were stepping-stones in the path to greater understanding and increased cooperation between Iran and these countries. Looking back to his childhood days, and studying events during the time that elapsed between his accession to the throne and the end of the year 1958 (during which these state visits were made), it can readily be seen that the Shah has been saved from many perils. And—surely protected by the Almighty—through dramatic and strategic moves, he managed to put the pieces of an endangered monarchy together and set it on a right course. It would appear that His Majesty is indeed a man of divine destiny.

10
Persian Year 1338

The Persian year 1338 (1959 by the Western calendar) was one of the most eventful years of His Majesty's reign. He made official visits to England, Holland, Denmark, and Jordan, as well as unofficial visits to France and Switzerland. It was a year of rapid development in domestic affairs in the country, and a memorable year as to personal affairs.

On April 29 the Counselor for Public Affairs, USIS, Tehran, sent a memo to offices of the agency in all European countries to be visited by the Shah officially, announcing the fact that I would be covering His Majesty's visits and, among other things, requesting that "pouch privileges for sending film negatives to Tehran" be provided. More about this later.

I arrived in London a couple of days ahead of the Shah (in early May) along with one press representative and two still photographers. We had been warned that because of certain red tape and strict protocol, freedom of the photographers would be rigidly restricted.

Along with the Iranian press attaché, we were invited to Buckingham Palace to meet an earl who was serving as the Queen's press officer at the time. In that meeting we discussed the press arrangements and were told in detail exactly where we would be permitted to take pictures and where such activity was forbidden. I particularly interrogated the official as to how we would be allowed to cover the Shah's arrival. Explicit instructions followed.

We were informed that a large contingent of aircraft of the Royal Air Force would meet the Shah's plane and escort it to Gatwick Airport, where the Duke of Gloucester would board the plane to welcome His Majesty to England on behalf of the Queen. The Shah and his party would then board a special train at Gatwick Airport that would convey them to Victoria Station in London, where they would be met by Her Majesty Queen Elizabeth, the Duke of Edinburgh and members of the British royal family.

At our meeting I commented that I must get adequate footage at Victoria Station as the two monarchs met, and would then like to follow them to Buckingham Palace. The Queen's press officer immediately said, "Oh, but that is impossible! You can't do that!"

"Why not?" I asked.

"Because our protocol dictates that nobody other than the official members of the two entourages will be permitted in the procession. Your press photographers, who have been officially introduced to us, will be confined to taking pictures from scaffolding erected at the station for photographers. You alone from the Iranian press party, and the official photographer to the Queen, will be permitted to photograph on the platform."

I said, "If I had four cameramen with me, I would photograph His Majesty's arrival at the station myself, and place the other four on the route to Buckingham Palace to get the continuity of the event. But I am alone. I will have to have freedom of movement!"

The man was adamant. "This is the way it is done here and we will expect you to conform to our regulations." He then added, "Movietone News is also covering the arrival, and they are placing six camera crews along the procession route, because they well know that cameramen cannot be allowed in the procession." I insisted that I *must* be in the procession because I was the only Iranian cameraman and did not have Movietone News Company's access to additional personnel. Furthermore, I had always been given such privileges in other countries.

He was patient with me, admonishing, "But this is England. We never break our line of procedure," thus closing the subject. I presumed at the time that what had been done in good old England for two hundred years would probably be done for the next two hundred.

The man *was* kind enough to add, "You are the Shah's official cameraman; we also have an official photographer for the Queen. You two have priority over the others. You may decide the spot you want to photograph from and we will do our best to arrange to assign you there. But I am afraid you cannot move around during the arrival ceremony, or follow the procession."

I could visualize the Shah arriving in all his charming dignity, greeting the no less charming Queen and her consort, the Shah reviewing the guard of honor, entering one of the royal coaches and proceeding through the mall to Buckingham Palace with great pomp and show. I decided that—one way or another—I was going to photograph the entire arrival ceremony.

Because of strained relationships between the two countries in the past, particularly during World War II, and the new status of equality that had at long last evolved, I wanted very much to show the Iranian people, through my coverage of this event, that their leader was being received in a manner befitting the head of a state with a long distinguished history. How to do it?

I mentioned the fact that I wanted to be at Buckingham Palace when the Queen and Shah alighted from the royal coach. The press officer said that it was traditional for a group picture to be taken as Their Majesties arrived, before they entered the palace. He agreed I should have this shot but explained it would be physically impossible to get me from Victoria Station to Buckingham Palace because all the roads would be closed to traffic.

Inquiring as to *how* I would get coverage of the entire arrival ceremony and the procession if I could not accompany it, I was told again that Movietone News had been given permission to photograph the event, that they had placed cameramen on the route of the procession and that it might be possible for me to buy footage from them.

The Queen's press officer put me in touch with the Movietone News people who agreed to sell me six hundred feet of film (approximately a six-minute showing) at a pound per foot, amounting to about $1,800 at the time. The price staggered me. My entire budget for the production of a documentary film on this visit, including my travel expenses, was less than that amount.

I appealed to the Iranian Embassy but found no help there. I was told that perhaps I should wait until the Shah arrived and talk to the Minister of Court, Grand Master of Ceremonies or someone else in the official entourage to see if the money could be supplied by the government. The suggestion was impractical.

I knew that my office (USIS Tehran) would not be interested in spending $1,800 for coverage of the Shah's visit to England. I had to find another solution!

The Shah was scheduled to arrive the following day at 12:30 P.M. I was at Victoria Station two hours ahead of time. I met the Queen's photographer and found we had been assigned to the best positions on the floor level of the station, close to the place where the royal family would stand to meet the Shah. I saw that if I stayed there all I could get would be the arrival of the train, the Shah as he alighted, and his greeting by the Queen, Prime Minister, and so forth. And so I declined the "preferred" position, giving it to one of the Iranian still photographers, and climbed up on the scaffold that had been erected for photographers. I found a good place where I could command a clear view of the Shah's arrival, a place that had also been chosen by a British cameraman working for Movietone News. I casually inquired of him, "What happens after this? Where do they go?" And he answered, "Well, the Queen introduces the Shah to members of the royal family and cabinet, and then they will go out on the other side of the station to review the guard of honor; then they'll enter the royal coaches, and drive through the Mall to Buckingham Palace."

"How do you get to the other side from here?" I asked.

"Oh . . . you just go down there," he pointed, "turn left, and there you are." Then added sarcastically, "But watch out for the secret police—if they see you there they'll arrest you!" A whistle informed us of the approach of the train. He turned to check his focus.

I photographed the train as it pulled into the station, the Shah getting off and meeting the Queen and Prime Minister. Then I quietly walked down and found my way to the front of the station, proceeding in a relaxed but confident manner as though I had been told to go there.

As planned, the Shah and Queen emerged on this side of the station, and the guard of honor saluted Their Majesties. I saw not a single photographer. (Movietone News cameras had been planted at strategic points along the route, but no cameramen were walking.) I felt sure all the British policemen conspicuously on duty were eyeing me coldly, wondering, "Is this single cameraman supposed to be here?" But I went on about my business without

Dome of the Shrine of Shah Nematollah Vali in Mahan, Kerman (*Photo courtesy of Audio Visual Department, Ministry of Information and Tourism, Iran*)

A fine specimen of Persian and Arabic script by the famous nineteenth-century artist Mirza Fathali, Shirazi (From Iran Today, *Vol. 1, No. 4, Autumn, 1959)*

Modern pottery-making in Hamadan *(Photo courtesy of Audio Visual Department, Ministry of Information and Tourism, Iran)*

Pottery by Chinese artisans made at the order of Shah Abbas the Great (1587-1629)

Wall of Vakil caravansary in Fars *(Photo courtesy Audio Visual Department, Ministry of Information and Tourism, Iran)*

Tomb of Hafez in Shiraz

Queen Farah is seen *on opposite page* congratulating Iranian *(top)* and Japanese *(below)* performers at the Ninth International Festival of Arts, August 1975. The festival is held every summer in the beautiful city of Shiraz and in Persepolis.

Lofty Mt. Damavand, north of Tehran (*Photo courtesy of Audio Visual Department, Ministry of Information and Tourism, Iran*)

Queen Farah is deeply involved in the lives of her countrymen. She is seen *opposite* being embraced by a villager and *below* visiting with a sick child.

College of Medicine, Tehran University

Palace of Chehel Sotun, Esfahan

Audience Hall, Chehel Sotun Palace

apology, photographing proceedings. Not one policeman made a move to throw me out or arrest me. I kept my camera rolling until the royal coaches pulled away.

I went back the same way I had come as fast as I could, but of course no one noticed me because newsmen were hurrying away to file their reports and everything was in a commotion.

I had a car and driver from the foreign office at my disposal. I jumped into the car and said, "Get me to Buckingham Palace!" The driver said, "Sorry—I can't, you know. The roads are closed." I insisted, "I don't care if the roads *are* closed—just get me there in five minutes!"

The driver probably thought, "This man is crazy so maybe I'd better humor him." He looked hard at me and then said, "Right, sir. Hold on!"

I grabbed the strap and away we went by a devious route. He drove at top speed but was a very good driver and within moments we were in the square in front of Buckingham Palace. Gates were open for the royal coaches. "Drive right into the grounds!" I ordered. "Park right here and wait for me," I said as I jumped out of the car, dashed out of the palace grounds and climbed up on the statue in the square.

Using my telephoto lens, I photographed the beautiful royal coaches as they approached and drove around the circle and into the palace grounds through the open iron gates.

Everybody was looking at the Shah and Queen and paid no attention whatsoever to me. I slipped into the grounds without being questioned. The guards could see my security card on my lapel and did not stop me. I went directly to the place where the Shah and Queen were alighting, photographing their every move; and then (with other photographers) got the promised portrait shot.

I immediately flew to my car and said to my driver, "Airport!" I had shot six hundred feet (six minutes in time) and on the way to the terminal I labeled all my cans and wrote a dope sheet for each roll of film. I got it all together in a small package at the airport, and put it into the hands of a pilot of a BOAC plane due to leave for Tehran within a few minutes. I stood there and as I watched the plane ease into the sky I "fell apart."

I knew that the Shah was to place a wreath on the grave of the Unknown Warrior at Westminster Abbey that afternoon but this

I would just have to miss. I had my driver take me back to my hotel, so that I could get some much-needed rest.

That evening the Iranian press representatives were entertained by the British press at a party. On my arrival I was greeted with a rumor that an Iranian cameraman had been guilty of infraction of the rules and had photographed the Shah and Queen—not only at Victoria Station but also in their coaches en route and on their arrival at Buckingham Palace. On being told this I said, "Really! He did *that?* I wonder who it was! He'll surely be along soon and we'll find out." I didn't want to admit that I was the guilty one because I might be forced to do something like that again during this trip if I had to beat the British protocol system.

But when the Queen's press officer arrived, he came straight up to me and said, "You are the one who broke British tradition today!" I had to defend myself.

"I had to do it, sir, believe me! I couldn't afford to pay Movietone News one pound per foot of film! I had to have that footage! I was forced to break your rules for which I humbly apologize!"

Unofficially, however, he understood my situation, for he related an incident regarding another photographer accompanying a head of state to London:

Several months previously, Konrad Adenauer, Chancellor of Germany, had visited England. His official photographer, who was very well known in his country, hoped to achieve an especially fine coverage of the visit. However, he too encountered the barriers I had met. In frustration, he took a picture of himself on the palace grounds with his cameras hanging on him and sent it to Bonn with this message, "Sorry I can't send you any pictures. This is England." The eloquent photo appeared in a leading magazine in Germany.

The film I had been brazen enough to make was picked up at Tehran airport, rushed to the laboratory, and the following day our television stations and many cinemas in Tehran carried five and a half minutes of the arrival of the Shah in London. Movietone News came along with a similar coverage two days later!

The Shah seemed to arrive in England under a good omen. He brought with him bright sunshine that lasted for the twelve days of our stay. Most unusual for London in the month of May!

His Majesty visited the Queen Mother at Clarendon House, and later met with members of the London County Council, Mayor, aldermen, and so forth, of the city of Westminster. The Queen and

Duke of Edinburgh gave a state banquet at Buckingham Palace and the Shah met high commissioners and other dignitaries in diplomatic positions for discussion of affairs of common interest.

I ran into a slight difficulty during my coverage of an evening of ballet at the Royal Opera House, Covent Garden. When a still photographer covers a story, he can describe what was seen by the subject of his story, but the cinematographer has to *show* what was seen. I had photographed the arrival of the Shah in the lobby of the theater, along with members of the royal family, and had taken my seat, carrying my camera with me of course. I never liked to be separated from it. I had successfully taken sequences at a performance of the Kabuki Theater in Japan, and so during the evening I decided to try catching some of the ballet performance on film. In the back of my mind I thought about the continuity of the coverage of the event. The Shah arrives at Covent Garden. Then what? Why did he come? What will he see? The first part of the coverage (arrival) would in a way be wasted if it were not followed by a bit of the performance. (The ballets programmed that evening, incidentally, were Delibes's *Coppelia* and Prokofiev's *Cinderella*.)

I did not think about the fact that my camera's whir and the sound made by winding it might be distracting. At the Kabuki Theater the situation was quite different from that at the Royal Opera House. The Shah and Emperor were sitting together in a loge as were the Shah and Queen here; however, partly because of the nature of Kabuki, and partly because of the architectural structure of the theater in Japan, my camera noise did not disturb members of the audience.

I quietly slipped out of my seat and up to a balcony close to the stage. I composed my picture and started my camera. It sounded like a machine gun in that quiet atmosphere, but I let it run perhaps forty seconds.

I had noted the complete silence and intense concentration on the ballet, but I did not reckon with the live acoustics of the opera house. During my years of photographing the Shah I followed a habit of checking his reaction to the action taking place, for cinematic continuity. When I stopped photographing the ballet performance to wind my camera, I automatically glanced at the royal loge. To my distress, I suddenly realized I had created a situation. All faces in that sea of white ties and tails, glistening shirt-fronts, elegant evening gowns and brilliant gems, were turned in my direction. No one was watching the performance. I made myself as inconspicuous as possible and crept out. Fortunately no more incidents occurred during the rest of our stay in England.

After that evening I thought of a mosque in Esfahan that has such acoustical properties that the voice of the Mullah reverberates seven times (as does one's voice in the tomb at the Taj Mahal in Agra). The mosque was built before the days of microphones and loudspeakers and these acoustical properties were depended upon to make the voice heard by thousands of Moslems who came to pray and to listen to the preacher. I thought surely there was some relation between the mosque and the Royal Opera House!

Following the visit to London, I accompanied the Shah to Amsterdam. The sojourn there proved to be a pleasant experience. His Majesty's schedule included meetings with the Queen and high officials of the Netherlands, and the traditional calendar of social events. I managed to make a short documentary of this state visit which eventually was shown all over the country in Iran. I was happily rewarded on May 16 when Queen Juliana conferred on me the Order of Orange Nassau.

Following our visit to Amsterdam, we flew to Copenhagen, the capital of Denmark. Each country we had visited had certain elements that I felt were important to portray to the Iranian people. In Saudi Arabia, I had to include—above all—the Shah's pilgrimage to Mecca and other holy places; in England, anything showing the Shah with the Queen as her highly respected guest was enough. In Denmark, it was a different story.

At that time (in 1959) sadly enough, many ordinary people in Iran had never even heard of Denmark. Some others knew it was a country in the Scandinavian area and that was all. I felt a keen responsibility to portray the country and its people in as complete a fashion as possible for educational purposes. This, representatives of the host country cooperated fully in helping me to achieve.

One day the Shah and the King of Denmark started their program by inspecting specific agricultural projects, advanced irrigation systems, and so forth. By midafternoon some of the cars in the procession had dropped out for one reason or another. Newspaper reporters, feeling they had gotten enough material for their daily reports, left the party. By early evening the rest of the entourage, having had enough of visiting farms, disappeared.

Heads of state at times honor one another by conferring the highest honors of their respective countries, but sometimes gifts are of a more personal nature. Having heard that this was the day the Shah and the King planned to exchange gifts, I did not return to my hotel when others left, for I wanted footage of this gesture of respect and friendship. I felt it would add human interest to my coverage of the visit, especially because in Iran the giving of gifts is an important part of friendship.

Our driver, my official host (a member of the staff of the Danish Foreign Office) and I followed the Shah's car with its motorcycle escort and found ourselves approaching a palace outside Copenhagen. When we arrived I was told that this was where the Shah and the King planned to spend the night, but that I could not follow him, for this was to be a private affair.

My host, who was sitting in the front seat with the driver, seeing my determination to follow Their Majesties inside, caught my spirit and advised me, "Put your camera down on the floor and sit relaxed."

"What for?" I asked.

"Never mind. It's all right. Just do as I say," he answered.

I did his bidding, removing the harness for camera support, placing it and my camera on the floor out of sight. I combed my hair and sat very straight in the back seat.

When we reached the entrance to the palace, the soldiers guarding it knew we had been in the King's procession, but they said, "This is as far as you go." My host did not blink an eye, talked to them quietly in Danish, pointing casually to me at one juncture, and to my amazement they saluted with their guns and indicated that we could enter.

When the car stopped in front of the palace, I picked up my camera and walked purposefully inside. No questions were asked. Perhaps the security men reasoned that if I had been given permission to enter the gate, I was expected.

The occasion was what I had thought it would be—a royal gift exchange. I got my coverage of the event and walked nonchalantly back to the car where my host was waiting.

"How did you get me in? How did you manage it?" I asked in great admiration.

With a slow smile he replied, "I told them that you are the Shah's brother and should be permitted to follow him." For Danes, who had seen few Persians, I suppose we all looked somewhat alike. It was easily conceivable that—by foreigners who had not seen either of us before—we might be thought to resemble each other enough to be brothers.

After my host's identification of his passenger, the guard had said, "Go on in!" But now I had to get out. My host advised, "We'll go out just as we came in. Hide your camera equipment." I departed from the palace grounds in dignity that might befit the brother of His Majesty the Shahanshah of Iran!

It is hoped that the reader will understand reasons for using such strategies. It is the first rule of thumb in newsreel filming that the cameraman obtain the story by whatever means at his disposal. In most cases, time permitting, a way can be found to make necessary arrangements for the coverage through official channels. However, sometimes this is not possible, as in the case just described. The newsreel cameraman must therefore rely entirely on his ingenuity and the evolving circumstances. My documentary of the Shah's visit to Denmark proved to be a highly informative and educational film for the people of Iran.

I felt highly honored to receive the Order of Knight of Dannebroz from the King of Denmark.

From Copenhagen the Shah and his entourage left for Paris. Because trips to France and, later, to Switzerland were to be unofficial, I requested permission to leave the party in Paris.

By 1959, I was considered an authority on filmmaking in Iran, but I was conscious of the fact that there was much more to be learned in the art and technique of this medium. I wanted very much to know how films were being made commercially in Hollywood. The summer of 1959 seemed to be an auspicious time for me to take a leave of absence from my duties in Iran for this purpose. Having received an affirmative response to my request (through the Chief of Protocol) to leave the official party in France, I flew directly from Paris to Washington, and a short time later I registered for the summer course in the Department of Cinema at the University of Southern California.

During my three-month stay in the United States, I received news from home of continued progress in national affairs. The Shah, in his book *Mission for My Country*, outlines a few of the projects initiated and tasks completed during the second half of our Persian year 1338, the year which fell in 1959-1960. A partial list follows:

A new school for the blind was opened.

Telephone communications were inaugurated in some of the towns in southern Iran.

Anti-tuberculosis centers were opened in the cities of Rasht, Mashad, Esfahan and Babol.

Radio-telephone communications were inaugurated between Iran and Italy.

Drilling began in the Persian Gulf on Iran's first offshore oil well.

An orphanage for 2000 children was constructed on the outskirts of Tehran.

New power stations went into operation in fifteen provincial towns.

Many new schools were opened in various parts of the country.

A mechanical agriculture center was opened in the province of Kurdistan.

Construction was started on the Shahnaz Dam.

Hospitals were enlarged, and dental clinics added.

Hundreds of rural houses were constructed by the government.

A sugar factory and a factory for making olive and sesame oil went into production.

Irrigation wells were drilled and canals built.

A veterinary station was completed in Esfahan.

Esfahan's new radio transmitter went on the air.

New grounds were laid out for Tabriz University.

Sanatoriums and clinics were established.

Research laboratories, power stations, new water systems in towns were completed.

A major bridge was constructed at Khorramshahr as well as a television station at Abadan.

Plans were set in motion for better use of Khuzestan's gas and other resources.[33]

Upon my return from Los Angeles, an interesting thing happened to me, reminiscent of tales such as "The Thief of Baghdad."

As I mentioned in the first part of this chapter, "pouch privileges" had been arranged for me so that I might send exposed film back to Tehran. Knowing I would be visiting the USIS offices and Iranian embassies in Europe, my wife sent letters to me in care of these official centers.

I had to carry with me on this trip many of my most important personal papers, because I planned to leave directly for the United States and the University of Southern California after I had discharged my responsibilities in Europe: passport, diplomas, transcripts of grades, identification cards, and so forth, and all these documents I kept with me in a briefcase.

---

[33]Mohammed Reza Shah Pahlavi, *op. cit.*, p. 141.

Immediately on my return to Tehran in September, my brother-in-law, who had been in Europe during the summer, delivered a German Ford he had bought for me there. A few days later, my cousin and I stopped at my house for a moment before dashing off to a newly-opened German exhibition, leaving the briefcase in the locked car. Ten minutes later as we returned I noticed with horror that my case with all my important papers had been stolen.

We immediately reported the loss to the police. I knew that placing an ad in the Tehran papers offering a reward for the return of the documents would be futile, for I reasoned that the thief was a member of the uneducated class and could not read a newspaper.

I repeatedly returned to the police to inquire if they had any trace of the lost articles. One day as I was talking to the Chief of Detectives, I noticed that a man sitting nearby was listening intently to everything I said. When I walked out he followed me and asked, "You had your briefcase stolen?"

"Yes—about two weeks ago."

"How much money did you have in it?"

"Oh, only a few American dollars, but it contained important documents that will be very difficult to replace."

In our conversation I learned that this man was a master lock-picker who wanted to reform. The police were considering hiring him to help them solve robbery crimes and to regain stolen property; however, they had not as yet called for his services. They hoped he would give them information on his friends' activities. This he could not do because of the code of honor among thieves; however, he was willing to work with the police in recovering stolen property (without revealing the identity of thieves) if they would hire him on a permanent basis.

He said, "If you will put in a good word for me with the police department I will find your case for you." I immediately responded, "If you can find it I will give you whatever you ask." Knowing he had no money I gave him twenty toomans (about $2.50).

Although he felt he could get my papers back, it was understood that I would not ask him to disclose the name of the man who took them. I did not really care who had taken the case—I just wanted to recover my documents.

The lockpicker asked a rather unusual favor: he wanted to see where I lived. I took him to my home, where we had a pleasant conversation over a cup of tea. My mother almost had a heart attack later when I told her that she had been a gracious hostess to a professional thief. She feared we would all be robbed and stabbed in our beds that night! My wife, who was not at home during the lockpicker's visit, was very much disappointed not to have been there to meet a real, genuine thief and wanted me to invite him back for tea again!

It would appear that the reason the man wanted to see my house was that there was an informal agreement among thieves as to which man "worked" each area of the city. Seeing the location of my home, my guest could be fairly sure as to the guilty person.

The next afternoon the man called to tell me he had tracked down the thief. He reported that the briefcase had been sold and the American money had been converted to local currency; however, all my papers were safe and would be returned to me. No— he would not bring them, but I would be receiving them soon.

"Come on over and have tea with me again; my wife particularly wants to meet you," I said. He declined the invitation but agreed to meet me at a café, where I gave him another twenty toomans. True to my promise, I then went to the police and gave them a commendation on behalf of my lockpicker friend.

The thief (I discovered later) put my papers in various envelopes found in my briefcase and dropped them at different post office boxes in the city. The envelopes were the ones I had received from my wife and friends, addressed to different centers in Europe and the United States. The Iranian postal clerks sent these envelopes as addressed even though the stamps had been canceled!

Some time later I received a note, with a letter enclosed, from a friend of mine, Earl Balch, who had been for many years American cultural attaché in Tehran, and who was at this time with the United States Embassy in Ankara, Turkey. The letter had come to him from a Joanna F. van der Maas, cultural affairs specialist in the Netherlands (where Mr. Balch had served between his assignments in Tehran and Ankara). It read as follows:

> Enclosed is a mysterious envelope and contents which I am rather at a loss what to do. The envelope was addressed by Jenny in March and I assume it then contained one of your circular letters. It now has come back to us with a checkbook in the name of Mohammad Ali Issari and a note. It looks as if USOM in Tehran has returned it to us, which makes me think that Issari is no longer there. Do you perhaps have his present address so that you can forward it to him.

Another letter came from Jack Evans who was with USIA in Washington:

Dear Ali: I am enclosing an envelope that was delivered to my office November 28, 1960. I don't know how it got to my desk. The mail room was unable to trace its source. It may not be important but I thought it best to forward all of it on to you. Best wishes and good luck.

Letters came to me throughout the year—from the Iranian embassies, USIS offices in Europe and from the United States, telling me they were sorry but it would appear they had failed to deliver mail to me at the time of my visit, and that perhaps the mail had been mislaid.

My wife and I received so many inquiries from puzzled people that we worked out a circular letter and sent it to all concerned to clarify the mysterious situation.

The first assignment with the Shah after my return from the U.S. was scheduled for the second of November when I accompanied His Majesty and party to Jordan, flying into the capital, Amman. King Hussein greeted the Shah as he disembarked and the traditional ceremonies took place.

On that first day, the Shah placed a wreath at the tomb of Malek Abdullah Hussein, grandfather of the present king. King Abdullah was really the builder of Jordan, the first king to take the throne after the country became independent of England following World War I. The present king ascended the throne after his grandfather lost his life at the hands of an assassin.

The Shah received heads of foreign missions, ministers, and other diplomats, attended a formal banquet given by King Hussein and visited religious shrines.

The following day our party made a short flight to Jerusalem to visit the old city's holy places. We made a pilgrimage to Mohammad's Mosque Al Aghsa and the Mosque of Omar, sometimes referred to as the Dome of the Rock. We then ascended the Mount of Olives, from which we could view almost all of the ancient city.

I became keenly aware on this visit that Jerusalem is indeed the religious center of the world, for Christians, Jews and Moslems have their roots here. We visited the tombs of many men and women from whom stem all three great religions: Abraham, Abraham's wife Sarah, Isaac, Isaac's wife and many others.

From Jerusalem we motored down to the Dead Sea, and then

to the Palace of Zarabad. Here I was a little startled with our greeting.

I was walking backwards photographing the Shah and King Hussein in this somewhat isolated place, when I heard gunshots behind me. What else could one think but that this was an assassination attempt on the lives of one or both heads of state? And there I was in the middle! But it soon became apparent that the Bedouin chiefs at this place were following an old Arab custom of welcoming dignitaries by shooting their rifles into the air and dancing wildly. This exuberant ceremony of greeting was a moviemaker's dream. The sequence I shot that day was a highlight of my coverage of the visit to Jordan.

The next day the Shah was honored with a very impressive parade staged by the Jordanian army. I noted with interest the pride the men exhibited in being members of these armed forces.

The units that passed in review included two troops of Camel Mounted Desert Police, brigades of engineers, signalmen, transport services, royal guards, King Ghazi's Sixth Infantry Battalion, four companies of Boys of the Jordan Arab Army School, detachments from the Royal Armoured Arm, Royal Artillery and Medical Corps. At the end of the parade, there was a rousing fanfare by massed buglers and the royal salute of twenty-one guns.

During our visit in Jordan, I repeatedly admired the gracious manner of King Hussein. Always considerate of those in the Shah's party, he spoke in English to those of us who did not understand Arabic, and appeared to meet his soldiers on common ground. At one of the maneuvers we witnessed, he joined groups of officers and chatted with them as equals. He became one of them!

We returned to Tehran after four days in Jordan. A month later King Hussein graciously honored me with the Decoration of Esteghlal.

The year had been one in which the Shah had made state visits to four countries; schools, dams, health centers, power stations, factories and communication centers had been constructed.

The latter part of this significant period was highlighted by events of a different order, for it was in December of that year (as has been mentioned in Chapter Four) that he was married to Farah Diba, who was to be the mother of the long-looked-for Crown Prince, and three other beautiful children.

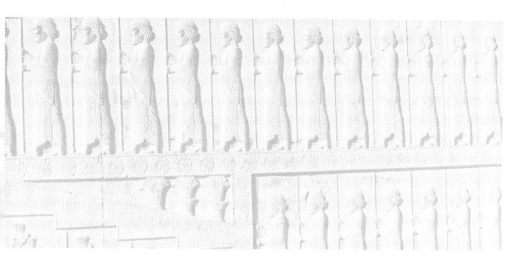

11
Year of Fulfillment

Early in December I received an office memorandum which read in part:

> We have emergency instructions from Washington to send a motion picture photographer to Kabul immediately, with a 35mm camera and Eastman color stock.
>
> We have made a reservation for you on the 0700 flight on Tuesday, 8 December which is the earliest flight there is. This is the Ariana flight.
>
> Can you begin immediately to secure clearance to leave and re-enter Iran, and to get an entry visa for Kabul, please? You will need to be in Kabul for the arrival and departure of the President, both of which take place on December 9th Wednesday, and you can return here as soon as that is over.

Our Information Officer cleared the way for me through the Embassy of Afghanistan in Tehran, and the Passport section of the Department of Police, for the necessary documents.

I arrived in Kabul on December 8 to photograph the visit of President Dwight Eisenhower to Afghanistan. Upon arrival I was given a press kit that included information as to the minute-by-minute execution of the program. The kit included instruction as to where photographers could obtain background material, information as to the location and facilities of press rooms, maps of all areas to be visited, precise time schedules for all activities and specific plans for procedures based on protocol with detailed instruction to the press.

179

In 1959, the "cold war" was at its peak, and Russians and Americans were seldom seen together in public. At Iranian diplomatic parties the most newsworthy picture a photographer could get was one of American and Russian ambassadors shaking hands or conversing with one another. I believe the atmosphere of cold relations was paramount in other countries of the world as well. Therefore, it was surprising to me to ride in a bus with Russian journalists and photographers and to notice the close relationship between the Americans and Russians residing in Kabul. Another interesting point was that Mr. Eisenhower, the President of the United States, inaugurated the use of the Bagram Airport at Kabul, just completed by the Russians.

The President's visit was so short that every minute had to be accounted for. Main events were traditional greeting ceremonies, talks between President Eisenhower and the King of Afghanistan, with his Prime Minister Daud, ambassadors and foreign ministers present; lunch at Chilstoon Palace, and inspection of the honor guard at Jeshyn National Parade Grounds, where the President boarded a helicopter to be returned to Bagram Airport. I photographed the entire program of the President's visit and sent the films to USIA in Washington.

There was nothing to keep me in Kabul after the President's departure, but I ran into transportation problems. As Bagram Airport was not completely ready to handle commercial planes, Kabul Airport with its limited runway and no facilities for instrument landing was still in use. It appeared that if there were a cloud in the sky, incoming planes would circle the field and fly away. My return home was delayed one week!

President Eisenhower went from Kabul to Pakistan and then came to Tehran. His American film crew was with him, of course, to cover his visit, but I managed to return to Tehran a few hours before his arrival and took charge of our local coverage there. We photographed his activities in Tehran side by side with the American motion picture crew and made a documentary of his visit for our local theaters and television.

President Eisenhower was so deeply admired because of his having led the Allies to victory in World War II, and because of his genial personality, that everyone wanted to be in a picture with him. As a result, officials crowded around him from all sides, obscuring him from the photographer's view, creating quite a problem for us.

The Shah presented to President Eisenhower a magnificent Khatam desk and chair—inlaid with tiny pieces of mother-of-pearl, ivory, gold, silver, ebony and various other fine woods. To my mind, it is the most beautiful kind of furniture. This desk and chair had probably taken twenty artisans several years to complete.

President Eisenhower graciously accepted it in behalf of the United States and said that it would find a special place in the Eisenhower Museum.

In February of 1960, the Shah and Empress Farah made a state visit to Pakistan. As usual I preceded them and their party, going by commercial airline. I had a very happy experience on the flight. I found myself directly across the aisle from Ali Khan (who, it will be remembered, was once married to Rita Hayworth), son of the Aga Khan, head of the Ismaili sect. The Ismaili sect (as was mentioned in Chapter Two) is an offshoot of the Shi'ite sect in Islam. We established rapport within a few minutes and my trip was therefore most pleasant.

On February 20, the Shah and Empress were greeted at the Karachi Airport by the Guard of Honor, President and Begum Ayub Khan, Iranian citizens of Karachi, Iranian Embassy representatives, cabinet ministers, Prime Minister Zulfikar Ali Bhutto, and others.

Apart from the political talks between the heads of the two countries, the events planned for the visit were of a social and highly entertaining nature. They included duck shooting at Chandu Lake, a visit to the newly completed Iranian Embassy, a beautiful horse and cattle show and a tattoo at Lahore. One of the very exciting features of the show was a performance by the Pakistani Bagpipe Band, one of the best in the world. Surely there must have been between two and three hundred players in that magnificent organization, playing together in unique harmony.

The Empress visited the Pakistani Girl Guides Association, and during the time set aside for official talks between the Shah and President and their flight over Warsak Dam, she visited the Fort and Badshahi Mosque, as well as Fatime Jinnah Medical College.

On the fifth day of our visit, Empress Farah began to show some signs of physical strain—after attending a Citizens Garden Party in the gorgeous Shalamar Gardens and lunch at Governor's House.

The calendar of visiting dignitaries is far more strenuous than the casual observer might realize. For example, the presentation to Girl Guides, an afternoon program, included formal presentations of the girls, an address, offering of friendship pins and Girl Guide literature, a ceremony of flags of the nations, a drill for deaf and dumb Girl Guides, the showing of international badges, a dance performance, a tambourine drill, presentation of the Jinnah Guide Badge, and taps. But Queen Farah had a special reason for showing excessive fatigue and slight illness.

The Empress could not keep up with the schedule planned for her. At this time it was disclosed that she was pregnant, and an official communiqué to this effect was released—news heartily welcomed by the people of Iran.

After our return to Tehran, I flew to Abadan to photograph the inauguration ceremonies of an important bridge. The port of Khorramshahr, which is the largest and most important in the country, faces the island of Abadan across the river Karun. However, previous to the building of the bridge, the only means of transportation directly between the two towns was by small boat. For centuries, if a man wanted to travel by road from Abadan to Khorramshahr, it was necessary for him to go by way of Ahwaz, capital city of Khuzestan—a detour of a hundred and fifty miles.

This much-needed bridge connecting Abadan and Khorramshahr was built with funds from the Pahlavi Foundation in 1960. It was a great pleasure for me to photograph dedication ceremonies, because the local inhabitants were exuberant over the forging of this new link between the two important centers. The Shah evidenced his own deep satisfaction in helping to make this development possible.

During the years 1958 to 1962, in addition to my work with the United State Information Service, and my own "on call" assignment as official cameraman to the Shah, I served as free-lance cameraman for various television networks in Europe, England and the United States. In this way I was able to spread throughout the world news of developments in Iran and of the activities of the Shah, the government and the people in laying the foundation for the "Great Civilization."

I worked with the United Press International, Hearst Metrotone News (Telenews), American Broadcasting Company, Columbia Broadcasting System, Independent Television Newsfilm/London, British International Newsfilm Agency (BCINA), Fox Movietone News/Paris and Movietone News/London. These networks covered about four-fifths of the world and sent news films to an average of sixty-three different countries. The work developed into a personal, thriving business, leading to the establishment of the Issari Newsfilm Agency. It grew beyond the time I had available to devote to it; therefore, I turned it over to my brother. The Issari Newsfilm Agency, under his direction, has grown to be the International Newsfilm Agency of Iran, and is still in the initial business of informing the world about Iranian affairs.

In May (1960) the Shah embarked on a rather extensive visit to three countries: Sweden, Belgium and Austria. (Empress Farah remained at home because of her pregnancy). The Shah arrived at Bromma Airport in Stockholm on the fifth and was taken to the City Hall, where he boarded the Royal Coach for a stately procession through the streets of the city to the Royal Palace. The usual festivities ensued—including a reception for the diplomatic corps, the State Banquet, the reciprocal banquet given by the Shah at the Grand Hotel where he was residing, a gala performance at the Opera and visits to two art galleries (the National Gallery and the Waldemarsudde Art Gallery).

The event that proved to be the highlight of our stay in Sweden for me was a visit to the Sodertorn Flight Squadron. A new fighter plane streaked out of a tunnel, flew, then landed with parachutes braking it to a quick stop—a new technological development in aviation to which we were introduced.

The feeling of goodwill between the two countries was evident from an address by Mr. Tage Erlander, Prime Minister of Sweden, at the banquet given by the Government of Sweden in honor of His Imperial Majesty, the Shahanshah, on the last day of our visit:

> It is a great honor and pleasure for the Swedish Government to have been able to welcome Your Imperial Majesty as its honored guest to Sweden.
> Personally I am very happy to have the privilege to convey this greeting to Your Majesty, remembering vividly the pleasant time which my wife and I spent as guests of Your Majesty's Government in your beautiful country earlier this year. We are deeply grateful for the warm reception in Tehran and for the hospitality and friendliness shown to us on that occasion by Your Majesty and Her Majesty the Empress, as well as by the Iranian Government.
> It is our sincere hope that Your Majesty has enjoyed your stay here. We regret that it has not been possible during the short time available to make the programmes for Your visit as full and as varied as Your wide personal interests would have indicated. However, we have tried to show

You some significant aspects of Sweden, past and present, and to give You an idea of the life and work of the Swedish people.

At the same time You have no doubt noticed that there is great sympathy and a genuine interest in Sweden towards Your country and that we wish Your great people every success in the efforts to build a modern Iran. This attitude has deep roots in the past and is strengthened by the continuous and increasing cooperation between our two countries in economic and many other fields. We are convinced that the visit of Your Majesty to our country will be a milestone in the long line of friendly personal contacts which form the basis for this cooperation and for the excellent relations which so happily exist between Sweden and Iran.

Excellencies, ladies and gentlemen, may I ask you to join me in a toast to the health and happiness of our welcome guest, His Imperial Majesty the Shahanshah of Iran, of Her Majesty the Empress, and to the prosperity and well-being of the Iranian people.

On May 11, jets of the Belgian Air Force escorted the Shah's plane to the airport at Brussels, where King Baudouin awaited him. He proceeded to Des Souverains au Cinquantenaire, where he was graciously received by the mayor of the city, and then continued to the royal palace. Wherever he went during his five-day stay, he commanded a horse escort as well as an escort of protective motorcycle police.

On this trip the Shah seemed particularly interested in visiting refineries and industrial sites. He was learning continuously, storing away in his mind ideas he might carry back to Iran that could implement further progress and modernization of his country.

Nothing occurred of unusual interest; all scheduled events appeared to be somewhat routine: luncheon with the Bourgemeister of Ostende, a meeting with the Bourgemeister of Bruges and the usual receptions. On May 16, he flew out of Brussels for Vienna.

The Shah's reception was no less than fantastic in Austria! Everywhere we went, we could feel the warmth of the people, and sense their obvious pleasure at his visit. In addition to court affairs and formal events, we spent a glorious morning visiting the Spanish Riding Academy and watching the world-famous "dancing horses."

Of course, the Shah was a guest also at the Vienna Opera, one of the greatest in all the world. *Don Giovanni* was the offering on that gala occasion.

We took the train to Linz, and then to Salzburg. The evening was certainly one to be remembered. The Shah and a couple of his aides were guests at le Château de Mittersill or Schloss Mittersill Club. This is an exclusive, elegant guest house, actually a private club, members of which are either financial tycoons or men and women bearing royal titles.

Members of this prestigious international club and their parties may stay here when they are in the area, amid as splendid accommodations as may be found anywhere in the world. A glance at the membership list may give some idea of the kind of people who belonged at that time. The roster included: Prince and Princess Alfred Auersperg, Countess Avogardo Bonfi, Her Highness the Maharani of Baroka, His Highness the Maharajah of Baroka, Prince de Beauviau-Craon, Marquis and Marquise de la Begassieri, H.E. Ambassador and Mrs. Angier Biddle-Duke, the Duke de Gramont, the Earl and Countess of Granville, the Earl of Hardwicke, Mrs. Randolph Hearst, Prince and Princess Alexander Hohenlohe, Prince and Princess Chlodwig Hohenlohe, T. H. Maharajah and Maharani of Jaipur, Prince Eduard Joseph Lobkowicz, Sir Charles Mendl, Count and Countess Warner Mörner, Mr. and Mrs. S. Stavros Niarchos, Mr. and Mrs. Aristotle Onassis, Sir Duncan and Lady Orr-Lewis, Baron and Baroness Hubert Von Pantz, Count Ferdinand Pecci-Blunt, Sir Francis and Lady Peek, Baroness Gottfried von Kramm, the Duke of Alba, T.H. Prince and Princess Sadrudin Aga Khan, Her Majesty Queen Juliana of the Netherlands and H.R.H. Prince Bernhard.

This elegant club serves as a sort of retreat for very important people who wish luxurious accommodations "away from it all." One can swim, ski (it is located in the Austrian Alps) or just rest in surroundings befitting members of the nobility.

The stay here was devoted to relaxation and entertainment. A beautiful folk dance presentation highlighted the evening.

Most of the Shah's entourage spent the night at a village inn a few miles away, joining him the next morning for the drive to Innsbruck, where His Majesty inspected industrial installations and talked informally with a large number of Iranian students who gathered at the Tyrol Hotel to meet him. The Shah enthusiastically outlined progress in Iran for them, and earnestly urged them to return when they had completed their course of study to aid him in implementing his plans for further modernization of Iran. After a day in Vienna, we flew back to Tehran.

The news that the Empress was expecting a child had spread like wildfire to every remote corner of the realm, initiating a time of great rejoicing and thanksgiving.

Many days before the actual birth of the baby, newsmen and photographers were alerted to the fact that the great day was imminent. The Ministry of Information set up a press room in the Mother Protection Hospital, where Farah was expected to deliver her baby.

This hospital, located in a poor section of the city (in the south part of Tehran), was chosen because the Queen wished her child to be born "among the masses" rather than in the northern residential area, considered to be the wealthy district.

Reporters and cameramen came to Tehran from all over the world, and kept constant vigil to photograph Farah's arrival at the hospital. My brother and a few young friends working in the Issari Newsfilm Agency with us formed my team to cover the events around the birth of the hoped-for Crown Prince of Iran. Five of us worked in relays to cover the hospital around the clock.

A week passed. All members of the press and the photographers were wearing down under the strain. Great numbers of the people of Tehran, knowing the birth was expected at any moment, pressed around the entranceway to see the Shah and Queen when they arrived.

On the morning of October 31, 1960, the Shah finally brought the Queen to the hospital—unfortunately during my breakfast break. However, my brother was on the job and was able to get coverage of the royal couple's arrival. Many photographers missed this event.

As word spread through the city, an even larger crowd gathered around the hospital to await the news, openly expressing hope that indeed the Shah would—at long last—gain a male heir.

The delivery of the child was supervised by Dr. Jehanshah Saleh, former Minister of Health, and one of Tehran's foremost obstetricians. At about noon, Crown Prince Reza saw the light of day. But not until one-thirty were a handful of us photographers given permission to photograph the little prince through the window of his nursery. Cameramen were admitted in groups of three and given one minute to take pictures of the baby held up to view by Dr. Saleh. Not all photographers were able to get in because of the time limitation set by the physician for the child to be "on display."

After I had made my footage of the baby prince, I rushed to the laboratory and the processing of the film was pushed at top speed. That evening at six o'clock, the people of Tehran were able to see our newsreel of the arrival of the Shah and Queen at the hospital, footage of the great gathering of Iranians excitedly greeting the royal couple and then awaiting the news, doctors rushing into the hospital, flowers being delivered, members of the royal family arriving and one minute of the Crown Prince himself —the future ruler of the Persian people. The following evening, copies of the film were made available to cinemas and were also sent to villages in the various provinces for mobile units to present to the people in the remote areas. They too were entitled to see their new Crown Prince at the earliest possible date. That same evening we sent duplicates of this film to various international news agencies in Europe and the United States, and in less than twenty-four hours, millions of people around the world saw on their television sets, news of the birth of a Crown Prince in the ancient country of Persia. Perhaps this is the most memorable newsreel I have ever made—thanks to my brother and a wonderful crew of dedicated and energetic young men working with me during those days.

Exultant celebrations throughout the country were the order of the day. We covered the proceedings when their Majesties left the hospital. Enthusiastic subjects and the staff of the hospital formed a lane through which the proud father and the nurse with the long-hoped-for heir in her arms walked toward the waiting car. The Shah said, "How happy I was when God gave us a son. I thank Him that my young wife is in good health and happy beyond measure." When Empress Farah emerged from the building she was greeted with tumultuous applause.

The people of Tehran honored the royal couple and the little prince with banners, flowers and endless demonstrations of great joy. The road to the palace was decorated with millions of carnations.

Almost three years later, on March 11, 1963, the Queen gave birth to a daughter, Princess Farahnaz, and on April 28, 1966, Iran rejoiced over the birth of another son, Prince Ali-Reza. Now the Shah has two male heirs! Their Majesties' youngest child is a daughter, Princess Leila, born March 24, 1970. All four are beautiful children of whom the Shah and Queen can be justly proud.

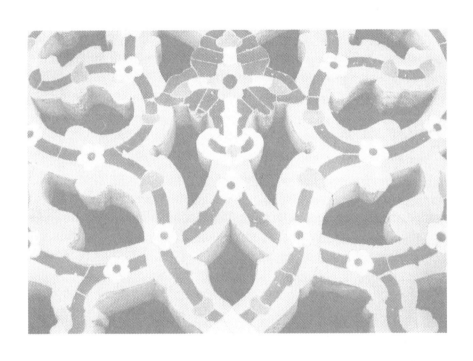

12
Iranian-American Friendship

After an announcement was made that Vice President and Mrs. Lyndon Johnson would arrive in Tehran on August 24, 1962, I was notified that I had been assigned to make a documentary of their visit to Iran. We knew that crews from the United States would accompany the Vice President to cover all aspects of his visit and that the Iranian government had also charged crews of cameramen to cover events, but I was to stay close by for a personal and complete coverage of the Vice President while he was in Iran.

I was also instructed to make a duplicate immediately of all footage shot by me and my crew, and to send it to Washington for use by crews accompanying the Vice President as they needed it.

When the press plane arrived, I was pleased to see in the party a press reporter whom I had met in the United States. When he saw me he called out, "Hi! Ali!" I responded by saying, "Welcome to Iran! It's nice to have you here. We've been looking forward to it!" He shrugged his shoulders wearily and commented, "Don't bet on it. He'll kill you!" Knowing how demanding had been my work with the Shah on state visits, often from six in the morning until two the next morning, I laughed. I felt sure that covering Mr. Johnson would not be nearly as difficult. How wrong I was!

An official itinerary had been carefully prepared. For instance, this was the itinerary for August 25:

12:30 P.M.–The Vice President will leave Saadabad Palace
1:30 P.M.–Arrive Varamin Experiment Station (Lunch)
2:00 P.M.–Leave Varamin
2:25 P.M.–Arrive Khoreen
2:55 P.M.–Leave Khoreen
3:15 P.M.–Arrive Gheshlagh
3:35 P.M.–Leave Gheshlagh
5:00 P.M.–The Vice President will address the members of the Iran-American Society

But Mr. Johnson's behavior was unpredictable. At any moment he might ask the whole caravan of official cars and escorts to stop along the way. The first such instance occurred on the road from the airport to Saadabad Palace, where he and his party were to stay during their visit. Thousands of people lined the route to greet him. Suddenly he asked the driver to stop. He got out and walked through the crowd, shaking hands with the people and (through his interpreter) saying, "Mrs. Johnson and I have come to Iran from America to extend friendship from our nation to yours," or something to that effect. When his car stopped, mine did also, and I had to jump out and be beside him within a few seconds, as my instructions were to give him a complete coverage. This became the procedure throughout his visit to Tehran.

In the afternoon of August 25 (part of the itinerary reported above) the schedule was a little tight: visiting several villages outside Tehran to see experimental stations established with American aid, and returning to Tehran to talk to members of the Iran-American Society in late afternoon. The Vice President cheerfully disregarded the planned schedule, stopping here and there whenever he saw something that particularly interested him. (Early in the visit the interpreter had been transferred to the Vice President's car to expedite matters, although this move was contrary to all the rules of protocol.) On his return from Varamin the same day, Mr. Johnson saw a man on the outskirts of Gheshlagh digging a *qanat.** He stopped the procession and walked across the field to speak to him. A second man was working at the bottom of the well, and of course we had to wait for him to clamber out to receive the Vice President's greeting. The thought occurred to me at the time that these poor villagers might not have even the vaguest idea as to

---

*A qanat is a kind of artesian well used in Iran for irrigation.

who Mr. Johnson was, and so hardly understood what was happening when he shook hands with them and said, "Mrs. Johnson and I bring greetings from America. We want you to know we are your friends," and so on. One might think he was embarking on an intensive vote-getting effort at election time in the States.

Nevertheless, his gesture of friendship was indeed well received by the people. For the first time, ordinary people felt their importance because the Vice President of the mighty country America got out of his car during official proceedings to shake their hands and to convey to them the friendship of his people. No other high official of a foreign country had ever done anything like that before.

However, security men were deeply perturbed about these unscheduled stops, and were noticeably concerned when, in the bazaar area of Tehran, Mr. Johnson saw a little shop where chandeliers and lamps were sold and asked to stop. The shop was tiny—only about five by ten feet square, allowing no room for security protection. Six or seven cars, carrying the American Ambassador, Prime Minister, other ministers, and so forth, followed the Vice President's car. When Mr. Johnson's car stopped, of course all the others followed suit in the crowded street. I jumped out of my car as I had done many times, and ran frantically to join him. He saw a chandelier that pleased him and promptly bought it. I was happy that it was not my responsibility to carry the chandelier safely through the dense crowd and into one of the cars in the procession. We had gone hardly a hundred yards when the whole scene was repeated.

Mr. Johnson was the only dignitary who visited Iran during my career there who cheerfully maneuvered the official schedule according to his own whims. My American friend's warning that the days would be rugged was substantiated. It was the most wearing period of filming I ever experienced.

After the very genial Vice President and Mrs. Johnson had departed, all of us in the press party gathered around a swimming pool, enjoyed a few beers, and together breathed a sigh of relief that now we could return to routine.

In September of the same year, a devastating earthquake hit the central section of Iran. My wife and I were returning home from a party one Saturday night (at about 11:30) when we felt our car shudder. The motor died, then started again. At home, getting out of the car we noted that water was splashing against the sides of our swimming pool. This meant one thing—an earth-quake somewhere in the area.

Early the next morning I called my boss to ask if he had received any news about a tremor. He had heard nothing officially. I then called the Department of Radio and received from the men there only the information that a small earthquake, somewhere west of Tehran—probably seventy miles or so—had damaged a few adobe houses. I then tried to call the University of Tehran to see if their seismograph had measured the tremor, but no one was available. Reporters for Associated Press and United Press International con-firmed the fact that a tremor had been felt somewhere west of the capital, but they did not think it destructive enough to report. Like people in some areas of the world, Iranians expect occasional tremors because the country is, in a way, an earthquake cradle.

My interest in finding out just what had happened guided me to my office, even though it was Sunday. Only one driver with his car was available to us on holidays, but the man I found there had not been assigned elsewhere, and the officer in charge had left for the day, so he agreed to go with me to the earthquake area to investigate. I put my camera equipment in the carry-all and we drove to Karadj (a small town about twenty-five miles northwest of the capital). I had only five or six minutes of film in my camera case, but not expecting to find anything worth photographing I had not bothered to stock up with more.

At Karadj we found the Red Lion and Sun Hospital had admit-ted a few people who had been wounded when their houses had been knocked down by the tremor. (Red Lion and Sun in Iran is the equivalent of America's Red Cross.)

We continued on to the end of the paved road at the foot of the mountains, then decided to follow the narrow mountain trail to the next village, Danesfahan, to see whether or not damage had extended that far. To our horror we discovered there an area of complete devastation. Only a couple of hundred people had sur-vived out of a population of about five thousand! Those who had escaped the holocaust were in a state of shock. They were weeping aloud as they dug frantically into the earth and rubble to extricate loved ones, most of whom had died through suffocation. Others had been hopelessly injured. We were apparently the first people to arrive from the outside.

As a news photographer my first impulse was to document the

event. I photographed what was left of the village and its inhabitants with the five rolls of film I had with me. Then I looked around to see what I could do for these people. The only medical supplies I had were in a little first aid kit in the car. We witnessed one heartbreaking scene after another: little children crying for their mothers who had been swallowed up by the angry earth; elderly people mourning the loss of their families; some villagers wandering in a daze, stumbling through the debris.

A couple of men who appeared to have overcome the shock of the disaster rushed up to me and said, "Sir, you've got to get help for us!" They begged me to take some of the seriously wounded to the hospital at Karadj. But how could I choose which ones should go? We finally crowded thirty-two people into our carry-all—some on top of others. I held a few children in my arms, and we tucked others between the driver and me.

Water comes from deep qanat wells in these areas, and the earthquake had disrupted the supply. I did not return to Karadj the way I had come, but drove north and around by way of Qazvin, in the hope of saving time. On the way we saw more devastated villages and everywhere the people were crying for water.

When I brought the wounded to the Red Lion and Sun Hospital at Qazvin, those in charge were astounded. Where had these people come from? The hospital had neither the facilities nor equipment to cope with a disaster of these proportions. By this time it was after midnight and the people were in need of food as well as medical attention. Unfortunately, I had only fifty rials (about sixty cents) in my pocket, for I had not anticipated the remotest possibility of a situation like this when I had left home.

I promised to send help and we drove on to Tehran as fast as road conditions would allow. I must have been a frightening sight to my worried wife when I presented myself at home at about two-thirty in the morning. I was covered with gray dust—clothes, face, hair, eyebrows. I briefly explained where I had been and said, "Let me take a shower and I'll tell you what happened." When I came out of my bath, I found my wife, Joan, had driven our car out of the garage, filled it with blankets, food, medicines, and so forth, and was ready to go to Danesfahan.

I said, "How are you going to get there over those impassable roads? And even if you do, you won't be able to accomplish much. What you have in the car won't help more than five people. We must get in touch with high authorities and ask for help for *hundreds* of people instead of giving it to—maybe five."

We sat down to discuss the problem over a cup of coffee. Where could we turn for aid? Finally we concluded that the first thing we might do would be to call the American Ambassador and apprise him of the situation, but it was then only 4:00 A.M. and we felt that we should not disturb him at that hour. We waited until 5:30. Fortunately, Joan was well acquainted with the Ambassador's secretary and both of us felt it wise to call her first.

The secretary said, "Ambassador Holmes has heard about the tremor but has had no information as to the extent of the damage." Joan immediately answered, "But we do have information! My husband drove out to the area and found terrible devastation and an enormous death toll in the one village he reached. If this village is an example of the destruction in the area, the calamity must be nothing less than catastrophic!"

With this information, the secretary called the Ambassador. As soon as I felt sure we had initiated some action for assistance in the area, I went directly to the laboratory, called the boys who worked there by telephone and asked them to come in for an emergency job. They responded and the film I had taken of the disaster area was soon being processed.

At about nine o'clock Ambassador Holmes called me for details. I told him what I had witnessed and then informed him that if he could wait a couple of hours he could see for himself part of what I had seen, on film. He said, "Good! I would like to see it myself and would like also to show it to the Country Team" (head of Point Four, head of USIS, and the American General in charge of the Military Assistance Advisory Group).

Shortly after viewing my five-minute coverage Ambassador Holmes called Washington with a request for immediate aid. It came first of all in the form of $20,000 in cash.

At six o'clock that evening my newsreel was shown on television. The next day scores of Iranians did exactly what Joan had done— filled their cars with emergency supplies and made a virtual caravan of Good Samaritans traveling to the disaster area. The Iranian Red Lion and Sun and other government agencies took immediate action, and help poured into the area from all directions.

Other countries responded generously. Hundreds of American army planes, based in Europe, brought in a 100-bed hospital, 195 doctors and nurses, medication, blankets, and food. The hospital set up at Qazvin was in operation in thirty-six hours. Church groups and private organizations around the world pledged themselves to help rebuild the villages.

Following is an excerpt from an article in the *USIA Correspondent* Vol. 4, No. 10, October 1962.

USIS TEHRAN ASSISTS EARTHQUAKE RELIEF
The September 1 earthquake which killed more than 10,000 persons in Iran and devastated a 6,000 square-mile area west of Tehran found USIS staffers and members of their families playing various roles in its aftermath.

On the official side, USIS Tehran, which was just recovering from a whirlwind visit by Vice President Lyndon B. Johnson, suspended practically all other activities to concentrate on publicizing the massive quake relief which poured in from around the world, including the United States, or which developed on the spot in Tehran.

USIS film cameraman Ali Issari went into the quake-rocked zone the morning following the temblor, before Iran was fully aware of the extent of death and destruction, and brought back the first films from the area. His film, which showed poignant views of victims and destroyed villages, had an electric effect upon those who saw it.

Plans for rebuilding through the joint efforts of the American and Iranian governments were set in motion. It was decided that the United States would send large quantities of wheat to Iran for which the government would pay a stipulated price. The money would then be turned back to Iran's construction bank to be used in reconstructing the villages. Building operations were to be turned over to an engineer-architect who would work along with American supervisors. The people of the area were to have a voice in the design of the villages.

The United States Agency for International Development (USAID) decided to make a film showing results of the whole concept of international collaboration in this project. I was asked to produce such a film. I fabricated a little story line about a small boy left homeless by the earthquake, and what happened to him afterwards.

The film opens with the little shepherd boy Hassan and his family—sister, mother and father—living a happy, though simple, life. His house is made of mud bricks, but there is love and respect within those walls. Hassan helps his father care for the sheep and goats; he has a good life. His favorite in the herd is a little white-faced goat that he calls *Boz*.

Just before going to bed one night, he slips out to the enclosure where the sheep and goats are corralled to see that his little pet is all right, and to place a strand of donkey beads his father has given him over the little goat's head. He is about to open the gate to the corral when he feels the earth shudder beneath him. A slab of wood strikes him on the head and he lies inert from the blow. In time he regains consciousness to find his home, his parents, and the sheep and goats (including of course his beloved pet) gone. He has survived only because he was out in the open. His home has collapsed, suffocating all of his family in it.

A hundred villages have been wiped out, and about twelve thousand people have been killed, trapped in their mud houses. Hassan is miraculously alive! But he is only eleven years old with no one in the world to whom he can turn. His only possessions are the strand of bright blue donkey beads and his father's little flute that he has pulled from the rubble.

Sobbing, he turns his back on the remains of his village and starts walking, not knowing where he is going—down the road and across the plains. He stumbles into the next village, where he finds that the Red Lion and Sun have already begun to distribute tents for families whose homes have been destroyed.

A father, with his own small son, stands at the entrance to his temporary tent home and watches the forlorn little figure pass. The man ponders the fact that he has more than he can handle, caring for his little family under these terribly adverse circumstances. He goes into the tent to relax with his loved ones and to give thanks that they are all safe, but he cannot rest. He goes out and calls to Hassan to come back. He gives him a bowl of food, invites him to lie down, covers him with a blanket, and the exhausted child falls into a deep sleep at once.

The United States Agency for International Development, in cooperation with the Iranian government, decides to rebuild the village in which Hassan continues to live with his adopted family.

A tall American supervisor arrives to talk with the Iranian engineer-architect, and to confer with the villagers. Hassan is deeply interested and "listens in" whenever he has the chance to do so. Noticing the eager youngster who seems to be following him around, the American engineer asks Hassan to help him rebuild the village. Hassan assists in laying out the plans for the village and the reconstruction of it. Despite the language barrier, a strong bond of friendship develops between them.

By spring, most of the construction has been completed and Hassan finds time to wander outside the village. Near his old village of Danesfahan, he sees a shepherd whom he recognizes, and who has in his small herd a white-faced goat Hassan believes is his pet. He kneels on the ground, hugging his long-lost friend. But a struggle ensues when the shepherd denies that the goat belongs to the boy, forcibly separating the child from it. The American chances to witness the scene and does not forget it.

Finally the work is done. Four villages are completely restored in the area. (Others have been constructed also with the financial help and personnel of other countries.) The American and Hassan make a final check on the houses—all small with only two rooms each. But Hassan has never known a house to have more than one room and he thinks them luxurious. Sanitary toilets, glass windows, concrete floors, electricity and a clean water system! What else could one ask for?

It is now the fall of 1963 as the project is completed and the people of the village are honored by a visit from the Shah who has chosen their village, Nodeh, and Danesfahan out of all the rest for formal ceremonies of dedication. The American Ambassador accompanies the Shah, visiting the new school at Danesfahan and inspecting some of the homes in Nodeh.

He speaks gracious words of thanks to the villagers for their cooperation, to the Iranian architect who designed the villages, the American women in Tehran who had raised the money for the construction of the school in Nodeh, to Iranian firms that had done the work, to the construction bank that had presided over the project, and to the American and his associates who had spent a year living in tents to supervise the construction.

It is time now for Hassan's friend from America to go home. But first he enters the house of the man who has befriended Hassan, and has a final cup of tea with the family. He has a surprise gift for the boy. He takes Hassan outside where a beautiful little white-faced goat is tethered—a new pet for the child who has helped him rebuild Nodeh. Hassan reaches into his pocket for the donkey beads he always carries with him, and slips them over the head of his beloved pet. He is as happy as can be.

But when the jeep taking the tall American speeds away, Hassan tearfully watches it, then runs after it, calling out to his friend. The driver stops the vehicle and waits for the child to reach it. Hassan smiles at his American friend through his tears

198   *A Picture of Persia*

and gives him—as a parting gift—his most precious possession, his father's flute.

The film ends with a quotation from the Persian poet Sa'di, written in the tenth century:

> All Adam's sons are limbs of one another
> Each of the selfsame substance as his brother.
> So while one member suffers ache and grief,
> Other members cannot win relief.
> Thou who art heedless of thy brother's pain
> It is not right at all to call thee man.

The role of Hassan was played by our own little houseboy—a child with rather poignant personal appeal and great native talent. He was not needed "on location" all the time, of course, and we took him out to the village whenever enough had been accomplished in reconstruction to fit him into the story. One day we decided it was time to shoot another sequence, but to my horror I discovered that—at his mother's insistence—he had had his hair cut. The barber had all but shaved his head. We had to wait several weeks before we could take another foot of film in which the boy played a part.

We had a problem of another kind with "Boz," our white-faced goat. We used the same animal throughout the film, not expecting him to change in any marked fashion. However, the wife of the film director (McNeil Withers, head of the Communications Division of Point Four in Tehran), who agreed to take care of the goat during the eight-month period, became very fond of him and fed him all too well. He got fatter by the day, and we were forced to put him on a diet before we could photograph him in the final scene.

The "tall American" was actually playing the role of construction supervisor in real life as well as in the film. He did a surprisingly professional, though natural, job of portraying the character in the film. Other members of the cast were real people in real situations, making the story very believable to the audience.

The film, which is about twenty-eight minutes in length, was shown to the Iranian people that they might see for themselves the magnitude of American and international aid to their country, both financial and technical, following the ravaging earthquake. The simplicity of the story line was especially appealing to the children, but adults saw the broader picture.

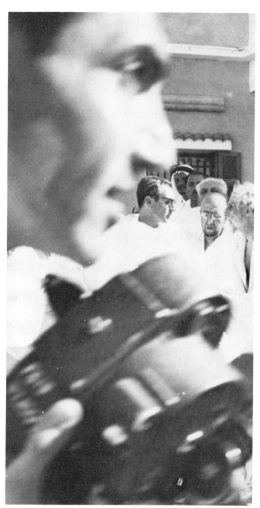

Mr. Issari and cameraman *(top right)*; being warned of the dangers of photographing an oil gusher *(center)*, photographing a tribal school *(lower right)*

Photographing Shah's pilgrimage to Mecca

Vice-President Johnson shaking hands with member of press on arrival at Tehran, 1962

The Shah, Empress Farah, President Celal Bayar of Turkey and Field Marshal Ayub Khan, President of Pakistan, alighting from carriage to attend horse and cattle show in Lahore, Pakistan, 1960

The Shah arriving at the Tokyo airport, where he is greeted by Emperor Hirohito and members of the Japanese government, 1958

Members of the Shah's entourage in Tokyo being served in true Japanese style, 1958

Author in a village to photograph scenes for "Literacy Corps" film, 1964

Members of the Syracuse University crew making films in Iran for use by cinema mobile units, 1952

President Dwight Eisenhower arriving in Tehran and being greeted by His Imperial Majesty the Shahanshah of Iran and high officials of the government, 1959

Vice-President Lyndon B. Johnson's visit to Iran, 1962

Photographing Eleanor Roosevelt during her visit to Iran, 1957

General Riahi, Minister of Roads, gives the Scheherazade bell to Dr. Jahanshah Saleh, Minister of Health, winner of the auction.

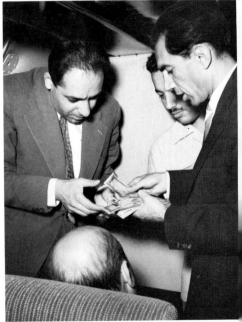

Author gives money raised from the Scheherazade bell auction to Dr. Khatibi, Secretary General of the Red Lion and Sun Organization.

Photographing the Crown Prince in 1963

Setting up the camera to photograph Qashghai tribal women baking bread
for the film *Tribal Tent School*, 1957

The Shah at a press conference in Sweden, 1960 (author in background)

Mr. Issari in pursuit of the news

We sent a copy of the film to the Agency for International Development in Washington, where it was shown to the Congressional committee in charge of the AID program. I am told that their proposed budget was approved in Congress, partly on the basis that they could see for themselves that funds were being appropriately used in situations such as the wake of the destructive earthquake in Iran.

The Iranian New Year (No-Ruz) starts on the twenty-first of March, coinciding with the coming of spring. For thirteen days the whole country celebrates the New Year and on the thirteenth day every Persian goes on a picnic, or in some other way marks the end of the holiday period with carefree festivities.

It was at this time (in 1963) that an American network requested footage on the royal couple to be screened on television the evening of the arrival of the Shah and Empress on a scheduled state visit to the United States. The network first planned to send a film crew of their own to Tehran to get this coverage, but they were advised by the Iranian authorities that competent, professional film crews were available in Iran to fill the assignment if they so desired. They concurred and I was asked to make the film, to be sent to the United States well ahead of Their Majesties' arrival.

Official photographers, at this time, were permitted to take pictures of the Shah and Queen only on public occasions. Filming them in informal situations was considered to be a form of "invasion of privacy." The American network, however, wanted a film taken "behind the scenes."

On the eve of the thirteenth day of No-Ruz (about midnight), I received a call telling me I would be expected the following morning at ten o'clock at the Queen Mother's palace—just outside Tehran. The Shah and Queen would be there and I would be permitted to photograph them for the American television network.

The next day, I presented myself to the Shah and Queen as ordered and reminded them that I was there to make a film for the American network and would like instructions as to what I could photograph. The Shah said, "Tell us what you want us to do and we'll do it." But I proposed that they proceed to enjoy the day as they wished and I would take what I wanted on film. Only a small number of people were present—members of the royal family and a few officials.

The Shah enjoys sports in general and in particular, tennis and volleyball. The Queen is also an accomplished sportswoman. Volleyball is the main sport when the family gathers. This was true the day I spent with them celebrating the end of the No-Ruz holidays. I photographed Their Majesties in quiet conversation, walking in the garden, playing with the little Crown Prince, in a game of volleyball with the other members of the royal family—all in an atmosphere of relaxed informality. It was a very pleasant assignment for me.

During the day, one of His Majesty's aides approached me and asked if I would like to accompany the Shah to the United States. This time he planned to make the trip without reporters and photographers, but arrangements would be made for me to accompany him. I agreed to go and said I would notify my boss at once.

The next day I outlined my plan to accompany the Shah to the United States to my supervisor and explained that, as before, the only cost to my office would be $12 a day *per diem*, for I would travel in the Shah's plane or go by commercial airliner at the expense of the court. I would send all footage back to Iran for showing in local cinemas and on television, and then on my return I would make a full-length documentary of the visit for showing throughout the country and via our cinema mobile unit operation. My boss agreed heartily to the plan, but told me he would have to clear the matter with his immediate superior. For some reason, obscure to me at the time, this man in charge of our operations (who was new on the job) refused to approve my travel.

A few months later I discovered the reason for the man's decision. Some time before the proposed visit, he had ignorantly requested Washington to arrange for a complete coverage of the Shah's visit in both still photographs and motion pictures, to be sent to Tehran for local distribution. He had done this without checking with my boss or me in the film section, to determine the most feasible plan for such a coverage. As it turned out, his arrangement with Washington cost several thousand dollars more than it would have cost had we done it.

I hardly knew how to tell the Shah's aide that I would have to decline the invitation to go to the United States, for I hesitated to say that I had run into a strange, puzzling situation at the office. I withheld my answer for a few days, not knowing what to say that might not be embarrassing to me and to the American Embassy in Iran. Three days before the Shah was scheduled to depart, I fell ill with pneumonia. The situation was saved. I sent word that I was physically unable to go.

The visit was highly publicized. President and Mrs. Kennedy seemed to enjoy the Shah and Queen Farah personally. The First Lady and the Queen were described by American reporters with extravagant adjectives, and it is said that President Kennedy commented at a glittering formal occasion something to the effect that he and the Shah had been definitely relegated to a secondary position with the spotlight on their charming wives, Jacqueline and Farah. Farah was beautifully gowned, wearing a diadem, necklace and bracelet decorated with emeralds, from the Persian crown jewels, valued at a little over one million dollars.

On the arrival of the film made in the States we invited the members of the Iranian press to view it. Their reaction to the film was unfavorable and all said as much later in their newspaper reviews. They agreed that it had been professionally done; however, the emphasis in the film was out of focus. The cameramen who had photographed the events of the visit had been so enamored of the charisma of the royal couple, what they were wearing, the Queen's jewels and the Shah's medals, that their emphasis had remained on Their Majesties rather than on what they saw and did—completely missing the reverse side of the coin. The filmmakers' point of view was all wrong. This film might have been of great interest to Americans, but not to Iranians who already very well knew their Shah and Queen. They wanted to *travel with* them and to *see* what they saw. We used a little of this twenty-minute motion picture in a newsreel, but the documentary did not merit (nor receive) a wide distribution.

I suspect that the Shah was not too well pleased with the film either. He has complained that far too often correspondents and photographers visiting Iran, dazzled by the pageantry of Persia's Oriental court, backed by thousands of years of tradition, have been more interested in the colorful setting than in his deep convictions as a head of state. The results have been reports for worldwide distribution composed of the most banal superficialities. He expresses himself pointedly as to his disappointments with the work of some American newsmen and cameramen covering important affairs of state, in his book *Mission for My Country:*

For some reason the Americans have specialized in such reporting. I marvel at the many instances I have seen of naive, even childish, reporting by big, well-dressed, self-assured, impressive-looking American correspondents. Sometimes I wonder if they have received the right training for overseas work. Happily there are exceptions, but it would help the Free World's cause if the exception could become the rule.[34]

It is evident to Iranians and those people throughout the world who have followed national developments since 1941, that the Shah is a man dedicated to improving the life of his countrymen. It is in this role that he prefers to be known, rather than (as foreign cameramen often depict him) in the role of regal monarch, ruling over his subjects from the Peacock Throne in ancient Persia. He says, "The plain truth is that I derive my chief satisfactions from grappling with complex economic and other problems."[35]

The years 1962 and 1963 were of vital importance in the cementing of ties between Iran and the United States. The friendly informal visit by Vice President and Mrs. Lyndon Johnson, the compassionate response of the American people to the tragedy of the devastating earthquake in Iran, and finally the gracious reception given the Shahanshah and Empress on their visit to the United States combined to serve as a warm clasping of hands, symbolizing friendship between the two nations across the world.

---

[34]Mohammed Reza Shah Pahlavi, *op. cit.*, p. 140.
[35]*Ibid.*

13

The Revolution of the Shah and the People (The White Revolution)

The Shah's statement, quoted at the end of the previous chapter, "The plain truth is that I derive my chief satisfactions from grappling with complex economic and other problems," was published in 1961. Progress during the next two years did not satisfy him. In 1963 he "grappled" with the disturbing existing problems with a bold move.

The position of the Shah in Iran is unique in the family of monarchies. He bears the responsibilities shared by other reigning personages, domestically and internationally. In addition, he is their leader in a less tangible or materialistic way; he is their leader in thought and spirit to a much greater extent than is the case with other rulers in their own realms. He is the ideal whom the average man strives to emulate. Nevertheless, the Shah's reform programs met with great opposition from the so-called ruling "thousand families."

At one time, preceding his "bold move," the Shah had said, "When this country needs a revolution, I will lead it." Abhorring bloodshed and violence, but noting a strong need for sweeping changes in the areas of justice, human rights and social patterns, he set about the gigantic task of effecting the sorely needed national "repairs" through a fearless single stroke. He undoubtedly knew he was taking grave risks in doing so, but he saw no other choice. This move was called "The White Revolution" (as opposed to

Red Revolution, meaning revolution with blood), and is now known as the "Revolution of the Shah and the People."

Facets of this "war" on injustice, domination of many by a few, and the disregard of human and national rights, were set in a six-point plan, and presented on January 9, 1963, before the National Congress of Rural Cooperatives held in Tehran. I was present to cover this important milestone in Iranian history in motion pictures for national showing. I was present also on the twenty-sixth of January of the same year, when a general referendum was held. At this time approval of the charter was declared by a ninety-nine percent majority vote. Since 1963, eight more points have been added, making it a fourteen-point plan. (More points have been added in recent years).

In his book *The White Revolution*, the Shah details the background against which he worked out the strategy for the Revolution. He writes of the vicissitudes suffered by the government from internal, treasonous dissidents, as well as the policies of foreign powers who hoped to create feelings of mistrust of the government, dissatisfaction with the status quo, and lack of faith in the country's future—particularly at the beginning of his reign.

He writes:

> First and foremost, I was the sovereign of over twenty million hardworking, noble citizens who had placed all their hopes in me. I watched them toil, and saw the rewards of their ceaseless efforts slip through their fingers into the outstretched hands of a group of parasites, whose only abilities were in concluding illegal deals and serving foreign powers.[36]

In the second year of his reign, the Shah declared a five-point program to attempt to meet the basic needs of all his people: health for all, housing for all, food for all, clothing for all, and education for all. Of course, this idealistic program could come to fruition only over a long period of time. He demonstrated his sincerity by handing over all his personal farming estates to the government so that revenue could be ploughed back into agricultural improvements, subsequently withdrawing them and selling them directly to the farmers (as has been stated previously).

Bills had been passed to better the lot of the peasants, but

---

[36]Mohammed Reza Shah Pahlavi, *The White Revolution,* Kayhan Press, Tehran 1967, p. 8.

intervention by irresponsible individuals who saw their interests threatened had rendered the legislation ineffective. Looking back over past failures, the Shah had come to the conclusion that decisive action was mandatory. He writes:

> It was essential that land reform should take place and the feudal landlord and peasant system be abolished; that the relationship between workers and employers should be regularized so that labour should not feel exploited; that women—who after all make up half the population— should no longer be included with lunatics and criminals and deprived of their social rights; that the scourge of illiteracy should be removed so that illiterates who do not know how to defend themselves should know their rights; that nobody should die of disease nor spend their [sic] lives in misery and wretchedness through lack of treatment or care; that backwardness in the villages should be ended.[37]

The *first* point of the master plan had to do with *Land Reform.* Unfortunately, in spite of the importance of agriculture in Iran since antiquity, peasants had been without rights. A village (which usually consisted of about a hundred families who worked the land with primitive implements) could be bought and sold, the peasants themselves being included in the sale "package" along with the land they tilled and planted.

In 1962, the average rural income was only approximately three dollars per month per family. In 1963, half the land capable of producing crops was in the hands of individuals, some of whom owned as many as forty villages. A few boasted of holdings of areas equal to all of Switzerland. These wealthy landlords rarely lived on their estates, preferring urban living in Iran, or residence abroad. Agents, who often sought private gain, made the peasants suffer to achieve it. And so, on this historic occasion (January 9, 1963) the Shah declared:

> So that no power can reinstate the regime of slavery among the villagers and plunder the nation's wealth for the benefit of a minority, I have decided as executive, legislative and judicial head of state to refer these reforms to a referendum. In this way, henceforth no individual or group will be able to cancel out, for their own private interests, the results of these reforms, which will free the farmer from the yoke of feudalism, ensure a brighter future, based on justice and progress, for the noble working class and a higher standard of living for honest and hardworking civil servants, members of the guilds and craftsmen.[38]

---

[37]*Ibid.,* pp. 17-18.
[38]*Ibid.,* p. 36.

Angry landowners sponsored and abetted violent demonstrations in the streets as late as June, 1963—a feared but expected reaction to their new status of diminished control (more about this later).

To assist in carrying out the aims of individual ownership by peasants working the land, a body called the Central Organization of Rural Cooperatives was established under the auspices of the Ministry of Agriculture and the Agricultural Credits and Rural Development Bank of Iran (now the Agriculture Bank of Iran).

Today there are approximately nine thousand cooperatives, about one for every six villages. These cooperatives purchase seed and fertilizer (and distribute it), oversee repair of qanats and assist in marketing produce.

The second of the six principles of the White Revolution dealt with *Nationalization of Forests and Pastures.*

Although Iran is not as heavily forested as European countries and the U.S., parts of northern Iran are covered with trees—perhaps thirteen thousand square miles. Other wooded areas are scattered.

In 1920 a small group within the Ministry of Agriculture sketched maps indicating the classification of forested areas as to whether they were government-owned or privately-owned; and in 1940 a Forestry Office was established in Tehran. Other measures took form, but for one reason or another they were not effective in preventing the wanton destruction of trees without long-range plans for reforestation. In Iran charcoal has been, for centuries, the principal household fuel. Because charcoal is produced by burning tree trunks, its production had ravaged much of the forest land.

The Shah, therefore, proposed nationalization of Iran's forests, which was to be followed by an extensive plan in the interest of conservation and scientific development.

The nationalization of pastures (included in Point Two) was a step forward. Preceding this time shepherds were often involved in difficulties with a small segment of people who held the whip-hand as landowners. It was proposed in Point Two that pastures be allotted to shepherds by authorized government agencies, and rental charges which poor shepherds had often been forced to pay for grazing and water rights were abolished.

The third point dealt with the *Public Sale of State-Owned Factory Shares as Security for Land Reform.*

The purpose of the move to make shares available in government-owned factories was to give the landowners the opportunity to invest capital realized from sale of their lands to the farmers, in sound industrial projects. At this time, fifty-five government factories that manufactured or processed products such as chemicals, textiles, sugar and other foodstuffs, were incorporated into joint-stock companies. These companies formed a corporation called the Government Factories Corporation.

It was the Shah's plan to attract capital for private investment both in established industries and in projects that he planned to develop in remote regions, utilizing local resources. He hoped to establish the Organization for the Expansion and Modernization of Iranian Industry, making the general public partners with the government, and dividing profits among a large number of investors with limited assets.

The fourth principle of the White Revolution dealt with *Profit-Sharing in Industry.*

This facet of the plan concerned workers, rather than investors. Although a plan to benefit factory laborers had been proposed many years before, it had not been as successful as one could wish. Better working conditions had been put into effect by legislation through the years, and in 1946, the working day had been reduced to eight hours and the working week to forty-eight hours by law.

However, the Shah felt that factory workers did not enjoy the same feeling of security as did the peasants who under the new laws owned their own land. Therefore, the fourth principle of the White Revolution proposed workers' participation in the profits of industrial and productive enterprises: workers were to receive up to twenty percent of the net gain of the factories in which they worked.

The fifth point concerned *Reform of Electoral Law.*

The Shah was keenly aware of the fact that the spirit of the Constitution of Iran, established sixty years previously, had not become fact. Men of influence (such as the wealthy landlords) and the so-called ruling class in general dominated legislation. Bills that might interfere with the personal interests of the few were maneuvered out of the legislature, sometimes without a word of public discussion.

Women, who composed half of the population, were not given a voice in the democratic process. The Shah looked with disdain on Article 10 of the law of elections to the National Consultative Assembly (known as the Majlis)which read:

> Those deprived of the right to vote shall consist of all females; minors and those who earn their living in a disreputable way; murderers, thieves and other criminals punishable under Islamic law . . .

History discloses that women have at times held a place of honor and esteem in Iran. During the Sassanian period the country was twice under the rule of queens: Pourandokht and Azarmidokht. With the passing of the centuries, however, women lost their distinguished status to the point that even the founding fathers of the Constitution classified them with the segment of population unworthy of the right to vote.

In the enlightened 1960s, the Shah considered it to be shameful discrimination for women, many of whom had distinguished themselves as educators, artists, poets, and even as members of the professions of medicine and law, to be deprived of a voice in shaping policies through their right to vote. Therefore, in his fifth point, he proposed the creation of a parliament that represented the whole nation, including the women of Iran. Today a number of women have been elected to seats in parliament, and in fact the way has been opened for a woman to hold the highest office in the nation.

The sixth principle concerned education and the proposed establishment of the *Literacy Corps*.

The deep yearning for education, far beyond the fundamentals of reading and writing, has been paramount in the lives of Persian people through the years, and is no less marked today. The Prophet Mohammad is said to have exclaimed, "If knowledge were to be found in heaven, the Persians would still strive to attain it."

It is recorded that the Prophet established a sort of Literacy Corps himself in the early days of Islamic influence. It is said that literate soldiers captured by Moslem armies (in the absence of funds necessary for purchase of their freedom) could go free if they served for a time as tutors for Moslem children, teaching them the rudiments of reading and writing.

Ancient Persians committed to memory long passages from the Koran and the beloved works of poets. Foreign visitors to remote areas of the country in recent years have been amazed to hear villagers quote at length from the works of Ferdowsi, Hafez and Sa'di in spite of their lack of any kind of formal schooling.

However, at the time of the White Revolution, only a small minority of the Iranian population could be termed *educated.**

The Shah's inspired idea as to a way in which literacy could be encouraged in the entire country was outlined in his Point Six: the use of high school graduates, eligible for conscription in the armed forces, as teachers in villages without schools, for the required period of service.

The plan, which proved to be eminently successful as time went by, was to expose the young men eligible for the program to an intensive four-month training course to prepare them for service in the villages. The course oriented the corps members to conditions and needs of the population in the areas to which they were assigned. Service was not to be limited to work in the classroom; members were expected to assist in whatever was needed to be done in the communities served. Through the years, the Literacy Corps has been responsible for building schools as well as repairing and remodeling existing ones; members have helped to carry out projects in road building, tree planting, qanat dredging; they have assisted in agricultural projects, and have organized village societies. In short, they have served as focal points of leadership among the untrained peasants in remote, underdeveloped communities. As a result of the wonderful work performed by these young men it is estimated that the illiteracy rate in the country has dropped below the fifty percent mark.†

It was my great pleasure to make a documentary film on the Literacy Corps, delineating the varied activities and achievements of the first group of corpsmen initiating the program in the far reaches of Iran. A letter which I received from the Ministry of Education reflects the way in which the documentary was utilized. Translation is as follows:

---

*Less than twenty percent.

†To reduce this rate further a paramilitary corps for young women has been established within the past five years. The recruits after four months of military discipline and teacher training are sent out to remote districts to conduct classes in areas Americans call the three Rs: reading, writing, and arithmetic. The first group of 1,775 girls went out into the villages in 1969. Since then the number of women in service in the Corps has passed 11,000.

Ministry of Education
No. 2075
Date: 24/10/43 (1/14/65)

Mr. Mohammad Ali Issari:
    The motion picture on the Education Corps which was directed and photographed through your initiative and effort has been received with great enthusiasm all over the country. In addition to serving as a training aid for the corpsmen themselves, it has acquainted a large number of people with the progressive program of His Imperial Majesty the Shahanshah, and has won the admiration of many audiences everywhere. We take pleasure in expressing our deep appreciation for your efforts and wish you further success in serving the Iranian people.

/s/
Minister of Education

It was estimated at the time that the film was seen by 15,000 corpsmen in the field or in training, and 100,000 other Iranians. The Ministry of Culture and Arts dubbed the film in English, Arabic, French and German, and submitted it for showing through Iranian embassies abroad.

Approximately eighty percent of the first group of young men working in the Literacy Corps have opted to remain with the Ministry of Education at the end of their required period of service, many requesting that they be permitted to stay in their villages in order to complete long-range projects. In subsequent years, an average of fifty percent have chosen to remain.

Well satisfied with the effectiveness of the Literacy Corps (at minimum expense to the government), the Shah sent a communication to every head of state in the world shortly before the Thirteenth General Conference of UNESCO opened in October 1964. In this missive he urged action to decrease illiteracy all over the world, and invited members of the organization to attend a World Congress in Tehran to deal with the problem. The invitation was accepted with enthusiasm, and in September of the following year the first World Congress on the Eradication of Illiteracy was held in Iran's capital city. At this time, attending members evaluated the Shah's ingenious plan to allocate a portion of the country's military budget to fight illiteracy, and as a result, other countries accepted the strategy and have put it to good use.

On January 21, 1964, the Shah issued the following decree: "In order to extend physical well-being, the treatment of the sick and public health, a corps of physicians and university and high school graduates shall be formed and named the Health Corps, which shall serve as mobile units in the villages and regions without proper health facilities."[39]

Three additional points were to be appended later to the Six-Point plan of the White Revolution. The first of these, or the Seventh Point, was the *Health Corps*. Again I was pleased to produce a documentary film on the activities and achievements of the members of the first group of Health Corpsmen, which enjoyed wide distribution. The program, which was launched in September 1964, has made a marked difference in the general health of Iranians living in remote regions. It is the kind of program I devoutly wished for the day the beautiful girl (mentioned in Chapter Five) in desperate need of medical aid, fell on her knees before me pleading for help.

The Corpsmen are composed of dentists, physicians, laboratory technicians and health education personnel. In addition to dispensing medication, applying treatments, and vaccinating large numbers of people to prevent such diseases as smallpox and cholera, they have assisted in upgrading sanitary facilities, digging wells, and so forth, and villagers have been taught preventive measures to stave off epidemics.

The establishment of the Health Corps has proved to be a tremendous step in the right direction.

The second added principle (or *Eighth Point*) was called *The Reconstruction and Development Corps*, which was actually an extension to the program related to Land Reform, and in some ways an adjunct to both the program of the Literacy Corps and the Health Corps.

Members of this corps were expected to conduct training programs in stock breeding, pest control, and general agriculture, and establish organizations made up of young farmers, for the purpose of initiating social as well as agricultural projects in communities. (Technical school and university graduates were required for this corps, because the work they were called upon to do demanded advanced training.)

The third principle to be added to the original plan (the *Ninth Point*) dealt with the establishment of *Houses of Equity* to provide

---

[39]*Ibid.*, p. 126.

justice for all. The basis for this proposal was simply that villagers and farmers were denied (but should have) benefits of justice equal to those meted out to urban dwellers. Quoting the Shah, "To do this we have chosen the most logical course of action: instead of making the villager come to the cities or the capital to secure his rights, we have taken justice to him in his village."[40]

In his book the Shah relates a story attributed to Ali (Mohammad's son-in-law), which shows this good and great man's feeling concerning justice, and which is somewhat relevant to the situation in Iran at the time of the White Revolution:

> One day Ali appeared before the Caliph Omar in a law-suit. When judgment had been given Omar asked him what he thought of the verdict. Ali replied: "I cannot say it was completely impartial, since in addressing me you used my title, whereas you called the plaintiff only by his name. This implied that you considered me above him."[41]

In Iran a poor farmer with no "title" or influential friends often received unjust treatment from the law.

The problems of the peasants are obviously not those related to big business, corporations, mergers, and that sort of thing; they are concerned with problems such as water or grazing rights for small herds of sheep or goats, or boundary lines of small plots of land. To go to a town or city to request legal counsel, file suit, or follow other procedures involving great expenditures of time and money was completely beyond their reach. The proposed plan was structured to eliminate any need for such action.

The new concept approved the settlement of legal differences in the villages through the help of local arbiters—trustworthy natives appointed by the villagers themselves. Judges (using the schoolhouse as a courthouse) were to receive no salary or payment of any kind. No set legal procedures were to be imposed, no particular steps were to be considered necessary for a settlement (as is true in court hearings). The judge was expected to give both sides involved in a difference equal chances to present their grievances, make investigations as he chose, call witnesses if he thought it wise or necessary, and try to reach prudent decisions.

Judges were to be honest, upright, reliable men elected be-

---

[40]*Ibid.*, p. 141.
[41]*Ibid.*, p. 143.

cause of these virtues by the people, to serve for a period of three years. They were to act under the supervision of the court of justice to which villagers would otherwise appeal.

The plan as proposed, approved, and put into action was officially added to the Six-Point plan of 1963, as the ninth principle on October 13, 1965. Although the first house of equity was formed in December 1963, in the village of Mehyar near Esfahan, as a prototype, by 1967 the number of such institutions had risen to eight hundred and many more have been established in the ensuing years.

Three more principles were added in 1967 to the nine discussed: *Nationalization of Water Resources, Urban and Rural Reconstruction*, and *Administrative and Educational Reform*.

Two more points were added in 1975, bringing the total to fourteen. The thirteenth point requires privately owned and government factories, as well as other large industrial complexes, to sell a percentage of their shares to workers first, with the understanding that unsold shares will thereafter be sold to the general public. In the case of government factories the percentage of shares to be sold to workers and general public is over ninety percent.

The fourteenth point, added in August, was initiated to protect the consumer from unethical practices of profiteering by big business. As a result, wholesale prices during that month decreased 2.8%, while retail prices went down 2.2%.

The White Revolution must stand as one of the Shah's greatest achievements during his entire reign to date. It was approved and put into action without bloodshed in spite of overt demonstrations by a segment of the people whose unethical practices were threatened.

Through these principles, His Majesty exhibited deep compassion for his people who were oppressed by a greedy few, ingenuity and foresight in pointing the way to solve problems besetting the many, and courage to face the consequences of his sweeping reforms. Quoting the Shah, "For the first time, the vast Iranian masses, in the villages, factories and elsewhere, need no longer fear that threatening shadow which was once called the power of the thousand families."[42]

---

[42]*Ibid.*, p. 152.

Since the Revolution's inception, approximately 125,000 young men and women, members of the Health Corps, the Literacy Corps and the Reconstruction and Development Corps, have been sent to remote villages of Iran to wage war against the farmers' common enemies: disease, ignorance and poverty. The achievements of the Literacy Corps alone are phenomenal. Through the years Corpsmen have been responsible for building more than 15,000 new schools as well as repairing and remodeling over 3,000 existing ones; members have helped to carry out construction and repair of over 144,000 roads, planted almost four million trees and installed over 7,000 postboxes. They have dredged 25,000 qanats, built more than 50,000 bridges, drilled almost 80,000 wells and built more than 3,000 mosques. But most important of all, they have taught a million children, and more than half that number of adults, to read and write.

Realizing that one facet of the life of the villagers still lacked fulfillment, in September 1968 the Shahanshah promoted the formation of a National Association of Rural Cultural Houses, ordaining the Crown Prince as its honorary president.

The basic idea of the project was to establish centers in rural areas in which the villagers could spend some of their leisure time and receive information about major happenings in the nation and in the world, as well as the latest news in the development of cooperative community projects. Here it was hoped that the villagers could learn more of their country's history as well as its goals for the future.

General social recreation was to be encouraged, along with a plan for organized athletics; native handicrafts, for which the Persians are noted, were to have a place in the overall program.

The project was planned to depend largely on voluntary participation and giving, backed by the Government under the general supervision of the office of the Minister of Land Reform and Rural Cooperation.

Within a year about a hundred and fifty cultural houses had been constructed and were in operation—a promising beginning.

Late in 1972, the farmers of rural cooperative societies proposed a movement to hold a national Congress to commemorate the tenth anniversary of the White Revolution, to review its achievements, and to work out plans for the next decade. Trade unions then issued a statement supporting the proposal, and were followed

Point Five (Equal and Universal Suffrage for Iranian Women): Women voting in Tehran, 1964 *(Photo courtesy Pars News Agency, Tehran)*

Point Nine (House of Equity): A scene in a village court, where the rule of enlightened modern law is brought to the villagers *(Photo courtesy Pars News Agency, Tehran)*

Point One (Land Reform): Village elder receives land deeds from the Shah at Khoramabad, 1964 *(Photo courtesy Pars News Agency, Tehran)*

Point Eight (Development and Agricultural Extension Corps): An extension corpsman and a farmer see the results of their effort—better crops *(Photo courtesy Pars News Agency, Tehran)*

Point Six (Education Corps): Villagers visit schoolhouse they have built themselves under the supervision of Education Corpsmen *(Photo courtesy Pars News Agency, Tehran)*

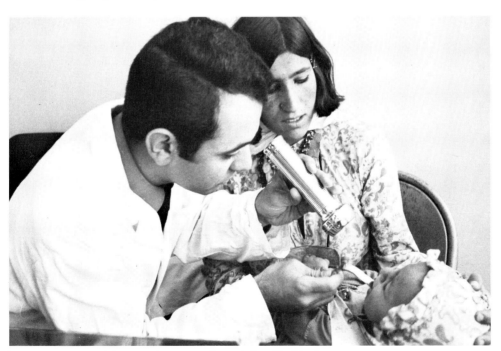

Point Seven (Health Corps): A member of the Health Corps examining a baby in a village *(Photo courtesy Pars News Agency, Tehran)*

Point Ten (Nationalization of Water Resources): Shah Abbas the Great Dam near Esfahan *(Photo courtesy Pars News Agency, Tehran)*

A view of the first steel mill plant in Esfahan, built in 1972 *(Photo courtesy Pars News Agency, Tehran)*

Shah and Queen at the inauguration ceremony of Shah Abbas the Great Dam, Esfahan *(Photo courtesy Pars News Agency, Tehran)*

A view of Abadan Refinery, the largest in the world *(Photo courtesy Pars News Agency, Tehran)*

Point Twelve (Administrative and Educational Reorganization): The Shah and Queen Farah presiding over Ramsar Conference for evaluation of educational reforms, 1975 (*Photo courtesy Pars News Agency, Tehran*)

Queen Farah inspecting a newly built kindergarten in Tehran, 1975 (*Photo courtesy Pars News Agency, Tehran*)

Iranian students studying abroad, who return to Iran during their summer vacation, are usually received by the Shah and Shahbanou. Their majesties inquire as to their progress, as shown in both photos taken in 1967 at the Sa'ad Abad Palace, Tehran. *(Photo courtesy Iran Press Photographers Association)*

Point Four (Profit-Sharing for Workers): Iranian minister of Labor hands over labor's share of corporate earnings in a ceremony in Tehran, 1973 (*Photo courtesy Pars News Agency, Tehran*)

Point Eleven (Reconstruction of Urban and Rural Areas): Ninth Aba District outside Tehran—an example of low-cost housing in Iran

The Shah, Queen and Crown Prince of Iran following coronation ceremonies at Golestan Palace, Tehran, October 26, 1967 (*Photo courtesy Iran
Press Photographers Association*)

Monument recording the twelve articles of the Revolution of the Shah and the People

Iran National Automobile plant in Tehran—second largest plant in auto-bus production in the world, 1975

Shahbanou Farah Dam in Gilan, 1975

New highway in Kurdestan, 1975

Modern farming technique in Khor-asan, 1975

Courtyard of Shah Abbas Hotel in Esfahan—one of the most beautiful and unusual hotels in the world

Qashghai tribal girls learning the fine art of tribal carpet weaving

One of the lounges in the Shah Abbas Hotel, decorated with magnificent Persian art

Qashghai girls weaving a tribal carpet in carpet-weaving school at Shiraz

by organizations such as the National Union of Guilds, educational councils, the Iranian Woman's Organization, local government authorities, and student groups. People in all walks of life enthusiastically supported the movement.

In an editorial published in *Kayhan International* on November 28, 1972, the writer made this statement:

> One point needs to be made again and again . . . The revolution is not something of the past; nor is it something ceremonial. Thus the opportunity offered by its tenth anniversary should see us work for the enlargement of the revolution's scope and aims.
>
> It should provide the entire nation with a new rallying point for the purpose of carrying out new revolutionary reforms in a number of new social and economic domains.

Thousands of teachers, students, industrial workers and farmers gathered at a meeting in Tehran to endorse the Revolution and to declare their willingness to participate in celebrating its tenth anniversary. They paraded in the streets of Tehran carrying slogans and playing trumpets and drums, thereby publicly demonstrating their support of the Revolution of the Shah and the People.

The Educational Council of Iran decided to build a 5000-student educational complex in South Tehran to commemorate the anniversary.

Similar activities celebrating the tenth anniversary of the Revolution took place across the country even in the most remote areas. Through public displays and constructive activities, the Iranian people in a united front reaffirmed their dedication to the continuation of the revolution's "scopes and aims"—looking forward with optimism to further social and economic reforms in the years ahead.

In a series of interviews by *Kayhan International* concerning the Revolution, Court Minister Assadollah Alam (Prime Minister when the Shah launched his Charter of the Revolution), commented that the liberation of Azarbaijan after World War II epitomized the unity of the Shah and the people. This historic event planted the seed for drawing His Majesty and his people more closely together. He further commented that previous monarchs had sought to reform the structure of Iranian society based on feudalism, but had not succeeded. He felt that the basic reason for the Shah's success was that he depended on the masses to implement his reform.

The Congress, initially proposed by the farmers, was held in Tehran between January 21 and 23, 1973, in the middle of the week of celebrations across the land, marking the tenth anniversary. It was attended by 5,000 representatives—863 from Tehran, and the remaining 4,137 from the provinces.

During the Congress, Premier Amir Abbas Hoveyda commented that what Iran had done in the past decade and what it would be doing in the years ahead should be considered "preparatory work for the era of the Great Civilization."

The term "Great Civilization" was not coined by Premier Hoveyda, but by the Shah, to describe the new type of society he has often said the Iranian people are capable of constructing. Hoveyda continued to say, "Those who say God is great and will look after the believers are right in the first part of their assertion. God, indeed, is great, but he does not look after believers who do not work, who do not contribute to life."

It would appear then, that the result of the efforts of the Iranian people to achieve the "Great Civilization," building on the foundation of the White Revolution, depends on the truth found in the well-known American adage "God helps those who help themselves." As the great Persian poet Sa'di has said,

> To leaven mortar of quicklime with the hands
> Is better than to hold them on the breast before the amir.[43]

---

[43]Edward Rehatsek (translator), *The Gulistan of Sa'di:* New York, G. P. Putna Sons, 1964, p. 109.

14

The Coronation

By the mid-sixties significant changes had taken place in Iran: the farmer had become a farmer instead of a serf as had been the case in the past; the worker enjoyed the privileges of a modern worker; illiteracy had been conquered to a great extent; problems of health and hygiene had been lessened and medical aid had become a right for all, rather than a privilege for a small segment of the population. Better housing, justice for the common man as well as for the man of wealth and influence, mass transit, free education and agricultural advances in such things as irrigation had come about as the result of the diligent efforts of the Shah, his government and the people of Iran to achieve a minimum standard of living for all.

Women of Iran had been given the right of franchise—a far cry from the days when they were never seen outside their homes with their faces uncovered. When Reza Shah in 1936 requested that his wife and two daughters attend an official ceremony with him, unveiled (referred to in Chapter Two), he made a brief speech. Among other comments regarding the place of women in society he said, "We must not imagine indefinitely that one-half of the community of our nation need not be taken into account."

Lifting of the veil, however, was more than a symbolic gesture for Iranian women. It marked the beginning of an era in the Pahlavi dynasty when women were to achieve equal rights with men. In

1966, a bill was drafted designed to grant wives greater rights and near-equality with their husbands. The bill, which eventually became law, deprives the husband of his inalienable right to divorce his wife at will, or to dominate her life as was the usual practice previous to this time.

As might be expected, the liberated women formed all types of organizations and societies where they could exchange information and opinions on important matters. In 1966, all these associations united under the name Iranian Women's Organization, under the patronage of Princess Ashraf, the Shah's twin sister. About seven hundred delegates attended the first general conference in Tehran on October 30, 1966. According to a 1973 publication entitled *The Revolutionizing of Iran,*

> The Iranian Women's Organization now has nine research and planning committees engaged in the preparation of draft projects. A legal committee undertakes continuous research into the legal status of women, supplying ammunition for campaigns to initiate new legislation on women's rights. An education committee studies new ways of promoting literacy among women. A health and family welfare committee supervises clinics, children's homes and family planning centres. An employment committee deals with the problems of employed women and questions of discrimination. An international affairs committee establishes contacts with women's organizations around the world. A cultural committee promotes and encourages women artists and musicians. A membership committee coordinates the activities of societies affiliated with the organization. A women university students' committee directs women graduates into more active participation in the Revolution. And a public relations committee acquaints the people with the importance and scope of these activities.[44]

In the early years of his reign, the Shah is reputed to have said, "It is not a mere pleasure to wear the crown of such a poor people." And so, it would appear that he delayed the day of coronation until the chain of events presented the right occasion. After twenty-six years on the throne, His Majesty decided that the time had come. The date was set for October 26, 1967, the fourth of Aban in the year 1346 Persian chronology, coinciding with his forty-eighth birthday.

A glance at the Constitution of Iran provides an insight as to

---

[44]Gregory Lima, Keith McLachlan, Pauline Jackson, Hushang Mehr Ayin, Amir Taheri and Kazem Zarnegar, *The Revolutionizing of Iran,* published by International Communicators Iran (INACO Ltd.), Tehran, 1973, pp. 104-105.

the significance of the occasion of the coronation. Article 37 (as amended December 12, 1925) reads:

> The (right of) succession to the Throne shall rest with the eldest son of the Monarch, whose mother must be of Iranian origin. If the Monarch has no male child, the nomination of the Crown Prince shall be made at the suggestion of the Monarch and with the approval of the National Consultative Assembly, on condition that this Crown Prince shall not be a member of the Qajar family; but at any time, if a son is born to the Monarch, he shall be Crown Prince by right.

The amending of Article 38 on September 9, 1967, paved the way for the memorable event that was to take place the following month during the coronation. It reads:

> In the event of the transfer of the Throne, the Crown Prince shall personally perform the functions of Monarch when he has reached twenty years of age (to be calculated on the basis of the solar year). If he has not reached that age, the Shahbanu,° mother of the Crown Prince, shall assume the Regency, unless another person shall have been designated by the Monarch for that office. The Regent shall form a Council composed of the Prime Minister, the Heads of both Houses of Parliament, the Chief Justice of the Supreme Court and four other sagacious, reputable personalities of the country to be selected by the Regent, and (the Regent) shall, in accordance with the Constitution, assume the duties of Monarch in consultation with the Council until (such time as) the Crown Prince reaches the age of twenty. In the event of the demise or resignation of the Regent, the Council shall temporarily carry out the duties of the Regency until another Regent—not a member of the Qajar family—is appointed by the Houses of Parliament. Remarriage by the Shahbanu Regent shall constitute resignation (from Regency).

Persian women had come a long way toward equality with men since 1936, when they were emancipated by Reza Shah. And the country, since 1941, when Mohammad Reza Pahlavi took the reins of government in that turbulent time, had passed through amazing changes affecting every stratum of society. It had been a time of unparalleled progress in Iranian history for both men and women. And now the stage was set for the long-awaited coronation.

As one writer has said, the sumptuous ceremony was "like a fairy-tale from the Thousand and One Nights." The seven-year-

---

°Shahbanu is the Persian word for Queen.

old Crown Prince Reza was the first of the three principals to enter the Hall in Golestan Palace. Wearing his full-dress cadet uniform with the golden laces for the first time, he proceeded with great poise to the left of the ornate Peacock Throne, said to be decorated with 26,733 jewels.

Exactly three minutes later, Empress Farah entered the Hall, escorted by six maids of honor, and took her place at the right of the throne. As is traditionally prescribed by protocol, another three minutes passed before His Majesty, the Shahanshah, entered, preceded by commanders of the Army, Air Force and Navy, and the chief of the Superior Commander's Staff, with drawn swords. His Majesty proceeded to the throne followed by a high-ranking Iranian general carrying his crown, and another carrying the crown for the Empress.

The Shah's 10,400-carat crown, which is the one that had been placed on the head of his father, Reza Shah the Great, in 1925, resembles those of ancient Persia. It gleams with 3,380 diamonds, 5 emeralds, 2 sapphires and 368 pearls.

Empress Farah's crown was created in the museum of crown jewels in Tehran by the well-known Parisian jeweler Pierre Arpels, who, following suggestions made by the extremely artistic Empress herself, created a design combining old Persian tradition and modern design. It is constructed of six circular ornaments, is 15 centimeters high and weighs 1,600 grams. The crown is luxuriously ornamented with 1,469 diamonds, 36 emeralds, 36 rubies, 105 pearls, and an indescribably beautiful hexagon emerald of 150 carats.

A fanfare of trumpets announced that the ceremony was about to begin, and the Imperial Flag was hoisted in front of the Palace. The highest clerical dignitary of Tehran, the Imam Juma, blessed the Shah, who then raised the Holy Koran (brought to him by a member of the Imperial Guard) to his lips, and touched it against his forehead. The Imperial Insignia were then presented to him. Next the glittering crown was extended to the Shah, who lifted it from its embroidered cushion, raised it, then lowered it slowly to rest on his head. Two officers brought forward a golden belt with an egg-sized emerald buckle, and the "all conquering" sword, jeweled with emeralds, diamonds and rubies. These he fastened on "with a dexterity that betrayed hours of practice" according to one reporter. He then received the gold scepter in his right hand.

A salute of 101 guns was fired to announce to the crowds outside the palace and throughout the capital city and all over the country that Persia had, at last, a crowned Emperor!

Farah then rose, looking regal in her sweeping white satin gown, and stepped forward to face the throne. The maids of honor followed, carrying the Coronation Cape. Farah slowly knelt before the Shah, lowering her head, and with the help of two attendants, she donned the Cape, made of deep-green velvet and trimmed with white mink. The Cape was a masterpiece of design, decorated with old Persian flower motifs, the Imperial Arms, and ornamented with precious jewels. It had been richly embroidered by Iranian seamstresses.

After the Cape was adjusted, Assadollah Alam, Minister of the Imperial Court, presented the blue velvet cushion on which rested the Shahbanu's magnificent crown. The Shah had said previously, "The most important day in my life shall also be the great day in the life of my consort." He made it so by carefully placing the crown on Farah's high-piled coiffure. The Empress showed her emotion and a deep awareness of the significance of the occasion through tear-filled eyes as she arose and resumed her place at the right of the throne. Prime Minister Hoveyda was the first to step forward to tender congratulations to the Imperial Couple.

To the music of the coronation hymn, the Shah walked into the garden of the Palace, treading the traditional red carpet, with other members of the party following. He was greeted with a smart salute of the Guard of Honor, and officials present bowed in respect to their newly crowned Emperor. The Shahbanu followed with her attending maids of honor.

When the strikingly handsome and winsome Crown Prince Reza appeared in the garden, looking every inch a prince, he too received an enthusiastic ovation. Soldierly in his cadet uniform, he marched in the procession, keeping step with the whispered cadence of a military aide.

The Shah, Shahbanu and Crown Prince then entered a golden coach, drawn by eight white horses, and drove through the streets as thousands of Persians expressed their joy by shouting "Long live the Shah! Long live the Shahbanu!"

As a matter of interest, the coach was a reproduction of the one used by the Hapsburg Dynasty in Austria. It was constructed by the famous craftsman Josef Kliemann in Vienna. To be flown to

Tehran, it had to be taken apart and the pieces packed in great trunks, and subsequently reassembled in Iran.

The priceless jewels worn by the Shah and Empress are the property of the state and usually rest in Bank Melli Iran (Central Bank of Iran), where they help back the country's currency. They represent the most valuable collection of crown jewels in the world, and so are a great attraction to foreign visitors in Iran.

Empress Farah now symbolized the epitome of the heights to which an Iranian woman might rise and what she might become: not only consort to the monarch, but in case of his demise, Regent —leader of her country.

Following is an excerpt from the address delivered by the Shah on coronation day:

> I thank God the Almighty that I am granted the privilege of serving my people to the best of my ability, as Shahanshah of Persia, and I ask Him for granting me His guidance also for the future for a continued successful service. It is the only aim of my life to improve the welfare of Persia and the Persian nation. It is my most profound desire to preserve the independence and sovereignty of my country, to transform the Persian nation into one of the most progressive and prosperous peoples of the world, and to renew the old splendour of this historical country. For this aim I shall, as I always did, stake everything, even my life.
>
> At this moment in which I wear the crown of the oldest monarchy in the world, and the Shahbanu was crowned for the first time in the history of Iran, I feel more than ever before united with my noble and patriotic people, and I pray that God's grace may protect it.[45]

To mark further that memorable day in October, 383 schools were inaugurated in Persia.

Iranians set aside an entire week to celebrate. The initial social event, which took place on the evening of the coronation in Tehran, was the inauguration of the new Rudaki Theatre, named for one of Persia's most highly honored poets, Abu Abdallah Rudaki, who lived from 858 to 941. As was fitting, the concert was performed by Persian artists.

The following day, the Shah and Empress were honored by a spectacle lasting four hours at the Amjadieh Stadium. In addition to a parade by military units, Girl Guides demonstrated gymnastics with thousands of replicas of the Imperial Crown. Also, six hun-

---

[45]Burda Druck and Verlag Offenburg, *Coronation in Tehran, The Imperial Couple of Persia*, printed in West Germany, p. 4.

dred boys, from sports clubs across the land, formed immense mosaic-style pictures of the royal couple and the crown with paper shields (in the manner of organized "rooting" sections at major football games in the United States).

At the invitation of the Minister of the Imperial Court Alam, the Shah and Empress were feted at a reception at the Royal Tehran Hilton Hotel, which was followed by a national festival. Dance groups from all over Iran were there—including tribesmen such as the Kurds and Turkomen—wearing their picturesque peasant costumes. Tribal women in bright dresses and wearing gold ornaments, and men in colored blouses and velvet vests and wearing turban or fez, danced to the flute and tambourine in the fast tempo and wild abandonment of the mountain people.

To climax the excitement of the evening, several tons of fireworks were shot into the air by master pyrotechnists, illuminating the night sky with Iran's national colors, green, white and red.

A few days later the Imperial Couple entered the shrine at Mashad (the tomb of Imam Reza, the eighth Imam of Shi'ah Moslems), to join in a celebration of thanksgiving.

The coronation marked the "coming of age" of the country, as one author expressed it, and symbolized to the world that Iran, under His Majesty's guidance, had become a leader in the family of nations in the Middle East.

In addition, the monarch had broken all precedents in Iran by crowning the Empress as Regent, thereby symbolizing his high regard for women in general, and recognizing the equality of the sexes in the area of intellect and the ability to cope with political and economic problems besetting a head of state.

Empress Farah has, without a doubt, lived up to the Shah's expectations of her as his consort. Her study in Paris (previous to her marriage) and her extensive travel throughout the world have given her an enviable international background; she has always been impeccably groomed; and from the day of her marriage she has appeared to be dedicated to helping her husband fulfill his hopes for the people of their country. Long before the coronation she participated in public events, and was deeply involved in bettering the life of all Iranians.

One of her greatest contributions to Iran lies in her patronage of the arts—particularly those reflecting the traditional culture of the Persian people. (More of this in Chapter Sixteen.)

Looking to the future when Crown Prince Reza will ascend the throne, the Shah and Empress exert rigid discipline over their son (as well as their other children) for "who later has to command, must first obey."

The Shah recalls, in his book *Mission for My Country*, his early education following the coronation ceremony (when he was six years of age). His father, Reza Shah, directed that he should be given a "manly education." And after the boy reached the age of nine, the two spent an hour or more together every day, as the Shah says, "to make sure I was well acquainted with everything that was going on."

Like his father, Crown Prince Reza has, since early childhood, received royal tutelage and frequently takes an active part in the ceremonial affairs of the country.

Headlines in the *Iran Times* (July 4, 1975) eloquently stated the relationship between the Shah and his eldest son at the time: "Prince Reza: 'I'm my father's apprentice.'"

The story under the headlines dealt with the graduation ceremonies at the Reza Pahlavi School, where the fifteen-year-old prince had just finished the first grade of comprehensive secondary school with the outstanding average of 17.11 out of 20.

In an interview with the reporter the prince (whose education includes politics and protocol in addition to the regular curriculum) said, "I am a political apprentice to my father. I ask for his views on all affairs. I know protocol procedures well."

The reporter reminded him that on one occasion nine years previously he had asked him if he knew what the term "Crown Prince" meant and received the reply, "It means I will grow up, and help my Dad." To this Prince Reza smiled and said, "Now I know much more about what I should do."

He particularly enjoys history and geography, and is deeply interested in electrical and mechanical engineering. During the year he had made a transformer and a radio entirely on his own.

His discerning mind was evidenced in his answer to a question put to him by the reporter as to what he considered the characteristics of a good friend: He commented: "You used the word *friend* which itself says all there is to say. There is no such thing as a bad friend."

Returning to the coronation year, 1967—an editor on the staff of *National Geographic*, Franc Shor, in his coverage of the coronation in the magazine, reminisced about a day eighteen years previously when the Shah had said to him, "I inherited a crown. Before I put it on, I want to earn it."

His Majesty *had* earned the crown on that day in 1967; and when he declared Empress Farah Regent and formally presented the seven-year-old Reza as Crown Prince, heir to the throne, he established without a doubt the continuation of the Pahlavi Dynasty, thereby fulfilling the wishes of his people.

15
Slings and Arrows

Challenges confronting an official cameraman are numerous and varied, whether he is accompanying his monarch on a formal state visit or a domestic inspection. Fundamentals of protocol, a knowledge of customs of the people of a host country, cognizance of the importance of irreproachable personal behavior, as well as one's mastery of his profession pursued under pressure and in trying situations, are all factors to be taken seriously.

The film reporter must, first of all, be alert at all times. He must be "all eyes and ears," watching and listening for anything that might be of general interest or of special significance. The manner in which heads of state meet (in a cordial or merely formally polite fashion), the amount of pomp surrounding a head of state's visit reflecting the degree of importance given to it, the overt shaking of hands between representatives of nations emerging from a cold war status—all such things can be regarded as symbolic of the state of relations between nations, and will be so interpreted by news reporters, analysts, writers of editorials, and by the common run-of-the-mill newspaper readers and television viewers.

The film reporter cannot indulge in the luxury of prolonged social conversation or general sightseeing while "on duty." He cannot allow himself to be diverted from the important job to which he has been assigned.

In addition, he must at all times present the truth. One might

227

think that merely photographing what one sees is synonymous with presenting the truth, but such is not the case. For instance in photographing and/or editing his film, the cameraman can come out with footage that depicts a state visit as a round of glamourous festivities, playing down the serious intent of the coming together of men dedicated to ironing out differences, working toward greater cooperation, negotiating trade agreements, signing treaties, and so forth. He can overemphasize poor conditions in a country, or present a false picture of general overall affluence.

In the case of coverage of a domestic event, the cameraman has the same responsibility for showing all sides of the story, allowing the viewer to arrive at his own conclusions in case there are areas of conflict. His task, indeed, is film journalism.

The film reporter must be able to make quick decisions as to whether a scene or sequence merits a place in the final coverage. (This was particularly true in the early fifties when we were forced to consider the cost of raw materials that had to be imported.) He cannot let that poignant scene, that significant facial expression or gesture, that moment of meeting, that surprise happening escape his camera. Such footage, if lost, can never be retrieved.

Above all, the film journalist must love his work, for he must be able to survive under great stress with the whip of time at his back. He must be willing to dedicate long hours to the job with little chance for rest on certain assignments, and must adjust to irregular demanding schedules, finding his personal satisfaction in imaginative, though truthful, coverage for his audiences.

The official cameraman (upon entering a country) is given (by his host country) a press kit, program of events, and a list of places to be visited, most of which may have little meaning for him at the time.* Therefore it is necessary for him to find answers to many questions in record time. If the situation between the two nations is in delicate balance, he is usually apprised by proper officials of his own country as to what is expected by all members of the entourage.

It is highly desirable that the film reporter arrive in the country to be visited by his head of state, a few days beforehand to acquaint himself with the geography of the area. For example, if he is

---

*Such programs, although prepared well in advance and with utmost care, are kept confidential by both countries until the time of arrival, for security reasons.

scheduled to be at a certain place to photograph the beginning of a ceremony at nine A.M., he should know how much time to allow to get himself from his hotel to that location at least half an hour before events begin. He must ask himself questions such as: will filming be difficult at this hour? Will extra lighting be necessary at the location? From what position can I get the best angle? In other words, he should have time to "case" the sites where he will be photographing if it is at all possible. Forty-five minutes after he has completed his nine o'clock assignment, he may be photographing another scheduled event—the laying of a wreath or something of the sort—with no time to adjust to the new situation, if he has not had an opportunity to see the place in advance. And so it goes during the day and into the night.

I am thinking particularly of the fifties and sixties during the time I photographed the Shah's official state visits with no assistants. I was my own light man, my own sound man, scriptwriter and advance man. I carried my own equipment, which became almost intolerably heavy during a long full day. I was never privileged to enjoy the convenience of the compact lightweight equipment of today's television newsreel crew—with one or two assistants on hand, and a station wagon full of back-up equipment.

It is a personal characteristic of mine that the project in which I am deeply involved takes my complete attention, and I have little consciousness of the passing of time or what may be transpiring around me that is unrelated to what I am doing. Upon my return from a state visit, as I viewed my film for the first time (with an eye to editing it), I said to myself, "Aha! So *that's* where I was! *That's* what the Shah did! *That* is what he saw!" and I thoroughly enjoyed my trip—sitting in my viewing room, looking at the coverage as it unfolded before my eyes.

In those countries where everything is done "according to the book," knowledge of customs and procedures is most essential for members of the entourage—particularly the press party. In spite of the tremendous importance of detailed briefings on state visits, we were not always thus informed. However, each of us realized that we were representing the people of Iran through our personal behavior as well as through the excellence of our work.

An important part of state visits is the exchange of gifts between the two heads of the countries. The visiting head of state presents gifts representative of his country. Gifts are also given to local officials. The Iranian party generally offered Persian carpets, silverware, handcrafted furniture, and other products typical of Iran. Sometimes it required two cargo planes to accommodate such gifts taken with us on formal visits.

Gifts are also presented to the members of the entourage as "souvenirs" of their stay in the country. The President of Turkey and the Shah had exchanged decorations and gifts during our visit there, and the press party had gone on to the airport to prepare for departure. While we were waiting for the Shah to arrive, the Chief of Protocol suddenly arrived and presented a Movado watch to each of us. There was no inscription or insignia of any kind on the timepiece, as is sometimes the case in such instances. It could well be that it suddenly occurred to the Chief of Protocol that the working press in the entourage had not been remembered, and he may have called his jeweler in Ankara and said, "Get me half a dozen Movado watches pronto! We forgot the press party!" We appreciated the gesture nevertheless, and I have cherished that watch, which I still use.

Perhaps one of my most treasured gifts from a head of state is a heavy solid gold Omega watch with a picture of King Saud on the dial. Unlike the entourage that goes with the President of the United States on his more important state visits, numbering perhaps two hundred (television, radio and press representatives), the group with the Shah usually numbered about twenty-five. A gift of that many solid gold watches from a man as wealthy as King Saud was nothing at all! (In years back, the kings and sultans in some of the countries of the Middle East gave *slave girls* as gifts!)

The film reporter must always think of the expediency of putting a film together because an item which is news today will be history tomorrow. For that reason and in order to economize on raw stock in my newsreel coverages, I often tried to "cut the film in the camera" rather than shooting perhaps three or four times as much footage as I would include in the finished product. Following this plan, I was able to save valuable time as well as film.

I remember one incident in which I exerted myself to complete a film and have it ready for viewing in the shortest possible time. In the late fifties, I accompanied the Shah to Tabriz, the capital of Azarbaijan, where His Majesty was scheduled to inaugurate the Tehran-Tabriz railroad linkage. The cross-country railway in Iran,

Persian miniature painting

Inauguration ceremonies of the 2500th anniversary of the founding of the Persian Empire by Cyrus the Great

(Photos courtesy of the Iranian Ministry of Culture and Arts)

Part of the parade, representing ten dynasties of Persian history, during the 2500th anniversary celebration

The seventh Asian Games held at Aryamehr Stadium, Tehran, 1974

Persian miniature painting

joining the Persian Gulf to the Caspian Sea, built during Reza Shah's era, had never been connected to important cities such as Tabriz and Esfahan.

Our party arrived in Tabriz one day before the inauguration ceremonies were to take place. The following afternoon at exactly four o'clock, the Tehran-Tabriz railway train arrived at the Tabriz station. I photographed the Shah's official inauguration of the new railway line in a ceremony that lasted about two hours, using the procedure of cutting the film in the camera. The nearest laboratory was more than seven hundred miles away (in Tehran). While the last part of the ceremony was in progress, I wrote out instructions for processing and for the addition of sound. The package was given to the trainmaster who was leaving on the same train back to Tehran. The film arrived early the next morning in Tehran, where it was picked up, developed, printed and the sound track added. The following evening it was returned to me by air to Tabriz.

A projector and the film were ready when the curtain came down on a play given at the officers' club with the Shah in attendance. We invited him and his party to an adjoining room where a number of people had already assembled, and presented the film showing His Majesty's arrival in Tabriz and the ceremonies involving the inauguration of the railroad line—events that had taken place less than thirty hours before. All things considered—our handmade facilities, the distance to the nearest (and only) laboratory at that time—it was a record performance. Reaction to the feat was somewhat like that of viewers watching television's first showing of instant replays on the football field or baseball diamond.

During my years with the USIS in Tehran, although my prime responsibility was film, I was called upon to cope with a number of different situations. One concerned a trip I made in 1964 with American Ambassador Julius C. Holmes down the Persian Gulf coast aboard the U.S. destroyer *Bache*. Because of some unusual circumstances, I had to play a dual role: that of still photographer and interpreter. The trip began at Khorramshahr, and during the week we made official stops at the ports of Bushehre, Khark Island, Bandar Lengeh, Bandar Abbass, Hormuz Island and Chahbahar. We then flew to the city of Zahedan, and back to the capital city, Tehran. Visits to these various places followed a similar pattern. The Ambassador and his staff were welcomed by the Governor, along with perhaps forty to fifty local officials. Visits were then made to the government offices and local facilities. The Ambassador was usually honored by a luncheon or reception; gifts were exchanged; and at departure time, another set of short speeches was delivered. In Bandar Abbass, for example, Mr. Holmes had to give no less than eighteen speeches to local officials, schoolteachers and children.

In an office memorandum (dated March 5, 1964) directed to Dr. Henry F. Arnold, Counselor of Embassy for Public Affairs, Ambassador Holmes outlined details of the Persian Gulf trip and commended my efforts in a very courteous and graphic manner: "As a photographer he was indefatigable and extraordinarily alert. He sought and used the proper angles for photographing regardless of the climbing, running or scrambling this entailed. He was assiduous in assuring that every local official of any import whatsoever was included in at least one photograph—in appropriate relation to the principals present."

The following statement from his memo is included (risking accusations of undue self-congratulations) to point up the grave responsibility of the interpreter in cross-cultural communications: "Mr. Issari performed with efficiency and despatch his ambidextrous job of interpreting and photographing. His interpreting—both of what I said and what was said to me—was prompt and accurate with all due attention to the nuances which provide the grace notes on such occasions."

The reason for my dual appointment in this instance was a rather odd one. Several people were added to the Ambassador's entourage at the last minute, leaving only one seat in the plane that was to take his party to Khorramshahr (the point of embarkation on the U.S. ship) for two people: the photographer and the interpreter. The problem was turned over to me, and after futile attempts to recruit someone to take the difficult assignment, I decided to step into the breach and offer my services.

It is difficult to translate for a man without knowing his thinking and the background against which his remarks are being made. I was faced with the handicap of not knowing Ambassador Holmes as well as I should in a situation such as this. At the beginning of the trip along the Persian coast, I saw him at meals with ship officials, but had no chance to talk with him personally and to know the man as I wished to know him. On our first stop (at Bushehre) I translated his speech into Persian as well as I could, but I did not feel satisfied with the job.

After we boarded the ship I said, "Mr. Ambassador, I would like to talk with you a few minutes—about my translating for you."

"Of course," he replied.

I continued, "I would like to ask your permission not to translate what you say word for word, but to try to convey to the Iranians the philosophy behind what you say. The thought does not really come through when I translate word for word, or even sentence for sentence. If you could tell me beforehand roughly what it is you want to tell these people—in a very few words—and then give me permission to give the people a free translation, I feel sure we can do a much better job of communicating."

He agreed wholeheartedly with the arrangement and went as far as to say, "If you think that something I say is inappropriate, don't translate it." The system worked out very well throughout the remainder of the trip.

A filmmaker must be aware of all the characteristics of his target audience in order to communicate with them effectively. Knowing some of the cultural differences between the Iranian and American audiences, I used different filmic techniques for the two.

For instance, it has been my observation that Persians are more lavish in their use of descriptive words. The American may say, "That's very nice," while the Persian may say of the same thing, "That's marvelous! It's really beautiful!" Visually, a Persian prefers a shot or scene to be longer in duration than does an American. For example, a twenty-minute documentary film made for a Persian audience could be cut down to fifteen minutes for an American audience without losing anything in either the audio or video content of the film. One reason for the failure of some foreign films with Persian subtitles in Iran is that Iranians generally seem to have slower visual perception.

On the other hand, I believe that Persians in one-to-one communication are highly perceptive and can usually jump ahead of the speaker, anticipating what he is going to say. In Iran we have a saying, "When you began *F*, I knew you meant *Farahzad*," meaning that the word was heard almost before it was uttered. Admittedly I am not a trained sociologist but these and other social and cultural differences which I observed were taken into consideration while making films.

With these cultural differences in mind, I always panned a scene differently for the two audiences. The Iranian writes from right to left, the American from left to right. An American watching a picture panned from right to left (with no action to follow) will feel as though he is swimming against the current rather than with it. The same will be true of the Iranian if the direction is reversed, making him view a scene panned from left to right.

In the very early years of movie distribution via mobile units, people in remote areas, who had never seen a film before, registered very surprising and varied reactions. (One example concerns the man mentioned earlier who insisted that the Shah had spoken to him directly from the screen.)

A strange reaction, although a bit humorous, is described in Peter Hopkinson's *Role of Film Development.** He tells the reader that about twenty years ago a professor from a university in Brussels carried out an experiment in Africa to test the influence of motion pictures on people exposed to them for the first time. In one film the villagers were shown (step by step) how a knife, measuring about six inches in length, was made on a blacksmith's forge. One village craftsman made such a knife after seeing the film three times, carefully watching the process. It was correct in every way, but was four times as big as the one depicted on the screen, for this was the way it appeared to the man.

The reaction of the people in the villages of Iran to the film on the malaria-bearing mosquito (referred to in Chapter Five) is, of course, a case in point. Mosquitoes in their village (they thought) were not gigantic like those in the city!

An official cinematographer must be something of a diplomat and know the intricacies of good public relations. Problems of protocol may sometimes be "sticky," when visitors are not aware that a given behavior is not acceptable in the host country (and can create problems for the official cameraman). The whole area of protocol is sensitive, although the system is based on good common sense.

In the early days of my career I discovered that American protocol is much more relaxed than that of the traditional, formal Persian court. The difference was noted particularly on a visit to Tehran by John Foster Dulles, Secretary of State of the United States. Like the Japanese, the Iranians are instinctively a very polite people. When Mr. Dulles conferred with the Shah, he in-

---

*This book was written under the auspices of UNESCO and published in France in 1971.

variably sat with his legs crossed—a sign of disrespect, according to Iran's strict rules of court behavior. To show the Persian people a picture of this high representative of the United States government in this disrespectful posture while in the presence of the Shah would have triggered an unpleasant reaction—a reaction based on an unhappy period of history. As far back as a century before, the country was under the political dominance of Great Britain and Russia. The Persian kings were forced to listen to and acquiesce to proposals from the British or Russian ambassadors, for ultimate power lay with these two countries. Fear of foreign influence still lingers in the minds of the people. And so, if Iranians had seen a picture of Mr. Dulles sitting informally in conversation with the Shah, they would have said, "See that! The United States is getting the upper hand! Mr. Dulles is telling the Shah what he can and cannot do!"

The Chief of Protocol felt that correcting the sitting posture of the Secretary of State for cameras was really not under his jurisdiction. The Ambassador and the Minister of the Court preferred that someone else do it. After all, picture-taking was not one of their main concerns at the time. Who was left? The cameraman! I felt sure that my pictures of the conference would not pass the censor if nothing were said. If I wanted footage, I would have to speak to Mr. Dulles myself. I didn't mince words, but bluntly stated, "Mr. Secretary, please don't sit cross-legged in front of the Shah. It is considered disrespectful in our country." He very graciously did what he was asked to do, and was not in the least offended at what I feared might be construed to be effrontery.

It became the practice for me to warn all visiting dignitaries ahead of picture-taking time to assume a posture of dignity and respect when in conference with His Majesty while cameras were present.

The official film reporter must also keep in mind all segments of his audience, not forgetting any group that may be influential, however small. He must exercise great care in photographing scenes that might run the risk of being misunderstood. For example, the Shi'ah religion forbids the consumption of alcoholic drinks. However, such beverages are produced in Iran for those who do not seriously adhere to this aspect of religion. Wines of Shiraz and Esfahan are famous. Iran also produces a vodka that vies in quality with that of its Russian neighbors.

Officially, drinking is not forbidden by civil law in most Moslem countries (with the exception of Saudi Arabia, where alcoholic drinks are neither made nor sold); however, the majority of orthodox Moslems never imbibe. The Shah, head of the state of a Shi'ah country, is forbidden by religious law to drink. At formal dinners (in the Western countries) where heads of state drink to each other's health, after toasts are proposed, it is obligatory that the Shah lift his glass even though it contains only water.

We had one unfortunate incident on one of our official trips, when a still photographer took a picture of the Shah at such an event with a glass containing a cola drink in his hand. After this picture was circulated a furor arose, spearheaded by the Mullahs who used it as a springboard for an anti-Shah campaign saying, "Look at this! Here is the head of your country who drinks, ignoring the law of Islam!"

As is well known by photographers and portrait painters everywhere, getting the best results is far easier if the cameraman or artist knows his subject well. It is rarely possible for a commoner like me to know a member of the royal family well enough to establish a significant rapport. Although I had traveled with Their Majesties on many visits at home and abroad, not until one particular day did I feel that I was able to do justice to the great beauty of Queen Soraya.

At this time the children of an orphanage in Tehran presented a play for the Queen, and it was my assignment to cover the event. While the play was in progress, I moved about quietly trying to find the best angle from which to photograph Soraya as she watched the play. I stepped down softly into the orchestra pit of the little auditorium (knowing the whir of my camera would not be heard enough to distract the audience or the players). I peered through my lens at the Queen, but decided the location was unsatisfactory. Coming up out of the pit, I again looked at Soraya through the lens, getting her face at a three-quarters or Rembrandt angle and liked very much what I saw. When I viewed the footage I took from that location, I saw Queen Soraya on the screen as she appeared to me in real life—for the first time. After that day, I always tried to photograph her from this particular angle.

Sometimes a spectacular sequence will evolve without any long-range planning by the cameraman. A happy set of circumstances afforded me the opportunity to photograph such a sequence. It came to me during the time when I was traveling in the country to make a documentary on tribal schools, mentioned earlier. I saw a caravan of nomadic tribesmen approaching me across the desert, riding camels, donkeys, mules and horses. I waited until they came to where I was standing, photographing them as they approached, and the entire caravan as it passed. I went wild, fascinated by the picturesque beauty of the scene. One of the most exciting shots I was able to get was that of a Qashghai woman on a camel. The terrain around her was yellowish brown; the sky was true cerulean with little patches of white clouds; the camel she was riding was large and brown. This woman wore several layers of petticoats—red, green and yellow, all showing their hems, under the edge of her wide gathered skirt. She was a natural beauty, bronzed by the sun. Her luxuriant hair was caught with bright scarves and her coinlike jewelry tinkled as she gracefully rode by. I stooped low, tilting my camera so that I had this gorgeous creature of the desert framed against the blue, blue backdrop.

During my career in Iran it was my great privilege to make films on many distinguished personages as well as numerous events of historic importance in the country, such as: the inauguration of the Karadj Dam—one of the first dams to be built in Iran; the wedding of Princess Shahnaz and Mr. Ardeshir Zahedi; the visit of Queen Elizabeth and the Duke of Edinburgh to Iran; Harold Lamb, the American writer, presenting his seventeen books on Iran to the Shah; various meetings of the members of the Baghdad Pact in Tehran; CENTO (Central Treaty Organization) activities in Iran; and the inauguration of the Royal Tehran Hilton Hotel.

The dignitaries I personally photographed included the Crown Prince of Japan in Iran; Averell Harriman; Adenand Menderes, Premier of Turkey; Mohammad Ayub Khan, Pakistanian Field Marshal (later president); India's Prime Minister Jawaharlal Nehru, during his four-day visit to Iran; Indira Gandhi (later Prime Minister of India); King Faisal of Iraq; King Hussein of Jordan; President Celal Bayar of Turkey; Iskandar Mirza, President of Pakistan; Princess Margaret of England; Trygve Lie and Dag Hammarskjöld of the United Nations.

Others of international note whom I photographed were: Eleanor Roosevelt, Jacqueline Kennedy, Ambassador Bowles, Dean Rusk, Chief Justice Warren, Gary Cooper, President Camil Shamoun of Lebanon, Prince Abdul Illah of Iraq, Konrad Adenauer of West Germany, Henry Cabot Lodge, the Sheik of Kuwait, Prime Minister Daud of Afghanistan, and Mr. John Foster Dulles.

I photographed King Baudouin and Queen Fabiola of Belgium,

King Phumiphol and Queen Sirikit of Thailand, President Lubke and Foreign Minister Willy Brandt of Germany, President Franz Jonas of Austria, and many others during their visits to Iran. The list of heads of state and high officials photographed abroad is even longer, but most of them have already been mentioned in previous chapters.

Over a period of ten years the stories I covered on the activities of the Shah (both in Iran and abroad) for our weekly newsreel exceeded 300 items, which were seen by an estimated audience of 250 million people. In addition, numerous film coverages were made on the activities of His Majesty and the Royal family, which were sent to international television networks and for theatrical showings around the world.

Work on one film with which I had had no initial association proved to be a great source of satisfaction to me.

The famous film entitled *Years of Lightning, Day of Drums* made by USIA after the assassination of President John F. Kennedy is a two-hour documentary, ably directed by Bruce Herschensohn for showing abroad. The film was sent to many countries where the language of the people was dubbed in by the most capable linguists available. I was greatly flattered to be asked to help with the translation in Iran, and to supervise the dubbing of the film locally. It was a most challenging assignment. How can one translate a statement such as "Ask not what your country can do for you, ask what you can do for your country" into another language, retaining its full impact?

Iranians adore movies, but they are far more interested in films with story-lines than in documentaries. Very few people in the USIS office in Tehran thought the Kennedy film would be well received if shown in commercial theaters and admission charged. One commented, "This film won't play more than two nights in Tehran theaters."

Unfortunately the film was ready for release during the month of August at a time when most people are out of the city because of the heat. But the man in our office was wrong. The movie was shown from two o'clock in the afternoon until midnight in one of the first-class theaters in Tehran for twenty-nine days.

I had a very strong interest in the film because of the devoted labor we had put into it, and so went on a sort of inspection tour the first few nights it was being shown. I was amazed and touched to see Iranian women (many of whom could easily have been illiterate with no knowledge about Kennedy except that he had been President of the United States) emerge from the theater, red-eyed from weeping.

For those who were not privileged to see the film, it covered Kennedy's funeral procession from the White House to Arlington Cemetery. The concept behind the film was to juxtapose the man's hopes, dreams and philosophy (as flashbacks) with views of the cortege. Dubbing this film in the Persian language was one of my proudest assignments and the source of tremendous inner satisfaction.

I was occasionally called upon to serve as photographer outside the circle of my regular duties with USIS and as the official cameraman of the Shah. One particular example had to do with an uprising in Iran spearheaded by a faction of Mullahs.

It was in the year 1963 when the unrest came to full bloom under the leadership of a Mullah named Ayatollah Khomeini, who had attained a place of power among the Shi'ah Moslems.

As has been previously stated, Reza Shah had moved to lessen the undue influence of the Mullahs, and it will be remembered that John Humphrey, the American filmmaker (as reported in Chapter Six), commented that the Mullahs seemed to him to be "holding the people in the religion, using them for their own ends, seldom using the religion to help the nation." As he admitted, there were a great number of Mullahs who were sincere and fine, upstanding characters; but there were some who craved power. The Shah continued in the path of his father, attempting to balance their influence in accordance with the place they deserved in the life of the people.

Clashes erupted in early June during the mourning month of Moharram. Khomeini and other religious leaders used their pulpits as platforms from which to deliver diatribes against the Shah's reforms. Mourners in the various congregations were moved to frenzy by the fiery oratory.

Dissidents from all levels, including the Communists of the country, gathered around the Mullahs. The movement gained momentum in places such as Qum, Mashad, Tabriz, Esfahan and Tehran. One day this leader, Ayotollah Khomeini, residing in Qum at the time, went to the preacher's stand in a mosque and made the very rash boast that he could bring the Shah down off his throne in

a period of twenty-four hours. Violent followers rioted, and went
as far as to burn schools. I hastily took my daughter out of the
model school she was attending in the northern part of Tehran—
which I thought might become a prime target.

The government of course attempted to curb demonstrations,
deploying soldiers in the streets, with manned tanks standing
guard. The Shah issued specific orders that there was to be *no*
bloodshed. Should the army or police forces resort to violence to
put down the demonstrations, eliciting retaliation in the form of
bloodshed, then who could be said to be right? Such was the philosophy of the Shah at this critical time. He wanted very much for
the demonstrations to be contained peacefully

On Friday morning, June 4, a friend of mine (close to the
court) came to me and said, "As you may have heard, the Shah
has given specific orders to the security forces that there is to be no
bloodshed. The Chief of Police would like to show him that they
are carrying out his orders, keeping the peace according to his
instructions. To prove this, we need to photograph the demonstrations and show him our tactics."

He continued by telling me the police had learned that the
rioters planned to meet at a certain mosque at four o'clock. Following afternoon prayers and speeches by their leaders, they would
walk *en masse* to the main square, where they hoped to gain
strength through the addition of numbers of sympathetic followers,
then go to the bazaar, where they would stage another demonstration in the evening.

The police planned to surround them completely in the main
square of the capital, and propel them to a large hall in the traffic
division of the police department. Here they hoped to reason with
them and persuade them to disperse.

My friend wanted me to photograph the entire procedure, the
film to be shown to the Shah the same evening. I demurred because
first of all I knew it would be a dangerous assignment, and second
I knew that I couldn't use any of the big heavy 35mm camera
equipment in my office without specific permission of my superiors;
and even if I could, it would take some time for processing and
printing the film. My friend overrode this excuse by telling me
he could get a Bolex 16mm camera with a zoom lens for this purpose, and could arrange for immediate processing of the 16mm
reversal film. He further implied that this was a matter of national

importance, and if he could not rely on me, he did not know where he could turn. He finally persuaded me to cover the event, for I well knew that there probably was no other cameraman available to do the job on this Friday morning (a holiday in Iran).

Three plainclothesmen from the police department and this friend of mine went with me to the mosque on Istanbul Avenue at the appointed time. I climbed up to a balcony in front of the mosque, waiting for the crowd to come out. After prayers and a number of inflammatory speeches (which we could hear over the speaker placed outside the mosque) accusing the Shah and his government of all kinds of wrongdoing, the people poured out of the mosque into the street. I began my coverage.

I did not have time to find high vantage points for filming as the crowd surged toward the main square. My friend accommodated me by lifting me up so that I could be above the throng with my camera. A perfect target for anyone with a hasty hand!

For some miraculous reason no one appeared to notice me. Fanatics who were willing to burn schools, endangering the lives of children, surely would have had no qualms about shooting a man who was photographing them, thereby—in their minds—securing a visual document for the police to use in identification and future arrests and indictments.

At the square I found a good vantage point on the balcony of the traffic department building, and photographed the crowd of three to four hundred milling people. I was pleased to see that the police, who had turned out in force, carried out their plan without a hitch. The people were herded into the police hall, where they calmed down and eventually dispersed peacefully.

I took the film to the laboratory, processed it, and gave it to my friend, who took it to the court for the Shah to view that evening. The police were thus able to show His Majesty that his orders were carried out and they had managed to disperse the crowd without bloodshed.

Khomeini and other religious leaders were subsequently charged with plotting against the government, aided by large sums of money sent into the country by a courier who admitted to having smuggled sums amounting to $700,000, to support the uprising. Khomeini was released from custody some time later, but on resuming subversive activities he was sent into exile.

The job of an official cameraman is not always glamorous. He

sometimes runs into complications beyond his control. As cameraman for the Shah I naturally enjoyed prestige and leadership in
my technical field, and had developed friendship and close associations with many government officials. However, this position did
not shield me from the "slings and arrows of outrageous fortune."

In 1961, the irresponsible action of one young Iranian triggered
a chain of reactions that eventually disrupted (for a time) my
assignment as the official cameraman for the Shah, and plunged me
into a period of disillusionment and despair.

On a Friday afternoon in January, 1961, I opened the new issue
of a magazine called *Sefid-o-Siah,* a small, somewhat leftist publication at the time, to the first article, which turned out to be a
scathing review of a movie on Iran. The article, which had been
written by an Iranian student in the United States, was entitled,
"The Most Disgraceful Film Shown about Iran Abroad." I wondered *who* the Iranian was who would make such a film! This is
what I read:

> In the first days of December, all the students of Weber College,
> Ogden, Utah, were requested to get together in the auditorium of the
> University to see a film about Iran. . . . We all wanted the people of the
> great country of America to know us well, as most of them still think
> very strangely about Iran. They think that in our country we do not have
> automobiles and we travel between cities by donkey and camels, that all
> Iranians wear turbans and in their harems they keep hundreds of beautiful
> wives and spend all their time in pleasure and dancing. . . .
> Finally the lights of the hall dimmed and went out and with the
> dimness came a great silence over the auditorium. . . . The strong lights
> of the projector fell on the screen and there was written in Persian and
> English, "A Mother for Shamsi—Produced by Mohammad Ali Issari.". . .
> In the first few minutes of the film, we, the Iranian students, got a
> terrible shock. . . . I wish that instead of this film they would have shown
> the old Mullahs with turbans on their heads and slippers on their feet,
> with their harems full of women. But alas, they showed things that, I
> swear to God, I, who have lived in Tehran for 19 years, having seen most
> of the northern and southern cities of Iran, never saw all this poverty
> and disgrace, as if somebody intentionally wanted to put side-by-side all
> the poverty and ruins in the worst possible way. . . .
> The story of the film was this: a poor woman who is the mother of
> little Shamsi travels from Tabriz to Tehran and instead of traveling by
> the most modern train we have, or an automobile or bus, she travels with
> a cart. I beg you to say, is there anybody these days who travels with a
> cart? . . . The photographer showed the mother of Shamsi in torn clothes,
> with her raggedly dressed daughter, sometimes riding in the cart, some-
> times near the water well where a number of people worse than they
> were pulling water from the well which was next to a toilet, and they
> drank it! . . . On one side of the well a number of people in torn, ragged

and dirty clothes are sitting in the sun and picking lice from their bodies and killing them, and their water jug is full of flies. Now imagine what an American seeing this film would think of our nation?

Finally the mother and Shamsi herself continue with their journey and come to the Jewish district in Tehran, and not in the good parts of it either. Among the garbage where dogs and cats search for dry bones, they search for food. Then, when they can't find anything they go to one of the dirtiest butcher shops. In this butcher shop, where a number of poor and unlucky people with bare feet are waiting to get spoiled and dirty meat which is covered with flies, where the photographer by the way presents his masterpiece by showing the flies on the meat, they buy some. I don't know how the great and complicated departments of the country permit the shipment of such films out of Iran. . . . We cannot look our American schoolmates in the face.

After the end of the film we all sat together and cried for our country. . . . We do not say that in our country there is no poverty. . . . but in this film nothing was shown except poverty and bitterly exaggerated dirt.

It is true that we ourselves should be aware of our poverty, and find a way to combat it, but why should we show these to foreigners who already look at us as low and miserable creatures? I now insist that you require the Propaganda Department to send a few films about Iran to our University so that in contrast to all these disgraceful scenes we can show some nice scenes about the big university we have, the factories, the dams, our engineers and laborers and how they all work together to build up our country.

The editor of the magazine had these comments to add:

This was a letter that we received this week from the United States and it caused us great sorrow. As the writer states, we do not deny the ruins and poverty of our country, and *Sefid-o-Siah* magazine, which is a critical publication, will remind the authorities wherever we see any poverty and corruption. But it is a fact that seeing a film in this shape, with its only aim to belittle our country outside Iran, can not give us any help. This is why we draw the attention of the concerned authorities to this subject.

The words "Produced by Mohammad Ali Issari," set in large print, leaped up at me from the page. I had never produced such a film, had never seen such a film (even to date I have not seen it) and knew absolutely nothing whatsoever about it. How could anyone write such a thing with no foundation? I felt certain that the readers of the magazine and the government authorities knew me well enough that they would not believe I had done such a disgraceful thing as was delineated in the article.

I knew, however, that it was wise to defend my position. I tried to call the editor of the magazine, but since it was Friday his office was closed and he could not be located. Although the magazine had a small circulation, by afternoon shocked friends began calling to ask, "Have you read the article in *Sefid-o-Siah?*"

One word in the article caught my eye: *Jewish.* I wondered if there could possibly be a connection between the story and the work I had done three years previously for an American-Jewish organization in Iran.

It was in 1958 that my boss called me one day and said, "There is a Mr. Dickman here from New York, representing the American-Jewish Joint Distribution Committee. He would like the services of a well-qualified cameraman in Tehran to shoot some scenes for him, showing progress achieved by the Committee in Iran. His organization is making a film to raise funds for their work abroad, and he would like some shots of the hospitals, clinics, kindergartens, and so on, they have built here for Tehran's Jewish population. I know of no one else who could come up to his expectations so I told him about you."

With my supervisor's blessing on the assignment, I accepted the job. It was agreed that, since the work would be an overload and not part of my regular work for USIS, the New York organization should pay me. I was happy to do this coverage as I knew of the excellent work the Joint Committee was doing to help the poor Jewish community of Tehran. I also knew of the importance that the government placed on this work because Mr. Hossein Ala, Minister of Imperial Court and Ex-Prime Minister, was the Committee's honorary chairman.

It should be pointed out here that although in some Arab countries there is no place for a Jew, Iran (which is not an Arab country) officially recognizes the various Christian, Jewish and Zoroastrian religions—even though it is a Moslem nation.

Mr. Dickman seemed very happy with my approach to photographing the scenes he wished me to film and returned to the United States with the processed film, entirely satisfied with what I had done for him. The following year (1959) when I was briefly in New York, he called me and during our conversation requested that I send him some pickup shots, including scenery of the capital city, the beautiful Alborz mountains north of Tehran, and so forth. This I did after my return.

At no time, however, did I photograph such scenes as referred to in the *Sefid-o-Siah* article. Having worked with the Board of

Censors in Iran for many years, I was well aware of what scenes were and were not acceptable. I suspected, assuming what the article said was true, that the footage I photographed for Mr. Dickman (none of which was mentioned in the article) was used in a film which someone else also had photographed, and I was credited as the photographer. For what other reason could my name be attached to it? It was an utterly confusing situation.

The next day, when I reported this to my boss, he said, "Don't worry about it," but I did. In Iran there is a press law that gives the victim of a published derogatory statement the right to deny it, and the denial must be presented on the same page of the next issue of the periodical. Consequently, I sent a detraction to the publisher of the magazine which included this paragraph:

> How such a film has been connected with me and credits me as its producer is a matter which will be unflinchingly pursued until the falsehoods are cleared.

The detraction appeared in the next issue but the above paragraph was changed to read as follows: "How such a film has been connected with me *and the Americans have credited me* as its producer is a matter which will be unflinchingly pursued until the falsehoods are cleared." The editor of the magazine then commented that he would print any new information uncovered by me or anyone else to bring out the truth. However, with the addition of the phrase "the Americans have credited me" in my detraction, and the political background of the publication, I realized the situation was being used for political propaganda rather than any attempt to get at the truth.

A newspaper friend, infuriated by the original article, accompanied me the next day on a visit to the editor, who admitted that he had made the mistake of not checking with me as to the truth of the matter before printing it.

The following day when my assistant and I appeared at Mehrabad Airport (with invitations in hand) to photograph the arrival of the President of Pakistan, we were stopped by a young officer of the Imperial Guard who barred my entrance, refusing to give any explanation for his act excepting to say, "It is an order."

On returning to my office, I called Theodore D. Feder, director of the American-Jewish Joint Distribution Committee in Tehran, and asked him if he knew anything about this film referred to in

the *Sefid-o-Siah* article. He replied in the affirmative, but insisted that the film was in no way derogatory to Iran and that the article was a distortion of the truth. He confirmed our conversation with the following letter:

> It would appear to me, as one who has seen the film ostensibly referred to in the article, that the writer was either unable to properly understand what he had seen in the picture, or *deliberately distorted* what he had seen, or may not have seen the original picture that was made here in Iran early in 1959. The fact that he mentions you as a producer is an indication that something is wrong, as nowhere in the titles and credits does your name appear as producer. We, and you, know you were not the producer.
>
> As I have explained to you, it would be utterly senseless for a welfare organization such as I represent, whose whole purpose in Iran is to work in the fields of health, education and welfare for thousands of people, to make a picture that in any way adversely reflects either on the people or the Government of Iran. . . .
>
> It is indeed unfortunate that such a letter was printed without the true facts having been ascertained. In my opinion there is nothing in the picture as produced that in any way could be called disgraceful or insulting to Iran.

At that time in Iran some students (with influential relatives) who were departing for the United States or Europe, were able to obtain press cards from their local journals with the understanding they would represent these publications at their destination. They wrote articles about America or Europe without pay, but the press cards gave them keys to open doors as well as to grant them exposure back home. It so happens that the student who wrote the article was a relative of the editor! It seems that he had been in Utah many months and had not sent back any stories for publication; and seeing *A Mother for Shamsi* gave him an opportunity to write something dramatic and sensational even at the price of distorting the truth, caring not for the consequences.

Within a couple of weeks after the date of publication of this article, I was interrogated by an agent of SAVAK (Iran's counterpart of the Central Intelligence Agency in the United States) about the magazine article. Shortly thereafter, I was called before the Information Department of the Ministry of Foreign Affairs, questioned by the police and then by the Ministry of Information. In every case, I denied that I had ever filmed any scenes that could even be conceived as being derogatory to Iran, nor had I ever seen the film mentioned in the article.

Copies of Mr. Feder's letter were sent to all these authorities, including the magazine editor, to support my case, but it was never published in *Sefid-o-Siah*. It was then that I was made well aware of the premise in Iran's conception of justice, during those days, that the accused was considered guilty until proved innocent.

I continued to receive official passes to attend ceremonies with the Shah participating; however, I was not permitted to enter. A strange, contradictory situation! This continued for a period of four months, during which the Shah did not appear in any of our weekly newsreels. I could film events in which the Prime Minister or other top Iranian government officials were involved, but I was not permitted to photograph events in which the Shah participated—although I was always invited.

I often wondered who had decreed that I was not to be permitted to photograph His Majesty. I could not conceive of the ban as having stemmed from the Shah himself, as it would be impossible for a man in his position, whom I had served for many years and knew well, to pass a sentence of "guilty" before all facts had been looked into.

Meanwhile, an Iranian friend serving in an official capacity in the United States, received a letter from the student in Ogden, Utah, repeating the accusations against me. My friend wrote me about it (in part) as follows:

. . . . This sentence quoted below was written by this student:

"A Jew by the name of Mohammad Ali Issari made a film of the Jewish district, located on Avenue Cyrus, which is, as you know, the worst and dirtiest spot in Iran. In this film he had tried to show Iran as a Jewish country. This film, which was obviously produced by foreigners for political reasons, tried to present Iranians and their country as backward and savage as possible," etc. etc.

My friend went on to say:

As I know you very well, I recalled the times when young, patriotic and brave people who fought the enemy could be counted on one's fingers, and you occupied your place in the very first row, alongside of us. It then suddenly dawned on me just who this Jewish Mohammad Ali Issari is!

In any case, I just wanted to bring this to your attention and in the meantime take the opportunity to express my deeply felt respect for you. . . .

Of course we did not take any action on this letter and ignored it.

At the end of February, 1961, I received a letter from Mr. Irving R. Dickman, Director of Public Relations for the American-Jewish Joint Distribution Committee in New York (the man under whose direction I had photographed the scenes in Tehran) telling me he had just read a translation of the article that had appeared in *Sefid-o-Siah* and was shocked by it. He informed me that some time previously the film had been withdrawn from public showings "to avoid any possibility of further misunderstandings." A portion of his letter follows:

> Let me assure you that *none* of the incidents mentioned in *Sefid-o-Siah* appears in the film. I am sure you found the article puzzling, because you know that no such things were ever photographed; if they existed, they would have been out of harmony with the purpose of the film. Shamsi and her mother are never shown traveling on a cart. They certainly are not shown drinking water from a well near a toilet, because we do not show anyone drinking, or any toilets in the film. There are *no* closeups of flies anywhere, neither in a butcher shop nor anywhere else. There is nothing which even faintly resembles a person picking lice.
>
> And it would have been unthinkable to show the mother and child looking for food in garbage, any more than people like them would do such a thing in real life. It is difficult for me to believe that the writer of the article was talking about "A Mother for Shamsi" and not some other film!
>
> Such scenes as these would have been completely foreign to the spirit of the film, precisely because the basic purpose was to show the *progress* now being achieved in the mahalleh, with the cooperation of a great many people in public life. The narration emphasizes that the people of the mahalleh no longer have to use water from the jube, for instance. We show how better food and medical care are making people healthier and happier. We stress what is, I think, a universal principle—that each man must help those who are unfortunate, those in need, and we show how such unfortunates are indeed being helped today.
>
> Perhaps most important, the film ends on a note of hope and confidence that for the people of the mahalleh life will be even better in the future.
>
> In the film titles, you were given the following credit: "PHOTO-GRAPHED in Iran by M. Ali Issari." This was done on our part because of the extraordinarily fine and sensitive photography which you did for the film and which we felt deserved credit and recognition of a professional nature. I must stress, however, that your work was entirely limited to the photography and that whatever you filmed was done under *our* direction, instructions and responsibility.
>
> Furthermore, the script and narration were prepared by us long after your connection and participation in the film had been completed, so that obviously you could have had no part whatever in the preparation of the script. You were engaged to perform your specialty—photography. As you well know, at no time were you called upon to participate in any part of the writing, editing, or production of the film. I would state for the record

that you are an excellent craftsman, but that you were in no way responsible for the finished film.

Further, to make this point crystal clear, at no time were you asked
to, nor did you, take any film which was in any way derogatory to Iran
or to its people. It did not even suggest itself; on the contrary, I recall
vividly your pride in your country, and I even think I acquired some of
my own affection for Iran and its people from you.

Through this letter, I now had proof that all the allegations in
the student's article were completely false as far as I was concerned,
and that my name had not appeared on the film as *producer*. I
sent copies of the letter to all the officials to whom I had given
explanations, but I received no conciliatory responses and my situation changed not at all. Needless to say, *Sefid-o-Siah*, which had
pledged to "bring out the truth," failed to print this letter also!

It suddenly occurred to me that a friend of mine—although
not in the country—might come to the rescue: Mr. Ardeshir
Zahedi, serving as Iranian Ambassador to the United States, and
known among his circle of many friends to be a *true* human being,
faithful to his vows of friendship. To give the reader an example
of his humanism we shall go back to the year 1953 at the time of
the fall of Mossadegh.

When the Shah left the country (as mentioned in Chapter
Three), he issued a decree appointing General Zahedi (Ardeshir's
father) as Prime Minister. Under the circumstances at the time,
the decree was not made public for fear of repercussions from
Mossadegh and his followers. The news somehow leaked out and
Mossadegh issued orders to arrest Zahedi and his son (who actively
supported the Shah), and all their friends. An army officer was
given the assignment; his orders, I was told, were to capture them
dead or alive. General Zahedi was well hidden in the homes of
highly trusted friends, but Ardeshir was mobile to unite the various pro-Shah elements and to act as liaison between his father and
these factions. I heard that several times during his movements,
this officer almost caught up with him, and in one or two instances fired at Mr. Zahedi, fortunately missing. When Mossadegh
fell and the Shah returned to Iran, this officer was given a jail
sentence. However, he was later released from prison under restrictions not to leave the capital city of Tehran. A few months
after he gained his freedom, he was involved in a car accident in
which both legs were crushed. Doctors in Iran decided in consul-

tation that if he were not taken to Germany where special medical technology was available, he would lose both legs, and perhaps his life.

The police refused to issue the man a passport until after the military court had removed his residential restrictions. Arranging for the military tribunal to convene and reopen the case would take months. At this time, Mr. Zahedi learned about the accident and the resulting complications. Within eight hours he had obtained special clemency from the Shah, a passport from the police, necessary visas and documents, and took them personally to his old enemy in the hospital. There he found that the injured man had no financial resources for the trip. I was told that Mr. Zahedi provided the necessary tickets, and informed the hospital authorities in Germany that he would be responsible for all the medical expenses involved. The next morning the injured officer was on a plane heading for Germany.

And so it was to this Good Samaritan that I wrote a letter explaining the entire charade, enclosing copies of the article and letters I had received, requesting that he personally look into the matter and report his findings to me. A few weeks later, Mr. Zahedi answered:

My dear friend,

Your kind letter of the 27th Dey received. I am extremely sorry to hear about all these complications. Thank you for letting me know the complete background and sending me copies of letters sent to you. Of course I will do whatever I can to straighten this matter. . . . I never had any doubt that you are completely innocent but your explanations made me even more confident. . . .

Whatever is in my power I will do to prove your innocence. I pray God Almighty for your health and success.

Ardeshir

P.S. I will write a letter to His Majesty in this regard. By the way, I am hoping to be in Tehran about the middle of April when I will personally talk to His Majesty about this. Give my best regards to all our friends.

A couple of weeks later, Mr. Zahedi did come to Tehran and called me, "Bring your camera and come over. An American high official from the United States is going to have an audience with His Majesty. You must photograph it." I told him I would not be *admitted*, but he insisted that I must meet him there.

When I arrived at the Shah's private palace, Mr. Zahedi was waiting for me at the gate. With him was a colonel attached to the Imperial Guard. In my presence, he told the colonel in no uncertain terms, "Mr. Issari is to be admitted at all times—before anyone else! He has merited preferential treatment through his very valuable services to His Majesty and his country!" He then left us to go to the Foreign Ministry. The colonel apologetically told me that he regretted the whole affair, and called the young officer who had first banned my entrance at the airport to escort me to the Shah's office.

That day, I was the only cameraman present to photograph the audience with the Shah. Bars were let down thereafter and I had free access to cover all events with the Shah as before. In fact, at times I was given special privileges on such occasions. Thereafter, we resumed in our weekly newsreel coverage of events in which the Shah participated.

A few weeks later I attended a party at the home of my brother, where I fell into conversation with the colonel with whom Mr. Zahedi had spoken in my behalf (who by this time had been promoted to the rank of lieutenant-general). I had been told that he was responsible for the whole fiasco, and I ventured to ask him, "General, I understand this was your doing. Are you the one responsible for banning me from the court?" He frankly admitted that such had been the case and added that he deeply regretted his impulsive action.

It seemed that he had become bitterly embarrassed during the showing of a film many years previously in the United States, in which Iranian farmers were pictured drinking water from the same jube as the one in which women were washing their clothes. When he saw the article in *Sefid-o-Siah*, remembering this experience, he became extremely angry and impetuously decided to use the power of his office to ban me from photographing the Shah.

While talking to him I felt myself getting angry, and so excused myself and left the room. I did have to admit, as I thought the matter over, that the general *had* apologized, and generals just don't apologize! But I was extremely grateful to Mr. Zahedi, who had not lost faith in me and who had finally untangled a web woven by a man who tried me in his imagination and found me guilty.

As one can readily see, the life of an official cameraman has its ups and downs, its frustrations, surprises, joys and achievements. But on the whole it was a very rewarding life. It has always been deeply satisfying to me to look back over the years I served as official cameraman to His Imperial Majesty, the Shahanshah of Iran, during which time I was privileged to mirror in film his many activities for the betterment of the country. I made nearly 400 newsreels of this type which were seen by approximately 145 million Iranians within the span of ten years.

In addition, I made many newsfilm reportages for television and movie theatres abroad, during this time. The number of audiences who saw these films across the world is difficult to estimate, but it must have run into millions.

By 1965, after the Ministry of Culture and Arts had started making their own local newsreels, I felt the motion picture division of USIS in Tehran had done its job. We had pioneered in introducing an era of film journalism and educational film production in Iran, through which we were partially responsible for informing, educating and motivating millions of Iranians to build a better and happier way of life for themselves. It was gratifying to me to know that I was a part of the process and that the industry we had helped create had become well established and was moving forward.

I regretted leaving His Majesty's service and my professional activities with the U.S. Information Service in Tehran, but my deep desire for higher education in my chosen field took precedence over my natural desire to stay in Iran. In August of 1965 I left the Land of the Peacock Throne in pursuit of Western technology in in the United States.

16

An Appraisal

Although I was deeply submerged in very demanding studies at the University of Southern California in Los Angeles, my heart was still in Iran. The thought occurred and reoccurred to me that I might be able to assist in developing the movie industry in Iran by applying advanced American technology to films set in a Persian background through which I could present my beautiful country to the world.

Iran is in the unique position of being able to furnish almost any kind of background for movies within an hour's flight time: magnificent mountains, forests, desert, snow. And sunshine is almost continuous!

The economic factor in making films in Iran, where the production cost is comparatively low, was another important consideration. At the time, extras in Hollywood commanded about $37 a day; in Iran the cost would have been only a few dollars a day. Costumes that might cost $250,000 in Hollywood could be expertly made in Iran for as little as $50,000.

I reasoned that if cooperative projects could be initiated to implement this idea, it would be of inestimable value to the young motion picture industry in Iran. The top Hollywood craftsmen coming to Iran for such projects could offer invaluable learning experiences to their counterparts and assistants. The movie industry would through this close association find nourishment for development and growth.

Several serious attempts at fulfilling this idea were made to bring about coproduction of feature motion pictures between Hollywood and the Iranian film industry, but to no avail. Iranian government film authorities (with little knowledge or understanding of the intricacies of coproduction) unfortunately were the stumbling blocks.

My first opportunity came in 1967 when an independent Iranian producer decided to make a movie based on a novel entitled *Mission in Tehran*. This book, written a few years after the Tehran Conference by a young and talented Persian writer Tooraj Farazmand, was based on the "traffic block" incident (described in Chapter Three). The plot dealt with a Hitler-inspired attempt to kill Churchill (considered the backbone of the Allies) while he was attending the conference in Tehran.

The protagonist is a British intelligence officer who infiltrates the German espionage network in Iran in the role of a lonely, ineffectual Polish musician. He pretends to be in love with a middle-aged woman entrusted by the Germans to make arrangements for Churchill's assassination, using a special agent parachuted to Iran for this assignment. But the three Allied powers in Tehran are looking for the agent, and a member of the Russian intelligence shoots the woman. She is rescued by her compatriots, but her last wish, expressed on her deathbed, is that her musician lover be cared for by the German high command as her reward for the valuable services she has rendered them. Eric, the highly competent German intelligence officer who is to be Churchill's assassin, takes the musician under his wing. But as Eric aims at Churchill with his high-powered rifle at the intersection blocked by the truck, he discovers that the "helpless" Polish musician is really a Lieutenant Harrison of British intelligence who has removed the firing pin from Eric's gun!

The film was to be done in the English language with an American cast, for worldwide distribution. I was to be the executive producer. Contracts were signed in Hollywood with American stars and crew and an advance party of four went to Tehran in June of that year for preproduction planning. Unfortunately, we were forced to return to Los Angeles at the end of August because of lack of funds for continuing the production. Although it was disheartening not to be able to see my dream come true, a new development came about that encouraged me to look forward to an even more significant project.

While I was working on plans for *Mission in Tehran,* I was approached on the possibility of doing a film of much greater proportions. I was informed by official government authorities in Tehran that a grand celebration was being planned to commemorate the 2500th anniversary of the founding of the Persian Empire, to be held in October of 1971. In exchanging ideas with these people, I suggested that an epic film based on the life of Cyrus the Great would be most appropriate for the occasion. I was persuaded to research the subject and develop a "treatment" (condensed story from which a scenario would be written) for their consideration.

I returned to the United States elated, and with an associate launched into a thorough examination of everything ever written about Cyrus, ferreting out sources in Persian, English and other languages. The more we read about this great man the more we admired and revered him. After two years, we had completed a 97-page treatment, ready for submission.

It was most gratifying to me—in the maze of Hollywood where thousands of scripts and treatments, many of them excellent, never find a reader—to gain the attention of top men in the film industry who wished to collaborate with me on this project. King Vidor— *The Big Parade, Northwest Passage, Duel in the Sun, War and Peace*—was willing to direct the film, and George Englund—*The Ugly American, Shoes of the Fisherman,* and so forth—agreed to produce *Cyrus the Great* with me. Richard Burton and Elizabeth Taylor (through their agent) showed interest in choice roles in the film, and—if all went well—I fervently hoped to sign Charlton Heston for the role of Cyrus. Metro-Goldwyn-Mayer, through George Englund, indicated that they were prepared to provide half the financing if Iran would provide funds for the remaining half. The film was to be photographed in 70mm with stereophonic sound, entirely in Iran, where some of the sites of 2,500 years ago would be recreated, with an estimated budget of ten million dollars.

It was my intention to release the film in all the capitals of the world simultaneously with the beginning of the festivities in Iran, thereby making the celebration a worldwide affair. I was told that Cecil B. De Mille had once said that he wanted every man, woman and child in the world to be able to see the life of Moses and the philosophy of the Jewish religion (through his *Ten Commandments*) for "a buck." In like manner I was hoping to show the glorious civilization of ancient Iran, and Cyrus, the founder of the Persian Empire, as a truly great human being.

In 1969 I went back to Tehran with a film treatment entitled *Cyrus, the Great,* and information as to Hollywood's proposal for cooperation in making the epic. Iranian authorities expressed willingness to underwrite half the costs of the film.

Eventually in Tehran, George Englund, Hugh French (Burton's agent), and I sat down with Iranian government officials headed by Senator Javad Bushehri to complete agreements. But unfortunately the relatively small amount of $100,000 (development money) proved to be a fatal stumbling block in the proceedings. This amount (to be used for establishing the production company, and for hiring attorneys to draw up contracts with stars, other actors, writers, directors, producers, etc.) the Iranians refused to pay, and the Americans thought it was not their responsibility. I was caught in the middle.

The impasse was never broken, and my years of research plus those months of careful negotiations proved to be totally in vain. I was particularly distressed, for I was confident that the film would not only return its initial cost several times over, but would also be a great vehicle to introduce to the world Cyrus and his philosophy of the humane way of life as he practiced it 2,500 years ago.

Mr. Englund seemed to feel as strongly about the project as I, which may be noted in excerpts from the letter he wrote to Senator Bushehri in his room at the Tehran Hilton, shortly before his departure for the United States:

> At a time in the world when there is so much despair and concern among the peoples of all nations, it would be refreshing indeed to see a major film about a man so farsighted and who recalls to us across the gulf of twenty-five hundred years the nobility of which human beings are sometimes capable. . . .
> I believe a film of the quality we have discussed would do more to publicize and give mass publicity to your twenty-fifth centennial celebration than any other single activity. Motion pictures are still the most extensive and most powerful means of communication on our planet. More people learn from them and are moved by them than by any other form of communication. The people in every part of the world could learn about Cyrus and the uninterrupted sovereign line that has descended from him when they see this film. . . .
> Let me say, Excellency, I am not seeking the captaincy of this project. It involves more work than you can possibly imagine and I already have a full and bristling calendar. But I did want to commend these thoughts to you . . . I wish also to compliment Mr. Ali Issari who gave birth to the idea thus far with wisdom and persistence. Good luck to

you, Senator Bushehri. I earnestly hope you can get the film made and most of all I wish you triumphant success on your Centennial Celebration.

In all fairness, I must say that Senator Bushehri and his advisors really wanted the film to be made; but they did not understand how film packages are put together. The Senator fully expected me to return with a different proposition for producing the film. He requested that I try to interest other companies or investors; however, I knew that it was too late to resurrect the project in time for the celebration.

The grand celebration marking the 2500th anniversary of the Empire (held as planned in October 1971) was perhaps the most lavish in modern history. Following is an excerpt from a news report on festivities in *Life* magazine:

> With thousands of years having gone by since the last really big party, it is understandable that the Shah of Iran and his Empress (Farah) wanted their nation's 2500th anniversary bash to be memorable. In this way they succeeded even before the festivities got under way this week; the preparations alone are the stuff of legend. The guests include fifteen presidents, four premiers, nine kings, eight sheiks, two sultans and two vice-presidents. The VIP guests are housed in fifty tents spread below the ruins of Persepolis, the greatest remnant of the ancient Persian empire. The tents are a fantasy out of *Arabian Nights*, with bedrooms, salons and kitchenettes, marble bathrooms, and chandeliers. Maxim's of Paris, which is handling *la restauration*, freighted in ten tons of champagne and wine (a month early so that fine vintages like the Chateau Lafite-Rothschild '45 would have a chance to rest), fourteen tons of other beverages, and eighteen tons of food.[46]

Each distinguished guest was met at the Shiraz airport with a brass band that played the national anthem of the country he represented. Heads of state were then taken by helicopter to Persepolis, where they were greeted by the Shah and the Queen, and then shown to their tents.

The dominant colors of the tents, made of a total of 43,000 yards of cloth both flameproof and waterproof, by Jansen of Paris, were blue and beige, adding the right touch to the glory of ancient Persepolis.

The party lasted four days and nights, with visitors from sixty-nine nations, who were housed in what was called Tent City in an

---

[46]*Life,* October 29, 1971, p. 35.

area of sixty acres. The occasion served as a salute to the Shah's thirty-year reign, as well as the anniversary of the establishment of the empire.

The celebration started at dawn when guests wound their way to the wide plain where lies the simple tomb of Cyrus the Great. After visitors were in their places, the Shah, the Queen and Crown Prince Reza advanced slowly on a strip of red carpet to face the tomb. The Shah ceremoniously placed a wreath at the tomb, and in the hushed silence of the windswept plain and that of the awed distinguished assemblage addressed the departed monarch: "O Cyrus, Great King, King of Kings." The eulogy ended with these dramatic words: "O Cyrus, rest in peace, for we are awake."

Six hundred guests gathered in the Royal Tent under a ceiling of pure silk hung with sparkling chandeliers for the five-hour banquet in the evening. The menu (served by a hundred and thirty-one highly trained waiters) consisted of delicacies such as quail eggs stuffed with caviar from the Caspian Sea, roast peacock with foie gras, saddle of lamb with truffles, arrangements of figs centered with raspberries, and champagne sherbet.

Following the banquet the guests gathered at Persepolis under the stars to watch a spectacle of light and sound depicting the history of the City of Persians, which ends with its destruction by fire at the hand of Alexander the Great.

Following the presentation, "rocket sites were suddenly flaming, rockets blasted from their moorings to soar over the ruins, bursting in the air. . . . The aerial fantasies that followed included shooting candles, sparkling parasols, bouquets of peonies, sizzling chrysanthemums and a sky-garden of other bursting, blasting, spark-raising marvels."[47]

The great parade in which 6,200 marchers representing ten dynasties of Persian history passed in review was the most memorable event of the celebration. Large numbers of scholars had spent years studying manuscripts, friezes and artifacts for details of costumes, armor, weapons and musical instruments—to be produced by Persian craftsmen. It has been estimated that approximately four million dollars was expended to research the authenticity of the garb, including the important accessories of the marchers in the grand parade.

---

[47]Jacques Lowe, *Celebration at Persepolis,* Creative Communications S.A., Geneva, Switzerland (no date indicated), p. 61.

The 2500th anniversary was marked not only in Persepolis but also in all parts of the country. Tribesmen celebrated with festivities of their own devising in the remote areas. And in Tehran the Iranian opera and ballet did command performances in Rudaki Hall. Receptions and gala dinners were held in the hotels in the capital city (nine of which had been newly constructed to accommodate the influx of visitors for the celebrations).

One of the major events in Tehran was the opening of the Shahyad Aryamehr Monument, probably the most impressive single structure yet achieved in the Pahlavi era.* Standing on an oval traffic island not far from the Tehran International Airport, it houses museums and exhibition halls. On the evening of the grand opening, the visitor looking out from the upper terrace was dazzled with miles and miles of archways glittering with decorative lights.

On the following day the sports-minded Shah officiated at the opening of the 100,000 seat, moat-surrounded Aryamehr Stadium, the first part of a great complex that was completed later and that hosted the Asian Games of 1974.

Cost for the celebration aroused some criticism. For example, fifty gold-threaded uniforms for members of the royal court cost $1000 each; and colored light bulbs cost about $840,000—close to a million dollars for light bulbs alone!

Unofficial sources have estimated cost for the festivities to be a hundred million dollars, an amount thought by many to be exorbitant. However, a fair portion of funds expended was allocated to improvements that will be permanent: hotels, roads, the Shahyad Aryamehr Monument and the Aryamehr Stadium, to name a few. The people of Iran donated money to construct 2,500 new schools—one for each year of the duration of the empire. (Funds received were adequate to cover the cost of building several hundred more schools than the 2,500 planned.)

Among critics of the vast amount of money spent for the celebration were groups of Iranians studying abroad, who have complained for some time that the royal household and other wealthy families spend millions of dollars in their villas in Switzerland and in casinos, while many Iranians "slowly waste away from lack of medical supplies and food." The target of their dissidence is the Shah himself, for—as has been true throughout history—everybody looks to the Shah for the final word; and if an Iranian is not in

---

*See picture on back of book jacket.

agreement with policies, he considers the Shah personally to be at fault. (This situation thrives in the United States, of course, but to a lesser degree.)

On the other hand, this cultural characteristic tends to promote excessive glorification of royalty, which has resulted in subconscious resentment of the monarchial institution by some, especially those educated in the West. This situation has been frowned upon by members of the royal family—notably Empress Farah.

Some Iranians who go to the West to study (particularly in the United States) see modern democracy at work, and the hallmarks of advanced technology throughout the land; they compare this highly modern way of life with that in their own country and grow discontented. They would like to see a complete change in Iran overnight, and blame the Shah for not accomplishing the miracle. The great majority of Iranians who studied abroad during Reza Shah's regime returned to assist him in furthering progress in the country; sadly, such is not the case today. I have often wondered if the tactics employed for enticing these young men and women to return to their country might be less than skillful.

A survey shows that there are more Iranian-born doctors in New York City and Chicago than in any city in Iran. Recently a study conducted by Dr. Hossein Ali Rownaghi of the Pahlavi University of Shiraz disclosed that most medical colleges in Iran lose more than half their graduate physicians to the United States. It is claimed that there are more than 1,600 Iranian physicians practicing in the United States alone, and between 1,200 and 2,000 Iranian physicians have decided to reside permanently in Germany.

These statistics reflect the trend in one profession alone; but the same is more or less true of educators, engineers, scientists and other intellectuals.*

The merciless criticism of the Shah and his regime is often voiced by young, inexperienced students who are influenced by certain factions to believe that Iran is made up entirely of a few extremely wealthy families and downtrodden peasants and laborers, and that it is a country in which protesters of government policies are in mortal danger.

Some of the most radical, fiery advocates of a change in regime

---

*In July 1973, at a press conference in Washington, D.C., the Shah stated that the "brain drain" from Iran toward the outside is almost at a halt now and the educated Iranian young men and women are beginning to come back.

have expressed themselves in violent terms in school newspapers and leaflets across the United States. Following is a quote from one such circular, unsigned:

> It is generally believed that Iran is a peaceful and stable country making rapid economic progress under the guidance of a benevolent, progressive leader—the Shah of Iran. Unlike what is normally presented by the conventional press, and the media in this country, Iran is NOT a free, stable and peaceful country on the road to prosperity. And the Shah is not a progressive leader working for the advancement and well-being of his people.

The writer continues by presenting so-called facts that while 47% of the total revenue from oil and other resources is being spent on a standing army of 250,000 and a secret police force of 65,000 men—both being used to suppress the Iranian people, there are many families whose utmost desire is a bit of bread. The circular claims that any form of political opposition is outlawed, and that there are 26,000 political prisoners in Iran, many of whom are being tortured by the most inhumane methods.

The author of another unsigned diatribe, which carried the headline "*Iran: repressive dictator rules,*" wrote of killings, mass arrests and tortures, pointing up the "striking example" of the horror of an uprising in the cities on June 5, 1963, which resulted in the slaughter of 18,000 Iranians by the Shah's army. This, I believe, is a reference to the uprising spearheaded by certain Mullahs described in Chapter Fifteen. As will be remembered, it was the Shah's strict order that the disturbances be settled peacefully—without bloodshed. However, as is the case in almost all major urban riots, there were many casualties during the period of violence; but they certainly numbered less than a thousand.

The reforms of the White Revolution are referred to as "pseudo-reforms" in this article. For example, the author states that a teacher in the literacy corps cannot expect a warm welcome in places where it takes one's entire physical strength to eke out a bare existence, and where hunger and disease threaten life itself. Having witnessed the reforms of the White Revolution in action, particularly the activities of the dedicated members of the literacy corps and the great enthusiasm with which the villagers in Iran have received these young teachers, it seems to me that such statements are completely without foundation.

The dissident further accuses the Shah's regime of domination of the universities and appeals to Americans (especially those in the

academic communities) to oppose any assistance to "such a dicta-
torial government, and to support the struggle of the Iranian people
in their fight against the Shah's regime." To withhold *educational*
assistance from any institution or government—no matter what its
political philosophy may be—at a time when better understanding
is desperately needed among the peoples of the world, and education is our last frontier, would seem to be unthinkingly short-
sighted.

These detractors are much like the "armchair coaches" who
sit securely in their homes viewing an athletic event on their television screens, and criticizing the directions given by the experienced coach, not fully realizing the overall game plan and the
complexities involved in mobilizing a team and directing it into
constructive channels of action. A view from the playing field would
probably make them appreciate the situation more fully.

In like manner, such people could accomplish a great deal
more for their country by working constructively to bring about
change *within* Iran's boundaries, instead of criticizing from their
comfortable seats on the perimeter of the action.

No one in Iran, including the Shah, claims that the country
has now reached a utopian state. Many things that are wrong must
be righted, as is the case in any other country. But in order to solve
these problems, time and the dedication of individuals are needed.

The Shah has also been the target of criticism in recent years
for his vast expenditures for advanced arms and equipment from
the United States—supersonic military aircraft, utility and gunship
helicopters, cargo planes, laser-guided bombs, tanks and frigates.
It would seem obvious that a country, many times almost defense-
less *and* overrun by occupation forces during two world wars in
violation of its position of neutrality, cannot now brush off lightly
problems related to its security and its defense against any threat
of aggression.

In an interview with reporters during his visit to the United
States in July 1973, the Shah, when interrogated as to the nature
of the threat against which he was arming his country, answered:
"But who is questioning France and Germany and Italy when they
have decided about the force they need to defend their countries?
. . . I hope that once and for all our problems will be looked upon
in the same light as theirs—not just those of another Middle Eastern
country."

To the comment made by a U.S. reporter, "It sounds as though your ambition is for Iran to become the strongest country in the area," the Shah spoke firmly, unequivocally, "It is not an ambition, it is inevitable."

The Shah deems it necessary not only to protect his nation against any aggression, but also to protect the Persian Gulf for the safe passage of oil tankers to the rest of the world.

Quoting an article in *Time* magazine (August 6, 1973), "At such desert-edge ports as Ras Tanura, Abu Dhabi, Kuwait, Dharan and Kharg Islands, scores of supertankers congregate like wallowing whales to suck up the crude oil. Daily they plow the gulf's warm waters and out through the Strait of Hormuz carrying 20 million barrels of oil—almost half of the non-Communist world's consumption."[48] The author of the article aptly dubs Iran the "top cop" of the Persian Gulf.

Mr. Ardeshir Zahedi, Ambassador from Iran to the United States, asked this question when interviewed by reporters (in January 1976): "If the outlet from the Persian Gulf through the Strait of Hormuz, which is only 12 to 14 miles across, were closed, what would happen to those tankers that pass through—one every five or six minutes—carrying oil to Japan, Western Europe and the United States?"[49] A vital question!

And so it seems that until such time as law and order pervade the world community, nations must continue to give high priority to their security and Iran is no exception.

Internally, the country of Iran is moving full speed ahead to take its rightful position with the most highly developed nations in the world. It is the Shah's goal for Iran, within a decade, to be where Europe is today, and to be her equal before the end of the century. The progress achieved during the last ten years is living proof that this ambitious goal is not unrealistic. Some economists predict that by the early 1980s Iran's gross national product will top the 190-billion-dollar mark and that the growth rate will surpass that of all the Western nations of Europe, with the possible exception of West Germany.*

---

[48]"Policeman of the Persian Gulf," *Time,* August 6, 1973, p. 30.

[49]*U.S. News & World Report,* January 12, 1976, pp. 52-53.

*Statistics on this page and the following pages are taken in the main from *Iran 75—Iran, Trade and Industry,* September, 1975.

Looking back now to conditions in Iran some twenty-five years ago, an overview of which has been presented in this book, and observing conditions of life in the country today, one cannot but marvel at the phenomenal improvements achieved in all aspects of life in this remarkably short span of time.

A country that was on the verge of bankruptcy in the early fifties and that had to rely for her daily existence on aid received from outside sources (chiefly the United States) is now one of the twenty richest countries in the world. An International Monetary Fund study made in 1973 puts Iran in thirteenth place among the twenty listed. According to the publication *Iran 75—Iran, Trade and Industry* of September 1975, in June of 1974 Iran's holdings in gold, international deposits and foreign exchange were known to be over 5.4 billion dollars.

The per capita income of the Iranian people, which was between 50 and 55 dollars in 1950 and less than $200 in 1961, rose to $1,200 by March 1975, and it is expected to rise to $1,520 by the end of 1978. Some economists are even more optimistic than those making the foregoing predictions, anticipating that the per capita income will be over $2,000 at fixed prices by that time. In simple terms, ordinary Iranians now have more money in their pockets than ever before and can look forward to even better times in the years that lie ahead.

The rate of growth of Iran's gross national product in the last few years has continued to be higher than that of any other nation in the world. The vast increase in the country's national income is of course due mainly to the development of the oil industry and other mineral resources, plus the quintupling of oil prices in 1973-1974.

However, Iran has not only used her wealth to raise the living standards of her own people, but has also shared her increased income with many other developing countries by giving them significant financial assistance.

In an interview with reporters of *U.S. News & World Report* in January 1976, Ambassador Ardeshir Zahedi stated that Iran has committed about seven percent of her GNP (about 11.9 billion dollars)[*] to economic aid, grants and loans over a two-year period.

---

[*]In 1974, United States economic aid to other countries amounted to about 0.33 percent of her GNP.

Of this total, 5.6 billion dollars has already been spent in aid to underdeveloped countries, international organizations and industrialized nations, and the figure is still rising. Loans and financial assistance have been given to Turkey (1.287 billion dollars), to India (1 billion dollars), and to Pakistan (nearly 1 billion dollars). Credit has been given to France in the amount of five billion dollars, and to England, Italy and Denmark in the amount of two billion dollars. Mr. Zahedi further added, "We have signed an agreement with your country for an Iran-United States joint commission providing 15 billion dollars that will come to America."[50]

In Iran, this sudden increase in wealth is being utilized to promote all sectors of the economy: to pay for machinery and techniques to develop agriculture, transportation and communications; to promote education through the building of better facilities and the training of skilled teachers; to continue the campaign for better health and welfare for all, and to promote the expansion of modern industries.

The government plans to replace the oil revenue (which was over 20 billion dollars in 1975) by non-oil revenue from industrial exports by the end of the century, at which time the oil wells are expected to decline in production.

Industry has enjoyed an annual growth of 29% since 1963. According to statistics released in September 1975, the motor industry achieved a growth rate of 35%; electrical machinery, 25%; metal manufacturing, 23%; rubber and tires, 20%; and clothing and footwear, a phenomenal 50% in one year alone! And the number of factories in Iran, not including oil and petrochemical plants, rose to 6,200 by the end of 1974.

This fantastic growth has given officials of the government a number of problems, one of which is a severe shortage of skilled manpower. Iran is now spending hundreds of millions of dollars both in the United States and in Europe (as well as in the country itself) to train Iranian technicians and other workers to meet the great demands for manpower in its rapidly developing industry.

It is estimated that during the Fifth Plan (which covers the period 1973-1978) Iran will experience a shortage of 560,000 skilled workers, 42,000 technicians and 16,000 engineers. The government is having to recruit much of its manpower from abroad (mainly

---

[50]*U.S. News & World Report*, January 12, 1976, p. 52.

from the Near and Far East) to bridge the gap until more Iranians can be trained in specialized fields. For example, in January 1976, 25,000 South Koreans were hired to modernize ports, build roads and construct houses.

In the fifties in Iran, illiteracy was common among the masses. On February 20, 1974, free education for all Iranian children from kindergarten through eighth grade, with a free meal for every child every school day, became the law. In April of the same year the Shah told his Cabinet that the government must also provide free education for secondary and university students.

In December 1975, he declared the concept of free education as the 15th Principle of the Revolution of the Shah and the People and expressed his "long-cherished wish" that no Iranians be deprived of the chance to continue their education because of lack of financial means. The 15th Principle of free education has been designed to give Iranian youth confidence and security in the future and to ensure adequate and well-trained manpower for the further development of the country.

During the past three years the number of students attending school in Iran rose from 5 million to 7.7 million; the number of universities from eight to nineteen and the number of other institutions of higher learning from 113 to 185.

One result of the rapidly rising rate of literacy was highlighted in a colorful feature article in a Tehran newspaper (in 1972) headlined: "Scribes are a dying race." The author wrote:

> Traditional scribes here are undergoing a subtle transformation. Very few of these professional letter writers, squatting on their stools outside the Central Post Office, are nowadays asked to write letters *per se.*
>
> The old-fashioned pens, inkpots and other paraphernalia of a scribe have been replaced by functional portable typewriters.
>
> And instead of writing, "I am well, my only sadness is being separated from you, how are you and your family" stereotyped letters for recently arrived illiterate villagers to their folks back home, most of the new breed of "scribes" are engaged in typing out legal documents. . . .
>
> "Since the campaign against illiteracy got into full swing there has been a considerable drop in the number of villagers coming to us to write letters for them," said Haidar Moqaddam, who has been a scribe for the past 16 years in the narrow lane beside the Post Office. The last eight years, however, have been with the aid of a typewriter.
>
> "There are still the lower class and 'nanny' type of maids who, with wet eyes, ask us to write beseeching letters to their sons to let their anxious mothers know how they are," Moqaddam said. And every so often there is the inevitable illiterate lover who is prepared to pay extra

for a more effective *billet doux* which will "warm the heart of the loved one" and presumably make the object of his affections adopt a more conciliatory attitude towards him.[51]

The developments in agriculture and the improvement in the farmers' status in Iran, during the last three decades, will stand as one of the most significant of the Shah's achievements.

As previously discussed, it was through the land reform program that large tracts of land were broken up into small units and sold to individual farmers, thereby moving the farmer from the status of serf to that of landlord.

The government is now encouraging the merging of small farms into production cooperatives through which the farmers can "pool their resources, share machinery and marketing facilities and receive training in new farm methods."[52] A far cry from the fifties when the villagers toiled under the yoke of the feudal system, working with primitive implements, and eking out a bare existence!

The development of aviation in Iran has received full backing by the Shah through the years; he is, himself, an experienced pilot. Iran Air has moved rapidly from the position of being a totally domestic airline in 1964 to that of international status serving the Persian Gulf states and offering 23 flights a week to major European cities, and transoceanic flights to New York, Peking and Tokyo.

Iran Air is going even beyond its expanding operation of moving people and freight; it is developing a computerized complete travel service that—in its own terms—will offer "a bed on the ground for every seat in the sky." The computer will be programmed with details of all hotel accommodations in Iran, and will give instant information on all tourist facilities in the country by mid-1977, when Iran is expected to take delivery of its first supersonic plane.

Expansion of the activities of Iran Air is greatly facilitating growth of the tourist industry in Iran, under the auspices of the Ministry of Information and Tourism.

Tourist offices have been opened in major cities across the world and the training of personnel to take care of foreign visitors has been given high priority.

---

[51]Khosrow Mehrabi, "Scribes are a Dying Race," *Kayhan International*, November 26, 1972.

[52]*Iran 75—Iran, Trade and Industry*, September, 1975, p. 60.

By the end of the Fifth Plan (1978) it is estimated that Iran will be host to a million foreign visitors annually. Esfahan and Persepolis are, of course, major attractions. The Caspian seashore and the Persian Gulf with its small coral islands, now developing as resort areas for golfers, horseback riders and deep sea fishermen, are luring more and more foreigners to Iran for their vacations.

Telecommunication came to Iran as early as 1857, when the British installed wire and poles across some of the world's most rugged terrain. By 1885 about a third of the world's entire telegraph service passed through Iran's network to India. In spite of this dramatic beginning, Iran's telecommunication service failed to keep pace with the needs of the country. As recently as 1960, to call someone by telephone only a hundred miles away necessitated going to the central telephone exchange to place the call. The caller often had to wait—sometimes for hours—before being able to make the desired connection.

Today most cities of Iran have direct-dial telephone communications with each other through 18,500 kilometers of microwave lines. Telephone communications between Iran and 22 countries of the world are now possible through the earth satellite tracking station. And the future plans of the government include the establishment of telephone connections between all the cities and towns in every province of the country—by the end of the decade.

Radio and television in Iran today are among the nation's "showcase" industries. The first radio transmitter was inaugurated in the capital city of Tehran on April 24, 1940, and television followed in 1958, as a privately owned operation. On March 20, 1967, the National Iranian Television organization was formally inaugurated, and in 1971 the radio broadcasting activities merged with it, forming the National Iranian Radio and Television organization (NIRT). This progressive unit has made unbelievable strides—in its life of less than a decade.

Problems of providing television coverage in a country such as Iran, spread over an area of 628,000 squares miles, and serving a population made up of people of many diverse heritages, are extremely complicated. But NIRT engineers and broadcasters (all native Iranians) have faced up to the challenge with fortitude and ingenuity. Today television signals cover most of the country.

Transmission and reception of programs to and from other countries of the world became possible through the use of telecommunication satellites as early as 1969. The Apollo 13 mission and the Apollo 14 landing on the moon were seen by the people of Iran simultaneously with people of the United States. NIRT provided live coverage of the 2500th anniversary celebration of the founding of the Persian Empire to millions of people around the world, in October 1971. Today both transmission and reception of events of international interest, via satellite, are common practice. Iran now boasts the most extensive television coverage in Asia (with the exception of Japan), producing more than 70% of its programs locally.

Educational programs are provided for children in grades one through eight in most Iranian schools today, and plans are being laid for the establishment of a "free university" for adults through television. The project is based on England's "open university" whereby working men and women can pursue their college education at home. The free university, the only one of its kind in Asia, is scheduled to begin operation in 1977, at which time 6,000 students will be accepted from 50 towns across the country, where educational centers will be established to provide guidance.

One of NIRT's most commendable projects has been the establishment of rural television clubs through which closed-circuit programs dealing with topics close to the life of the farmer, such as agriculture and public health, are presented. Other activities of NIRT include: a Music Workshop, a Theatre Workshop, publication of a weekly magazine, the Center for the Preservation of Traditional Iranian Music, a Chamber Orchestra, and the internationally famous Shiraz Festival of Arts.

According to archaeological findings, Iranian artistic creativity dates back thousands of years—as far back as the Neolithic Age.

> Dubbed "the land of poets, roses, arts and oil," Iran can boast of a legion of profound scholars and poet-thinkers, such as Avicenna, the 'Renaissance man' who interpreted Greek medical science for the academies of Europe; Razi, the founder of modern chemistry; Ferdowsi, one of the world's greatest epic poets; Sa'di, the poet-traveler whose insights in international thinking predate the spirit of the United Nations; Hafez, possibly the world's profoundest interpreter of the journey of the soul in short poetical form; and Omar Khayyam, mathematician, astronomer and poet, who developed the modern Persian calendar, an achievement of the 13th century which is still considered the most accurate solar calendar ever devised.[53]

[53]*NIRT*, NIRT Publication Department, Offset Press, Inc., Tehran, October, 1972, pages not numbered.

In keeping with her distinguished past, Iran today is nurturing a favorable environment for artistic expression. Under the patronage of Her Majesty Empress Farah, national pride in Iran's artistic traditions has been revitalized. She has been mainly responsible for a tremendous cultural revival in the field of drama, music, poetry, folk arts and crafts.

One of the many projects in the field of art of which she is an active patron is the Shiraz Festival of Arts, sponsored by National Iranian Radio and Television. The Festival was inaugurated in 1967 as a means of bringing together the arts of East and West, and to provide an outlet for performances of a truly avant-garde character. It features international performers along with Iranian artists, emphasizing the experimental in its programming.

A unique aspect of the Festival is that the offerings are presented in a variety of settings—from the ruins of Persepolis, to Hafezieh (the garden tomb of Hafez), to a reconstructed caravanserai, to modern auditoriums in Shiraz.

An appraisal of progress made in the country during the last quarter century would not be complete, however, without a fuller statement of the inestimable contribution made by the Queen. In a recent Columbia Broadcasting System documentary on the Empress, the narrator aptly referred to her as a priceless treasure whose magnificence lies in her warmth, genuineness and her closeness to the people of Iran. He said, "Wherever she goes, whatever the security precautions, she is assaulted with affection. The most underprivileged among her countrymen revere her—not just as the holy wife of their god-like sovereign; they worship her as the champion of the oppressed—their voice in the exalted and remote regions of the palace."

Empress Farah says that her great problem is, "I *care* for everything. There are so many things to be done in our country and I'm involved in everything." The seemingly tireless Queen has a staff of over 100 people who help her with activities of about 26 societies, councils, institutes and foundations. She has her own private office in downtown Tehran, where petitioners can reach her by mail or in person. Through Farah and her staff common people, who would hesitate to request aid through government channels, apply for small loans, entry into hospitals, and help with personal family problems.

The Shah frequently demonstrates his faith in the Queen as

a diplomat, assigning her responsible missions. She visited Peking as Iran's representative to open dialogue with the People's Republic of China, where she sat across the table from the late Chou En-lai, ably discussing trade and cultural exchange.

To present a complete picture of the progress in Persia is beyond the scope of this book. The country, under the able leadership of her monarch, has survived years of turmoil on both the national and international level to achieve internal stability and world recognition.

In being chosen to replace Canada as one of the four members of the International Commission of Control and Supervision in Vietnam, and being assigned to join the United Nations Emergency Force for coastal patrol duty in the Egyptian-Israeli sector, Iran is receiving increased prestige on the world scene.

The Persia of the 1970s has indeed become a land of promise, pressing courageously forward toward the "Great Civilization." Her people can now confidently say, "O Cyrus, rest in peace, for we are awake."

Bibliography

Books

Winston Churchill, *Closing the Ring:* Boston, Houghton-Mifflin, 1951.

William O. Douglas, *West of the Indus*: Garden City, N.Y., Double-day and Company, 1958.

D. R. Denman, *The King's Vista*: London, Geographical Publications, Ltd., 1973.

Burda Druck and Verlag Offenburg, *Coronation in Tehran, The Imperial Couple of Persia*: printed in West Germany.

W. B. Fisher (Editor), *The Cambridge History of Iran*: Cambridge, Cambridge University Press, 1968.

Richard N. Frye, *Persia*: New York, Schocken Books, 1969.

Peter Hopkinson, *Role of Film Development:* France, UNESCO, 1971.

Clement Huart, *Ancient Persia and Iranian Civilization*: London, Routledge and Kegan Paul, 1927.

Gregory Lima, Keith McLachlan, Pauline Jackson, Hushang Mehr Ayin, Amir Taheri and Kazem Zarnegar, *The Revolutionizing of Iran*: Tehran, International Communicators Iran, 1973.

Jacques Lowe, *Celebration at Persepolis*: Geneva, Switzerland, Creative Communications S.A. (no date indicated).

Mohammed Reza Shah Pahlavi, *Mission for My Country*: London, Hutchinson, 1961.

Mohammed Reza Shah Pahlavi, *The White Revolution*: Tehran, Kayhan Press, 1967.

NIRT, NIRT Publication Department, Offset Press, Inc., Tehran, October, 1972.

Edward Rehatsek (translator), *The Gulistan of Sa'di*: New York, G. P. Putnam's Sons, 1964.

Roger Stevens, *The Land of the Great Sophy*: London, Methuen and Co., Ltd., 1965.

Harry S. Truman, *Memoirs of Harry S. Truman*, vol. 2, *Years of Trial and Hope*: Garden City, N.Y., Doubleday and Company, 1956.

P. N. Vachla, *Iran, Ancient and Modern*: Consulate General of Iran in Bombay, 1956.

Donald N. Wilber, *Iran Past and Present*: Princeton, New Jersey, Princeton University Press, 1967 (seventh edition, 1975).

————, *Riza Shah Pahlavi: The Resurrection and Reconstruction of Iran*: Hicksville, New York, Exposition Press, Inc., 1975.

Foreign Relations of the United States Diplomatic Papers: The Conference at Cairo and Tehran 1943: Washington, United States Government Printing Office, 1961.

Rubaiyat of Omar Khayyám: New York, Hartsdale House, 1932.

Springs of Persian Wisdom: New York, Herder and Herder, copyright by Leobuchandlung, 1970.

Magazines

Teresa Barbieri, "Secrets of Royal Wives": *The Women*, April, 1967.

Article by Jim Kartes: *American Cinematographer*, June, 1972.

Iran 75—Iran Trade and Industry, September, 1975.

Life Magazine, October 29, 1971.

"Policeman of the Persian Gulf": *Time*, August 6, 1973.

U.S. News & World Report, January 12, 1976.

Newspapers

Khorsrow Mehrabi, "Scribes are a Dying Race": *Kayhan International*, November 26, 1972.

Kayhan International, November 28, 1972.

Kayhan International, December 14, 1972.

Index

275

FRANCE

GERMANY

CZECHOSLOVAKIA

SWITZER-
LAND

AUSTRIA

HUNGARY

RUMANIA

YUGOSLAVIA

ITALY

ALBANIA

BULGARIA

BLACK SEA

GREECE

TURKEY

MEDITERRANEAN SEA

LEBANON
ISRAEL

TUNISIA

ALGERIA

LIBYA

EGYPT

RED

MALI

NIGER

CHAD

SUDAN

UPPER
VOLTA

NIGERIA

CAMEROON

CENTRAL
AFRICAN
REPUBLIC

ETHIO

PRESENT DAY

IRAN